Social Security Law in Spain

Social Security Law in Spain

Third Edition

Thais Guerrero Padrón

María Isabel Ribes Moreno

Co-authors

María Teresa Velasco Portero

Cristina Sánchez-Rodas Navarro

Olga Fotinopoulou Basurko

María Gorrochategui Polo

Cristina Aragón Gómez

Daniel Pérez del Prado

María Arántzazu Vicente Palacio

Carmen Jover Ramírez

This book was originally published as a monograph in the International Encyclopaedia of Laws/Social Security Law.

Founding Editor: Roger Blanpain
General Editor: Frank Hendrickx
Volume Editor: Willy van Eeckhoutte

Wolters Kluwer

Published by:
Kluwer Law International B.V.
PO Box 316
2400 AH Alphen aan den Rijn
The Netherlands
E-mail: lrs-sales@wolterskluwer.com
Website: www.wolterskluwer.com/en/solutions/kluwerlawinternational

Sold and distributed by:
Wolters Kluwer Legal & Regulatory U.S.
920 Links Avenue
Landisville, PA 17538
United States of America
E-mail: customer.service@wolterskluwer.com

ISBN 978-94-035-1848-0

e-Book: ISBN 978-94-035-1858-9
web-PDF: ISBN 978-94-035-1868-8

The Authors

Thais Guerrero Padrón. Author of General Introduction and Parts X and XI. ORCID: 0000-0002-4814-6266

She is Associate Professor of Labour and Social Security Law at the University of Cádiz (Spain) and Vice-Dean at the Faculty of Labour Sciences of the University of Cádiz. She holds a Bachelor's in Law from the Complutense University of Madrid (1989) and a PhD in Law from the University of Cádiz after having defended the thesis 'Discrimination on Grounds of Sex in the Spanish Social Security Law; Legal Causes. Analysis Based on Directive 79/7/CEE' (2000). For thirteen years she has been an arbitrator in elections for employees' representatives, designated by the Public Office (Junta de Andalucía). She has great experience as Professor of Labour and Social Security Law in the Labour Relations and Human Resources, Law and Business Management Degrees, and in master programmes in Mediation, Human Resources and Gender. She has participated as a researcher in several I+D+I Projects and has been a speaker in national and international conferences and seminars. She has been External Evaluator in a doctoral thesis competition on international migration organized by Granada University. She has published many articles, her research activity being focused on domestic and European social protection issues, equality and discrimination, and European Union (EU) migration and asylum policy.

María Isabel Ribes Moreno. Author of Parts I and II. ORCID: 0000-0002-1685-7354

She is Associate Professor of Labour Law and Social Security Law, Head of the Faculty of Labour Sciences at the University of Cádiz (Algeciras Campus). She holds a Bachelor's in Law from the University of Sevilla, Master's in Company's Legal Advice from I.E. (Madrid) and a PhD in Law from the University of Sevilla (with honours). She is the author of a monograph and has published more than forty scientific papers and book chapters related to different issues, including maritime labour law and all aspects of social and working conditions of seafarers, posted-workers, workers in port services and general workers.

The Authors

She has conducted many reports and conference presentations on different issues. Since 2000, she has been a researcher in various research and development projects. She has carried out research stays at some of the most prestigious universities, such as the University of Oxford, London School of Economics and Political Science and the University of Sheffield. Professor Ribes has experience teaching in different areas of labour, employment and social security law, giving lectures for master and bachelor degrees and Jean Monnet Module (574698-EPP-1-2016-1-ES-EPPJMO-MODULE) in different universities. She is a mediator in the Extrajudicial Autonomous Service of Resolution of Labour Conflicts of Andalusia, Member of the International Network Maritime Work Watch (MWW), the Community for Labour and Occupational Research and Study (CIELO) and the INDESS (University Institute of Research for Social Sustainable Development) at the University of Cádiz.

Co-authors

María Teresa Velasco Portero. Author of Part III. ORCID: 0000-0001-6501-3679

She is Official Professor of Labour and Social Security Law in the Department of Law of Universidad Loyola Andalucía. She obtained her degree in Law from the University of Córdoba (Spain) and doctorate in Law (unanimous *cum laude* distinction) from the University of Deusto-Bilbao (Spain). She is Member of the TRESS programme, a project funded by the EU and coordinated by the University of Gant, and European expert in Equal Opportunity Between Men and Women and Social Security Coordination in Europe.

Cristina Sánchez-Rodas Navarro. Author of Part IV. ORCID: 0000-0001-9780-7860

She is Full Professor of Labour and Social Security Law at the University of Sevilla (Spain), where she has developed her academic career since 1992. She has been a national expert in the Madame Curie Project financed by the European Commission ('Social Protection in Europe: Convergence, Integration, Accession and the Free Movement of Labour', 2001–2003), and in the European Commission project 'Organising and Training on Social Security' (TRESS, 2005–2012). She has participated as a speaker in the activities of a Cooperation and Twinning Project with the Republic of Slovakia, aimed at the training of officials of the higher bodies of the Slovak Administration in the rules of coordination of the social security regimes, to facilitate Slovakia's accession to the EU. She is a member of the group of sixteen independent experts created ad hoc in 2009 by the European Commission (Research Directorate General, European Research Area) to provide advice for the design and implementation of the Community Research Policy. She has managed several research projects related, among others, to the European coordination of social security systems, the illegal migrants in the EU, the social protection in Europe and the free movement of workers. She has more than a hundred publications in various languages (Spanish, German and English).

Olga Fotinopoulou Basurko. Co-author of Part V. ORCID: 0000-0002-0395-9933

She is Full Professor of Labour and Social Security Law at the Basque Country University/Universidad del País Vasco/Euskal Herriko Unibertsitatea (Spain). She is an expert in maritime labour law. She has published up to hundred contributions as books (as editor or unique author), book chapters and articles in different national and international labour and maritime journals in relation to a wide and complete field of knowledge in labour and social security law. She has attended and participated in national and international conferences in relation to different issues. She coordinates the transnational labour law and transport research group at the University of the Basque Country and has been Principal Investigator (PI) in several national projects. At this time, she coordinates the national coordinated project titled: 'Labour law responsibility to face climate change and the realization of a just transition from an integrated perspective of environmental impact'. She has extended experience regarding teaching in Spanish and European Universities in all the fields of law. She is also Founder and Member of the International Network Maritime Work Watch (MWW).

María Gorrochategui Polo. Co-author of Part V. ORCID: 0000-0001-7276-2977. She is a PhD student at the Basque Country University (UPV/EHU). She obtained a double degree in Spanish and French Law at both Complutense University of Madrid and Panthéon-Sorbonne University of Paris, Master in International Law and Master in Private Law from Carlos III University of Madrid. After several years of professional experience as labour adviser for a telco company and as labour lawyer in several law firms, she joined the university to write her thesis on 'Collective bargaining and international collective actions: the maritime industry as a paradigm for other land-based industries', under the supervision of Prof. Fotinopoulou Basurko. Her areas of research focus predominantly on labour law and particularly, on transnational labour relations' collective aspect. Member of different funding projects, since the beginning of her research activity, she is the author of some publications related to her research interests.

Cristina Aragón Gómez. Author of Part VI. ORCID: 0000-0003-0849-8299

She is Lecturer of Labour and Social Security Law at the National University of Distance Education. She obtained her degree in Law from the Complutense University of Madrid, Master's in Human Resource Management in the speciality of Labour Relations, Master's in Private Law and Doctor in Law from the Carlos III University of Madrid (recognized with the extraordinary doctorate award). She is the author of a monograph entitled *The Contributory Benefit of Social Security* (2013) and has published more than thirty collaborations in collective works and academic journals. Throughout her professional career, she has taught multiple training seminars for professionals and companies and has worked as labour relations technician for an insurance company and as a legal adviser for companies in the labour area of a law firm.

Daniel Pérez del Prado. Author of Part VII. ORCID: 0000-0001-7106-6769

He is Associate Professor at Carlos III University of Madrid, has PhD in Law (with honours), and is also an economist. He is the author of three books and several articles on different topics but frequently analysed from an interdisciplinary perspective. He is specialized in social law and labour economics. He has participated in national and international conferences and meetings, has taken part in a number of research projects, some of them of international scope and has carried out research stays at some of the most prestigious universities, such as the University of Cambridge, Aalborg University, Université Libre de Bruxelles, University of Ghent, Université de Lyon 2 – Lumière, University of Leuven (KU Leuven). He is a member of the research group 'Economic Changes, Labour Law and New Society (DTCENS)', the Institute for Law and Economics at University Carlos III, the

CIELO Community and the Labour Law Research Network. He is also an expert of the European Commission (EX2013D148731). Professor Perez del Prado has extensive experience of teaching in different areas of labour, employment and social security law, giving lectures for master and bachelor degrees and specialized seminars, in both Spanish and English.

María Arántzazu Vicente Palacio. Author of Part VIII. ORCID:0000-0002-6559-4386

She is Full Professor of Labour and Social Security Law at the Jaume I University of Castellón, to which she belongs as teaching and research staff since 1991. She has developed an intense research activity with more than eight monographs, and up to 200 academic contributions, including chapters of books and articles in journals specialized in the most diverse subjects of the extensive labour legal system. She is an expert in the social security system. Her principal lines of research, in addition to the social protection system, have been the study of temporary hiring, labour legal treatment of maritime labour; occupational risk prevention and collective bargaining. Recently, she has participated, as PI, in different research projects financed by public and private institutions. She is the co-author of several university textbooks in the field of labour law (ten editions), occupational risk prevention (three editions), trade union law (two editions), and social security law (two editions), among others. She has also taught in different doctoral and master's programmes. She was the Director of the Department of Labour Law and Social Security for more than ten years and Vice-Dean of Labour Relations for eight years. Currently, she is an external evaluator for various quality agencies, both in research and in the evaluation of university studies.

Carmen Jover Ramírez. Author of Part IX. ORCID: 0000-0001-7096-4487

She is Associate Professor of Labour Law and Social Security Law at the University of Cadiz. She holds a degree in Law from the University of Córdoba and a doctorate in Law from the University of Cádiz (2004). She is a researcher in different I+D+I Projects. Her scientific activity has been focused on gender, especially on 'work-life balance'; social protection; sanctioning of labour law and gig economy.

She has made some research stays in 2016 and 2017 at Hull University (UK); in 2005, at the Instituut Amsterdam for Advances Studies (University of Amsterdam); in 2009, at the University Autónoma of Asunción (Paraguay).

Co-authors

Table of Contents

List of Abbreviations

BOE	Boletín Oficial del Estado (Spanish Official State Gazette)
CB	Contribution Base
CBCC	Contribution Base for Common Contingencies
CCAA	Autonomous Communities
CPI	Consumer Price Index
EC	European Community
ECJ	European Court of Justice
EEA	European Economic Area
EES	European Employment Strategy
EU	European Union
FOGASA	Wage Guarantee Fund
GDP	Gross Domestic Product
GRT	Gross Registered Tonnage
GSSA	General Social Security Act, adopted by Royal Legislative Decree 8/2015 of 30 October
ILO	International Labour Organization
IMSERSO	Institute of Social Services and the Elderly
INE	Instituto Nacional de Estadística
INGESA	National Health Management Institute
INP	Instituto Nacional de Previsión
INSS	National Social Security Institute
IPREM	Public Indicator of Multiple Effect Income
IRPF	Personal Income Tax Regulation
ISFAS	Social Institute for the Armed Forces
ISM	Social Marine Institute
LJS	Law 36/2011 of 10 October, which regulates the Social Jurisdiction
LMP	Labour Market Policies
LPAD	Law 39/2006 of 14 December, on the promotion of personal autonomy and care for dependent persons

List of Abbreviations

LPGE	General State Budget Law
MCSS	Mutual Societies for Social Insurance
MISSM	Ministry of Inclusion, Social Security and Migrations
MLSE	Ministry of Labour and Social Economy
MO	Ministerial Order
MSCBS	Ministry of Health, Consumption and Social Welfare
MSRA2030	Ministry of Social Rights and Agenda 2030
MUFACE	Mutuality of Civil Servants of the State
MUGEJU	General Judicial Mutuality
MWW	Maritime Work Watch
NHSA	Royal Legislative Decree 16/2003 on Cohesion and Quality of the National Health System
OECD	Organisation for Economic Co-operation and Development
OL	Organic Law
PI	Principal Investigator
RAI	Active Insertion Income/*Renta Activa de Inserción*
RB	Regulatory Base
RD	Royal Decree
RD-Law	Royal Decree-Law
RETA	Special Scheme for Self-Employed Workers
RETM	Special Social Security Scheme for Seafarers
RPDA	Consolidated Text of the General Law on the Rights of Persons with Disabilities and Their Social Inclusion
SC	Spanish Constitution
SESS	Secretary of State for Social Security
SOVI	(extinguished) Compulsory Old Age and Invalidity Insurance
SPEE	National Public Employment Service
SPS	Public Health Service
STC	Spanish Constitutional Court Ruling
TGSS	General Treasury of the Social Security
TRADE	Self-Employed Economically Dependents/*Trabajadores autónomos económicamente dependientes*
UN	United Nations
VAT	Value Added Tax

General Introduction

Thais Guerrero Padrón

§1. General Background

1. The Spanish Social Security System is to some extent a hybrid public system, in which the influence of the classic Bismarck's and Beveridge's models is evident, although with a clear predominance of contributory over universal protection.

2. According to the General Social Security Act, adopted by Royal Legislative Decree 8/2015 of 30 October (hereinafter 'GSSA'), the contributory model of protection guarantees coverage to individuals who meet certain professional conditions of affiliation, registration and contribution periods.[1] In this way, its scope of application includes all Spanish citizens who reside in Spain and foreigners who reside or are legally in Spain, carrying out an activity in the national territory and being included in some of the following groups:

- employed workers who provide their services under the conditions established by Article 1(1) of the Workers' Statute, in the various branches of economic activity. They may be in an equivalent situation to them, whether temporarily depending on production requirements, temporary or full-time, even intermittent employment, and including remote workers; any case, irrespective of the workers' professional group, the kind and amount of the remuneration they receive, and the usual or special nature of the employment relationship;
- self-employed workers, whether owners of individual or family businesses, of over 18 years of age and that meet the requirements as expressly established in the Statute and in its implementation regulations;
- workers who are members of workers' cooperatives;
- students;
- civil and military state employees.[2]

3. There is also another non-contributory or assistance model, which tends to ensure sufficient benefits and assistance to prevent states of need when individuals are lacking (enough) income. This second level protects Spanish citizens and foreigners residing in Spanish territory (the latter, with 'legal residence'), who lack the

1. Published in Official State Gazette (Boletín Oficial del Estado) (hereinafter 'BOE') No. 261 of 31 Oct. 2015.
2. Article 7 of the GSSA.

common working conditions and meet the requirements of the non-contributory modality. It is clear that the level of this 'universal' protection is substantially lower than the aforementioned, or at least different in terms of economic content and social protection.

4. In addition to the protective action of social security, Social Services and social assistance complements the general protective action of social security. On one side, Social Services focus on elderly and people with disabilities protection. On the other, social assistance grants certain services or aids when the affected person lacks the indispensable resources to face special situations of need.

5. The Social Security System is based on a public dimension: the rights and obligations that give rise to the system are 'public', insofar as they originate from the Law and not from agreement between private citizens, and the system is 'public' too, insofar as it is entrusted to entities that are subordinated to the State.

6. Outside the statutory and compulsory social security, there are complementary, voluntary and private nature social protection, whose purpose is to provide workers with benefits intended to supplement the benefits provided by statutory social security schemes. This category includes both benefits of pension schemes and voluntary managing entities called *Mutualidades* as well as specific measures approved on collective agreements. It must be stressed that in no case can they replace the public benefits of social security schemes.

7. In its contributory modality, the Spanish Social Security System is structured into a General Scheme and different special schemes.

8. The General Scheme, regulated in Title II of GSSA, extends to the majority of employed workers in industry, services and agriculture. There is a uniform administrative treatment in this scheme relating to social protection (affiliation and termination of affiliation), with special economic features (contributions) typical of each group, category or position. This factor will result in a specific social protection economic level.

9. Some groups of employees, who were protected under special schemes in the past, have been integrated into the General Scheme so that they have now practically the same protective action as subjects included in its personal scope. Nonetheless, there could be differences related to registration, contribution and collection. This has recently been the case for domestic and agricultural employees. Their integration has been possible through the so-called 'Special Systems', which establish different rules for these groups in terms of affiliation, registration, contribution or collection.[3]

10. The integration mentioned above is a manifestation of the trend towards homogenization followed by Spanish social security, which will probably

3. Article 11 of the GSSA.

determine, in the near future, the protection of all workers by only two schemes: one for salaried workers and the other for self-employed workers.

11. There are special schemes in those professional activities in which, by their nature, their peculiar conditions of time and place, or by the character of their productive processes, such establishment is necessary for the adequate application of social security benefits.[4] Workers integrated into special schemes are governed by their own and different rules, and there is a tendency to approach the level of coverage of the General Scheme. To be more precise, special schemes are provided to cover the following groups:

- self-employed workers (Title IV of the GSSA);
- sea workers (Law 47/2015 of 21 October);
- students (Law of 17 July 1953);
- coal mining workers (Decree 298/1973 of 8 October);
- civil servants, in particular, of the State administration (Royal Legislative Decree 4/2000), the justice administration (Royal Legislative Decree 3/2000) and the military personnel (Royal Legislative Decree 1/2000).

12. Self-employed workers constitute an important group in social security, which participates in the same tendency to equate or approach the rules of the General Scheme. The activity they carry out, the effective working time and the level of their income probably justify a lower protective action on average than that of the General Scheme. Overall, the importance of this sector is generating an analysis of its situation and possible regulatory changes, where their specific circumstances of work must be evaluated. In this field, agricultural workers are a traditional group of self-employed workers. Since January 2008, they have been included in the Self-Employed Special Scheme through a 'special system' with regard to affiliation, registration, contribution or collection matters. They participate in the same problems as self-employed workers of industry and services, highlighting their particular level of income and their social contributions. These circumstances have a decisive influence on their level of social protection.

13. The Special Scheme for Sea Workers includes subjects, whether employees or self-employed workers, who perform sea fishing activities. Although there is a tendency towards a homogeneous regulation with the General Scheme, the nature of their activity, the 'technical' stoppages and other vicissitudes linked to the working environment determine important aspects of their registration to social security and contributions. In terms of benefits, there are some differences with respect to the General Scheme, for instance, regarding retirement pension.

14. Something similar occurs with the Special Coal Mining Regime, whose existence is justified by the historical relevance of this productive sector in the Spanish economy, although, at present, its permanence responds to political factors. This scheme is a sample of privileged social protection.

4. Article 10 of the GSSA.

15. With regard to civil servants, they have historically consolidated specific norms of social protection, probably because of the 'public' nature of the employer (the State), which has also caused certain restrictions in fields as diverse as access, promotion, remuneration, collective bargaining, union integration, strike and other aspects that justify those differences. The trend towards their integration into the General Regime has been evident since 2011 so that new civil servants entering the public sector will join the General Scheme. This integration is relative since now it only affects the pension branch, but not other benefits such as healthcare, social services and other economic benefits managed by their own managing entities (*Mutualidades*).

16. Lastly, the students' social security, with its own regulations and the absence of any type of work and contribution connection, evidences the universality of the Spanish Social Security System.

17. In its general guidelines, the protective action of social security guarantees the receipt of benefits when the specific requirements for their recognition are met. Depending on the benefit concerned, the responsibility for their payment falls on the Managing Bodies and the Partners Entities.

18. The Social Security System is administered by the public authorities through Managing Bodies, such as the National Social Security Institute (INSS), the Social Marine Institute (ISM), the Institute of Social Services and the Elderly (IMSERSO), the National Public Employment Service (SPEE) and the National Health Management Institute (INGESA). This does not prevent a specific partnership of individuals in the management of certain matters, such as the Mutual Societies for Social Insurance (*Mutuas Colaboradoras con la Seguridad Social*, hereinafter 'MCSS') and the companies themselves.

19. The management of economic aspects falls on the responsibility of the General Treasury of the Social Security (TGSS). In essence, its patrimony is financed by contributions from workers and employers, and the progressive contributions of the State, which are allocated permanently in the general budgets. Other sources are the amounts collected in concept of surcharges, fines or similar, and the income, earnings or interest and any other product of its heritage resources.

§2. Historical Background

20. Associating the birth and evolution of social security with labour law is a common phenomenon that allows us to understand its precarious appearance, unstoppable development and decisive consolidation. The evolution of work systems, mainly during the nineteenth century, the workers' movement, mechanization and trade union strength, contributed to the birth of an incipient social security, prompted by the International Labour Organization (ILO) conventions and a clear humanitarian sense.

21. Going further the precarious formulas of solidarity (workers' aid, mutual help, brotherhoods, beneficence), the starting point of the current configuration of social security in Spain is the Social Reforms Commission of 1883, which is dedicated to the study of the improvement and welfare of the working class.

22. The first social insurance regulated in Spain is the Act on Accidents at Work (1900).[5] A lack of knowledge of the new means and instruments of manufacturing caused a multiplication of accidents at work that this Act intended to prevent and alleviate. Since then, the employer is responsible for the damages (death or disability) that occur in his factory or industry, although the voluntary nature of this social insurance is going to limit the effective protection against accidents at work. Maritime and agriculture sectors granted this protection in 1919 and 1932 respectively. From 1932, insurance against accidents at work will be compulsory.

23. The ageing of the labour force, the death and survival benefits, sickness protection and other precarious forms of social protection, including basic protection against unemployment, would give rise in our country to the configuration of the so-called 'Unified Social Insurance', as an integrating project of social protection.

24. With regard to instrumental evolution, in 1903 the Social Reforms Institute appeared as the driving force in the area of social protection, and in 1908, the Ministry of Labour was created. The latter granted specific powers in this area to the new National Welfare Institute (*Instituto Nacional de Previsión,* hereinafter 'INP'), with functions of research, administration and social protection, and specifically the mission of managing the social insurances introduced as compulsory in industry and agriculture.

25. In this way, social insurances are gradually appearing, covering different risks: in 1919, the *Retiro Obrero* (old-age pensions); in 1929, the Maternity Insurance; in 1938, the Family Subsidy; in 1939, the Old-Age Subsidy; in 1942, the Compulsory Health Insurance; in 1946, the Family Plus; and in 1947, the Compulsory Old Age and Invalidity Insurance (called *SOVI*) and the Professional Illness Insurance. Specific groups joined the social insurance schemes, such as agricultural workers (1943), sea workers (1941), students (1953) and domestic workers (1944). In 1955, the Old Age, Invalidity and Death Insurance was merged (1955), and in 1961, a basic National Unemployment Insurance was created.

26. The social insurances managed by the INP provided minimum protection to workers that justified the appearance of the *Mutualismo Laboral*, which is a form of complementary protection on a corporate-professional basis, managed by the *Mutualidades Laborales*, whose regulation was approved in 1954. Additionally, special protection created for civil servants called *Mutualismo Administrativo* was introduced, as well as other non-integrated mutual aid societies (*Mutualidades* and *Montepíos*) for certain professional groups.

5. Published by Gazette of Madrid No. 31 of 31 Jan. 1900.

27. The evolution of the protective action of social security is reinforced when social insurances are unified (invalidity, old age, maternity, sickness and death) and when accidents at work insurance become compulsory. In this project, the right of everyone to social security enshrined in the Universal Declaration of Human Rights (1948) and the messages of ILO Convention No. 102 concerning minimum standards of social security (1952) encourage governments to an updated review of social protection.

28. In Spain, the Social Security Bases Act (1963) constituted a milestone in this process.[6] It began an integrated planning of the different aspects that intervene in social protection. Its guidelines, according to the Law, were as follows:

- tendency towards unity;
- the participation of stakeholders in the governance of management bodies;
- the suppression of the possible profit motive;
- a joint consideration of protected situations or contingencies;
- transformation of the financial regime;
- an accentuation of the State's participation in sustaining the system;
- preferential concern for recovery and rehabilitation services.

29. The implementation of the latter took place through the Social Security Act of 1966[7] and its development, undergoing relevant reforms. The most significant was the Act 24/1972 of 21 June, on the Financing and Improvement of the General Scheme of the Social Security,[8] which introduced important modifications in terms of contributions for all contingencies, setting a maximum and minimum contribution limit for all professional categories. This regulation gave way to the Decree 2065/1974, approving the first Codified Text of the GSSA.[9] Notwithstanding, important new reforms were carried out later.

30. Royal Decree-Law (RD-Law) 36/1978 on the Institutional Management of Social Security, Health and Employment[10] implied the extinction of the INP and the '*Mutualidades Laborales*', and created the managing entities of social security, which were dedicated to managing the social security benefits. Thus, the INSS handled the economic benefits of the system, the National Health Institute managed health services and the IMSERSO managed complementary services for the social security benefits. The sea workers had a specific entity called ISM to manage their benefits and services. To culminate this period, the Spanish Constitution of 1978 (hereinafter 'SC')[11] incorporated certain contents related to social security that have influenced the evolution of the system towards a universal model of social protection.

6. Act 193/1963 of 28 December, Published in BOE No. 312 of 30 Dec. 1963.
7. Decree 907/1966 of 21 Apr. 1966, approving the first text of Law 193/1963 of 28 Dec. 1963 on Social Security Bases, BOE No. 96 of 22 Apr. 1966.
8. BOE No. 149 of 22 Jun. 1972.
9. BOE No. 173 of 20 Jul. 1974.
10. BOE No. 276 of 18 Nov. 1978.
11. BOE No. 311 of 29 Dec. 1978.

31. If the objective in the 1970s was to improve and extend protection measures, in the 1980s and mid-1990s, the protection was conditioned by the economic context. In fact, increasing public spending and guaranteeing the future viability of social security requires further reforms. Changes in the rules for calculating pensions, reinforcing their professional and contributory nature, were set up. Other reforms were settled as the automatic revaluation of pensions at the beginning of each financial year, based on the Consumer Price Index (hereinafter 'CPI'). The new General Health Act 14/1986 of 25 April extended healthcare to all citizens, while non-contributory old-age and disability pensions, family protection benefits and social services were established under Law 26/1990 of 20 December, on non-contributory social security benefits.[12] Finally, the process of homogenization of social security systems began, disappearing some special schemes. Employees covered by these schemes were integrated into the General Scheme (as railwaymen, footballers, commercial representatives, artists and bullfighters), and those who were self-employed did so under the Special Scheme for Self-Employed Workers (RETA) (book writers). These and other reforms led to the enactment of Royal Legislative Decree 1/1994 of 20 June, the second Codified Text of the GSSA.[13]

32. In the second half of the 1990s and beyond, there was an expansion of the personal and material scope of the Social Security System, improving its quality. The process of homogenization continues with the disappearance of the special schemes for agriculture and domestic employees, and their integration into the main two schemes aforementioned.

33. The economic crisis at the end of the first decade of the twenty-first century and especially the serious problem of the ageing of the population have originated the revision and readjustment of rules. Important reforms are being carried out, mainly affecting pensions and unemployment protection. The contribution has been intensified, and the requirements for access to benefits, the calculation of their amount and the setting of their duration have been tightened. This process has culminated with the publication of Royal Legislative Decree 8/2015 of 30 October, which approved the (third and current) Codified Text of the GSSA. The regulation in force updated and amended previous regulations.

§3. Sources of Social Security Law

I. General

34. The legal system of Spanish social security is made up of international and domestic rules. In a wide sense, the first category includes, on the one side, regulations, directives and decisions of the European Union (EU) in the field of social

12. BOE No. 102 of 29 Apr. 1986 and BOE No. 306 of 22 Dec. 1990, respectively.
13. BOE No. 154 of 29 Jun. 1994.

security, binding Spain as a Member State of the EU. On the other, numerous bilateral and multilateral conventions have been ratified by Spain, having in consequence legal effects. Conventions of the United Nations (UN), the Council of Europe, the ILO,[14] the Ibero-American scope and others are in this situation.

35. Domestic sources are governed by rules of legal rank (Organic Laws (OL), Laws, Legislative Decrees and Decree-Laws) and implementing Regulations (Decrees, Royal Decrees and Ministerial Orders (MOs)). Over them, the SC takes up a prominent position as the fundamental law of our legal system.

36. Several Articles of the SC refer to social security, for instance, Article 25.2 (appropriate social security for inmates), Article 39(1) (social and economic protection of the family), Article 43 (the right to health protection), Article 49 (services for the physically, sensorially and mentally handicapped) and Article 50 (adequate pensions and social services for the elderly). Undoubtedly, the main one is Article 41, which states:

> The public authorities shall maintain a public Social Security system for all citizens, which will guarantee adequate social assistance and benefits in situations of hardship, especially in cases of unemployment. Supplementary assistance and benefits shall be optional.

37. Article 41 of the SC is a governing principle of economic and social policy, which enshrines a social security model of a remarkable assistance character. Nevertheless, it does not enshrine a 'constitutional social security right'. This way, the legislator has a wide margin of action in the conformation and development of the Social Security System. It may explain its current contributory character, although it is evolving towards a universal or assistance model.

II. Legislation

38. The Spanish Social Security System is affected by continuous reforms justified by the economic and social context, which may alter its content. The economic precariousness in employment, the ageing of the population and unemployment rates are some of the issues addressed by rules of precise social objectives, which inevitably interfere with the general lines, structure and protective action of GSSA. Examples of recent reforms are the RD-Law 28/2018 of 28 December, on the Revaluation of Public Pensions and Other Urgent Social, Labour and Employment Measures, and Law 3/2019 of 1 March, on the Improvement of the Situation of Orphanhood of the Daughters and Sons of Victims of Gender-Based Violence and Other Forms of Violence Against Women.[15] In addition, it should be noted that it has become habitual for annual General Budget Acts to make

14. ILO conventions ratified by Spain: https://www.ilo.org/dyn/normlex/en/f?p=NORMLEXPUB:11200:0::NO::P11200_COUNTRY_ID:102847 (accessed 30 Jul. 2019).
15. BOE No. 314 of 29 Dec. 2018 and BOE No. 53 of 2 Mar. 2019, respectively.

adjustments in social security regulations. For instance, Law 6/2018 of 3 July on the General State Budget for 2018 has included new provisions on paternity leave or unemployment protection, among others.[16]

39. In spite of this, the current GSSA continues to be the basic reference regulation. In essence, the GSSA contains the general rules of the system, which are common to all social security schemes (Title I). It develops in detail the General Regime (Title II) and the Special Regime for Self-Employed Workers (Title IV). It also included the unemployment protection for employed workers (Title III) and the 'cessation of activity', which is the unemployment for self-employed workers (Title V). Finally, GSSA regulates non-contributory benefits (Title VI).

40. Notwithstanding the rules mentioned in each specific Part of this book, the significant laws are as follows:

- RD-Law 36/1978 on Institutional Management of Social Security, Health and Employment.[17]
- Law 14/1986 of 25 April, on General Health.
- Law 26/1990 of 20 December, on Non-Contributory Social Security Benefits.
- Law 16/2003 of 28 May, on the Cohesion and Quality of the National Health System.[18]
- Law 39/2006 of 14 December, on Promotion of Personal Autonomy and Care for Dependent Persons.[19]
- Law 40/2007 of 4 December, on Social Security Measures.[20]
- Organic Law 4/2000 of 11 January, on the Rights and Freedoms of Foreigners in Spain and Their Social Integration.[21]
- Law 27/2011 of 1 August, on Updating, Adaptation and Modernisation of the Social Security System.[22]
- Law 36/2011 of 10 October, on Social Jurisdiction.[23]
- Royal Legislative Decree 1/2013 of 29 November, approving the Consolidated Text of the General Law on the Rights of Persons with Disabilities and Their Social Inclusion.[24]
- Law 47/2015 of 21 October, on Social Protection for Maritime-Fishing Sector Workers.[25]
- Royal Legislative Decree 3/2015 of 23 October, Approving the Codified Text of the Employment Act.[26]

16. BOE No. 161 of 4 Jul. 2018.
17. BOE No. 276 of 18 Nov. 1978.
18. BOE No. 128 of 29 May 2003.
19. BOE No. 299 of 15 Dec. 2006.
20. BOE No. 291 of 5 Dec. 2007.
21. BOE No. 10 of 12 Jan. 2000.
22. BOE No. 184 of 2 Aug. 2011.
23. BOE No. 245 of 11 Oct. 2011.
24. BOE No. 289 of 3 Dec. 2013.
25. BOE No. 253 of 22 Oct. 2015.
26. BOE No. 255 of 24 Oct. 2015.

III. Regulations

41. Regulations are rules issued by the competent authority to develop the laws in order to allow their enforcement. These have the form of Royal Decrees of the Government (RD) or are MOs issued by the corresponding ministry (MO). In the field of social security, there are a large number of regulations. The matters regulated by some of them have been incorporated into the current legal text (GSSA of 2015), as the social security of self-employed workers or certain aspects of the management and administration of social security.

42. Some important regulations on the field of social security are the following:

- RD 84/1996 of 26 January, Approving the General Regulations on Registration and Affiliation of Companies and Registration of Employees, and Deregistration, and Amendments to Their Details Relating to Social Security.[27]
- RD 2064/1995 of 22 December, Approving the General Regulations on Contribution and Payment of Other Social Security Charges.[28]
- RD 1415/2004 of 11 June, Approving the General Regulations on Collection of Social Security Contributions.[29]
- RD 1192/2012 of 3 August, on the Status of Insured Person and Beneficiary for the Purposes of Health Care in Spain, Charged to Public Funds, Through the National Health System.[30]

43. With regard to benefits, the most significant regulations are as follows:

Temporary Incapacity:

MO of 13 October 1967.[31]
RD 625/2014 of 18 July, on Certain Aspects of the Management and Control of Processes for Temporary Incapacity in the First 365 Days of Duration.[32]
RD 1430/2009 of 11 September, on the Development of Law 40/2007 on Temporary Incapacity.[33]

Permanent Disability:

MO of 15 April 1969.[34]
RD 1300/1995 of 21 July, on the Development of Law 42/1994 in the Field of Incapacity for Work.[35]
MO of 18 January 1996, on the Development of Royal Decree

27. BOE No. 50 of 27 Feb. 1996.
28. BOE No. 22 of 25 Jan. 1996.
29. BOE No. 153 of 25 Jun. 2004.
30. BOE No. 186 of 4 Aug. 2012.
31. BOE No. 264 of 4 Nov. 1967.
32. BOE No. 176 of 21 Jul. 2014.
33. BOE No. 235 of 29 Sep. 2009.
34. BOE No. 110 of 8 May 1969.
35. BOE No. 198 of 19 Aug. 1995.

1300/1995.[36]

RD 1971/1999 of 23 December, on Recognition of the Degree of Disability, modified by RD 1169/2003 of 12 September.[37]

Old-Age Pension:

MO of 18 January 1967.[38]

RD 1131/2002 of 31 October, on Gradual and Flexible Retirement.[39]

RD 383/2008 of 14 March, on Reduction Coefficients for Firefighters' Retirement.[40]

RD 1851/2009 of 4 December, on the Retirement of Workers Affected by Disability.[41]

Survivors' Pension:

MO of 13 February 1967.[42]

RD 1465/2001 of 27 December, on Modification of Survivors' Benefits.[43]

RD 296/2009 of 6 March, Amending Some Aspects of Survivors' Benefits.[44]

Family Benefits:

RD 1335/2005 of 11 November, on the Development of Law 26/1990 on Non-Contributory Benefits.[45]

RD 1368/2000 of 19 July, on Lump-Sum Cash Benefits for the Birth of a Third or Successive Child and for Multiple Births.[46]

Maternity, paternity, risk during pregnancy and risk during breastfeeding:

RD 295/2009 of 6 March, Regulating the Economic Benefits of the Social Security System for Maternity, Paternity, Risk During Pregnancy and Risk During Breastfeeding.[47]

Care of children who are hospitalized with cancer or serious disease:

RD 1148/2011 of 29 July.[48]

Unemployment:

RD 625/1985 of 2 April, Implementing Law 31/1984 of 2 August, on Unemployment Protection.[49]

36. BOE No. 23 of 26 Jan. 1996.
37. BOE No. 22 of 26 Jan. 2000.
38. BOE No. 22 of 26 Jan. 1967.
39. BOE No. 284 of 27 Nov. 2002.
40. BOE No. 81 of 3 Apr. 2008.
41. BOE No. 307 of 22 Dec. 2009.
42. BOE No. 46 of 23 Feb. 1967.
43. BOE No. 313 of 31 Dec. 2001.
44. BOE No. 69 of 21 Mar. 2009.
45. BOE No. 279 of 22 Nov. 2005.
46. BOE No. 181 of 29 de julio de 2000.
47. BOE No. 69 of 21 Mar. 2009.
48. BOE No. 182 of 30 Jul. 2011.
49. BOE No. 109 of 7 May 1985.

RD 426/2003 of 11 April, on Agricultural Income.[50]
RD 200/2006 of 17 February, Amending Certain Aspects of the Management and Control of Unemployment Benefits.[51]

Permanent non-disabling injuries:

MO of 15 April 1969.[52]
Order ESS/66/2013 of 28 January, Updating the Amounts for Risks Materialised from 1 January 2013.[53]

Non-Contributory Benefits:

RD 357/1991 of 15 March, Implementing, in Respect of Non-Contributory Pensions, Law 26/1990 of 20 December, Establishing Non-contributory Social Security Benefits.[54]
RD 1400/2007 of 29 October, on Supplements to Non-Contributory Benefits for Residents in Rented Housing.[55]

IV. Adjudication

44. The wide, various social security regulations, and their concurrence with other matters, especially those related to labour, often give rise to interpretation problems that require a unitary and legal decision. The structure of our judicial network, in terms of awareness of conflicts arising in the field of social security, is organized into Social Courts and Social Chambers of the Superior Courts of Justice, the National Court and the Supreme Court. The latter is the highest body of our judicial system and the promoter of case law.

45. In Spain, case law is not a formal source of law. Notwithstanding, the Civil Code highlights the value of the Supreme Court's case law as a complement to the legal system.[56] Its notion is referred to the doctrine repeatedly upheld by the Supreme Court in its interpretation and application of statutes.[57]

46. In the field of social security, case law is a high-value interpretative instrument that assists in clearing up numerous legal questions of confusing regulation or interpretation. Sometimes, conflicts may arise from a simple material analysis of a physical or administrative evidentiary fact that, in general, clarifies the controversial question (e.g., issues of waiting period, age of the interested party, Contribution Bases (CBs), responsible entity or person, and similar cases). When more serious conflicts appear, as related to the management of social security or its protective action, the solution is not always uniform and regular, being necessary the case law

50. BOE No. 88 of 12 Apr. 2003.
51. BOE No. 53 of 3 Mar. 2006.
52. BOE No. 110 of 8 May 1969.
53. BOE No. 26 of 30 Jan. 2013.
54. BOE No. 69 of 21 Mar. 1991.
55. BOE No. 260 of 30 Oct. 2007.
56. Civil Code, published by Gazette of Madrid No. 206 of 25 Jul. 1889.
57. Article 6(1) of the Civil Code.

intervention. Therefore, the case law of the Supreme Court guides the solution of conflicts promoted in identical situations and binds the lower courts. Thus, if their sentences deviate from the doctrine established by the Supreme Court, such action justifies the challenge of those sentences.

47. In addition to the jurisprudence of the SC, doctrine of the Constitutional Court must be highlighted. Its function is of a different nature, as long as, on the one hand, it exclusively interprets the precepts and principles of the Constitution that affect fundamental rights and public freedoms. On the other hand, the Constitutional Court may order the elimination from the legal system of illegal or unconstitutional rules.

V. Labour Agreements

48. Based on the free autonomy of the parties, Article 85(1) of the Spanish Workers' Statute establishes that 'In compliance with the law, collective agreements may regulate matters of an economic, labour and trade union nature and, in general, any other matters that affect the conditions of employment and the scope of relations of the workers and their representative organisations with the employer and the business associations … .'[58] This is not the case with social security law, which is characterized as a branch of public law, in which collective and individual autonomy does not have the same recognition.

49. Article 3 of the GSSA states:

> Any agreement, individual or collective, by which the worker renounces the rights conferred by the present law, shall be null and void.

50. In addition, Article 43(1) of the GSSA states that 'The contributory modality of the protective action that the social security system grants to persons covered by Article 7(1) may be voluntarily improved … ,' and its paragraph (2) adds, 'With no exception other than the establishment of voluntary improvements, in accordance with the provisions of the previous section, social security may not be the object of collective bargaining.'

51. In consequence, collective agreement is not a source of social security law, but it is situated in the complementary social protection, i.e., outside the statutory and compulsory social security system. Therefore, collective agreements can introduce voluntary improvements in social security benefits, but not replace them.[59]

52. In collective bargaining, there is a progressive increase in measures (benefits or indemnities) complementary to those generally provided for in the Social

58. Workers' Statute, approved by Royal Legislative Decree 2/2015 of 23 October, BOE No. 255 of 24 Oct. 2015.
59. Article 43 of the GSSA.

Security System. Typical voluntary improvements usually consist of additional compensation in situations of healthcare and in matters of temporary incapacity, maternity or paternity and risk during pregnancy. They are also lump-sum settlements in terms of permanent disability (variable according to the degree of incapacity), widowhood and orphanhood, and in certain cases, of early retirement. Finally, collective agreements often include life insurance of variable content, taken out with an insurance company and financed by the employer as an insurer.

Part I. The Institutions

María Isabel Ribes Moreno

Chapter 1. Introduction

53. In Spain, social security is public and its management is owned by the State, as provided by the SC. Therefore, the Spanish Social Security System requires public protective action for all citizens.[60] In this sense, the GSSA set out that the State is committed to establishing 'the ordination, jurisdiction and inspection of the social security'.[61]

54. The current organizational system parameters are contained in RD-Law 36/1978 on Institutional Management of Social Security, Health and Employment, which simplified and rationalized the system. Thus, the management is carried out in accordance with a decentralized system of functions entrusted to different management bodies, attributed to different Ministries such as the Ministry of Inclusion, Social Security and Migrations (MISSM), the Ministry of Labour and Social Economy (MLSE), the Ministry of Social Rights and Agenda 2030 (MSRA2030) and the Ministry of Health, Consumption and Social Welfare (MSCBS). The development of the legal regime of management of social security is articulated around the managing entities, created to carry out the management and administration of the benefits granted by the social security, assisted and supplemented by the so-called common services and the collaborating entities.[62]

55. The SC sets out that the State is responsible for 'basic legislation and the financial framework of the social security, without prejudice to the implementation of its services by the Autonomous Communities'. Furthermore, the SC also allows the Autonomous Communities (hereinafter 'CCAA') to assume powers regarding social assistance and health and hygiene, as provided in its Article 148(1)17) and 148(1)20) and 148(1)21).

56. Finally, although the design of social security management is public, the regulations do not expressly prohibit the participation of private parties. Notwithstanding, the Law expressly prohibits the organization of social security to serve as

60. Article 41 of the SC.
61. Article 4.1 of the GSSA.
62. Articles 66–102 of the GSSA.

a basis for commercial profit-making operations.[63] Therefore, this private intervention is materialized through collaborating entities, such as mutual collaborators with social security or non-profit companies, acting in the management of the public social security service, specifically for concrete benefits. Additionally, voluntary improvements in the protective action of the General Social Security Scheme may be established by employers.[64] In this case, the management may have been assumed by the company, or by the management entities of the social security, Labour Foundations, *Montepíos* or mutual benefit societies or insurance entities of any kind, although these functions are in Spain completely residual.

§1. Ministerial Departments

57. Even though all competencies on labour and social security matters have been traditionally assumed by a single Ministry, the current Government attributed part of its functions into two, the MLSE, for labour and employment matters, and the MISSM. The main functions related to the management of social security are performed by the MISSM. The MISSM assumes the State competences of management that means the supreme direction of the administrative management of social security.[65]

58. The administrative body responsible for the development of these functions is the Secretary of State for Social Security (hereinafter 'SESS') and Pensions. It is the highest body of the department under the control of the MISSM. The SESS manages and supervises the Managing Bodies and Common Services of the Social Security and supports and manages the Social Security legal department. The SESS also promotes and directs the legal management, planning, economic and financial analysis of the Social Security System, and the direction and coordination of the management of financial resources and social security expenses, as well. Finally, it plans and supervises the management carried out by the social security collaborating bodies.

59. The Managing Bodies attached to the MISSM through the SESS and Pensions are: the INSS and the common services, as the TGSS, the Legal Service of the Social Security Administration and the Information Technology Management of the Social Security. The ISM, also attached to the MISSM, is the Managing Body of the Special Social Security Scheme for sea workers. Furthermore, the SPEE is attached to the MLSE, and the administrative body responsible for its functions is the Secretary of State for Employment and Social Economy.[66]

---

63. Article 4.3 of the GSSA.
64. Article 79.2 of the GSSA.
65. The basic organizational structure of MISSM are provided in Royal Decree 497/2020, of 28 April (BOE No. 121 of 1 May 2020).
66. Royal Decree 499/2020 of 28 April, modifying and developing the Organic Structure of the MLSE (BOE No. 121 of 1 May 2020).

60. Nonetheless, as a consequence of the autonomy of healthcare and services, these benefits have been assigned to another ministerial department. Consequently, although the GSSA includes healthcare in its protective action, it does not include regulations about its organization. Thus, the MSCBS is the one that holds the competences on this protective action having a managing entity for this purpose.[67]

61. The management body attached to the MSCBS has less importance due to the transfer of functions to the CCAA. It is the INGESA attached to the Ministry through the General Secretariat for Health.

62. After the Ministry restructuring due to the current Government, the MSRA2030 assumes the functions of attention to the Dependency and Disability. The IMSERSO is attached to the Ministry to that purpose through the State Secretariat of Social Services.[68]

63. Eventually, the specific schemes for civil servants are administered by special public organizations. These management bodies are in charge of the so-called External Special Regimes, such as the Mutuality of Civil Servants of the State (MUFACE), the Social Institute for the Armed Forces (ISFAS) and the General Judicial Mutuality (MUGEJU), linked to other ministries related to their competencies.[69]

§2. CCAA'S COMPETENCES

64. Article 147(1)7) of the SC sets out that the State is responsible for basic legislation and the financial framework of social security. Nevertheless, the CCAA can intervene in its management by developing the basic legislation and assuming its implementation as stated in the SC. Notwithstanding, the intervention in the management of social security by the CCAA is limited.[70] Some Statutes of Autonomy incorporate certain competences, but in practice, the State assumes all of them.

65. Moreover, the SC granted the CCAA competence regarding health and social protection.[71] Most of the competences related to healthcare are transferred to the CCAA, which exercises them through their health services.[72] Similarly, the CCAA

67. Royal Decree 1087/2003 of 29 August, establishing the Organic Structure of the Ministry of Health and Consumer Affairs (BOE No. 208 of 30 Aug. 2003).
68. The Organic Structure of the Ministry of Social Rights and Agenda 2030 is set out in Royal Decree 452/2020 of 10 March (BOE No. 63 of 12 Mar. 2020).
69. With regard to its ministerial relationship, the General Mutual Fund of Civil Servants of the State is dependent on the Ministry of Public Administrations; the Social Institute of the Armed Forces is attached to the Ministry of Defence and the General Judicial Mutuality to the Ministry of Justice.
70. Limited to the management of non-contributory benefits for disability and retirement.
71. Article 148(1)21) and 148(1)20) of the SC.
72. With the exception of the autonomous cities of Ceuta and Melilla, which competences are not transferred and they continue with the State healthcare.

has a prominent role regarding social protection and social services, assuming the management of welfare benefits, the integration of people with disabilities, the social services for the elderly, etc.

Chapter 2. Public Institutions

66. Therefore, the management and administration of the Social Security System in Spain has a concrete formula of organization, with several management entities and common services. They are state entities of public law, with legal capacity for the fulfilment of their purposes, since they have their own legal personality, with a specialized autonomous administrative organization and their own budget.[73]

67. The management entities are attached to the respective ministerial departments, as referred by Article 66 of the GSSA, which provides that:

> The management and administration of social security shall be carried out, under the direction and supervision of the respective ministerial departments, subject to the principles of simplification, rationalization, cost savings, financial solidarity and cash unit, social efficiency and decentralization (…).

The managing entities are the following:

- the INSS;
- the INGESA;
- the IMSERSO;
- the SPEE;
- the ISM;
- the MUFACE, ISFAS and MUGEJU.

68. Just as was stated earlier, some of the managing entities, such as the INSS, the INGESA, the IMSERSO and the SPEE, deal with issues arising from the General Regime. Other entities have the function of managing some special regimes, such as the Special Regime of sea workers that are articulated through the ISM. Similarly, the different bodies of civil servants manage their own special external regimes, which are not included in the GSSA. They are set out in the Act 6/1997 of 14 April, on the Organization and Functioning of the Administration.[74]

69. On the other hand, there are certain organizations that are considered common services, since they manage common functions to the different management entities. Traditionally, the TGSS has been the only one that provides these common services. However, nowadays, there are two more common services such as the Social Security Information Technology Management and the Social Security Legal Service.

70. Nevertheless, regarding the problem generated due to the decentralized regime in different managing entities to the citizens, the aforementioned Act 27/2011[75] set out an institutional change in the organization. Thus, in order to

73. The legal regime applicable to the management entities is regulated in the Additional Provision No. 13 of the Act 40/2015 of 1 October of Legal Regime of the Public Sector.
74. BOE No. 90 of 15 Apr. 1997.
75. Additional Provision No. 7.

improve and simplify the demands of citizens, the Government was authorized to create the so-called State Agency for Social Security Administration. The purpose of the Agency was to carry out, on behalf of the State, the management and effective application of the Social Security System. The Agency should have managed the affiliation, quotation, collection, payment and management of economic benefits, excepting those to unemployment coverage. Once the Agency had been created, it would have integrated some management entities and common services such as the INSS, ISM, TGSS, the ISM, computer management and the legal service of the social security. Unfortunately, after the entry into force of the Act 40/2015 of 1 October, on the Legal Regime of the Public Sector,[76] the constitution of the Agency was put on hold. Nevertheless, the third final provision of Law 21/2021 of 28 December,[77] guaranteeing the purchasing power of pensions and other measures to strengthen the financial and social sustainability of the public pension system, reinitiated the process of setting up the Agency.

§1. Management of Social and Welfare Benefits

I. National Social Security Institute

71. The INSS is the most important management body in the Spanish Social Security System. RD 2583/1996, 13 November, and subsequent amendments govern its regime of organization and functions.[78] Overall, the INSS assumes the management and administration of the economic benefits of the public social security system, except for non-contributory disability and retirement pensions and for unemployment.[79] In this case, the INSS recognizes and controls the right to the contributory economic benefits of the Social Security System (such as retirement, permanent disability, death and survival,[80] temporary disability, birth and childcare benefits, risk during pregnancy and risk during breastfeeding, caring for minors affected by cancer or another serious illness, economic compensation for permanent non-disabling injuries and school insurance) and of non-contributory economic benefits (per child or dependent minor; birth or adoption of a child, large families, single-parent families and in cases of disabled mothers; and for multiple births). Recently, it has also assumed the management of the minimum vital income, notwithstanding the collaboration of the CCAA and local entities, under the corresponding agreements.[81] Additionally, it assumes the recognition and control of status as an insured person and beneficiary, whether as a holder, relative or beneficiary, for the purpose of healthcare coverage, and the management of the Special Mutual Insurance Fund for social security civil servants.

76. BOE No. 236 of 2 Oct. 2015.
77. BOE No. 312 of 29 Dec. 2021.
78. BOE No. 3 of 3 Jan. 1997.
79. Attributed to the IMSERSO or to the Services of the CCAA when transferred. The unemployment is assumed by the SPEE. Article 66 of the GSSA.
80. Widowhood, orphanhood, in favour of relatives and death grant.
81. Law 19/2021 of 20 December, establishing the minimum vital income (BOE No. 304 of 21 Dec. 2021).

72. Accordingly, the INSS carries out the management and operation of the Register of Public Social Services.[82] However, this Register, which integrates public social benefits of an economic nature aimed at individuals or families, is being replaced by the Universal Social Card. It will systematize all information on public social benefits – contributory, non-contributory and welfare – of economic content, financed from public resources that citizens receive managed by the General State Administration, CCAA, local and other entities. The public administrations, entities and public bodies responsible for the management of public social benefits of economic content that have been incorporated into the Universal Social Card are obliged to provide the INSS with updated information, and the recognition of the right to healthcare.

73. Other duties, among others, assigned by regulations are:[83] internationally, the participation in negotiating and executing international social security agreements, as well as membership of associations and international organisms.

II. National Health Management System

74. This management body assumes competences related to health services, in accordance with the provisions of RD 840/2002 of 2 August.[84]

75. Its functions consist of the administration and management of health services. However, since the assignment of competences on these issues to the CCAA has taken place, public entities have been set up in their territories to carry out the management and INGESA functions on this matter are residual. Nowadays, INGESA only assumes the management of health services in Ceuta and Melilla.

76. However, given the existence of different Public Health Services (SPSs) in the different CCAA, INGESA performs coordination functions and the aforementioned activities related to health interests of the State or higher than the CCAA, as well as the activities that are necessary for the normal operation of its services.

III. Institute of Social Services and the Elderly

77. As with the INGESA, the IMSERSO maintains merely residual functions. Its regulations are currently in RD 1226/2005, 13 October,[85] which establishes the organizational structure and functions of the Institute for the Elderly and Social Services.

---

82. Article 72 of the GSSA.
83. Article 1 RD 2583/1996. A complete information about the powers of the INSS: http://www.seg-social.es/wps/portal/wss/internet/Conocenos/QuienesSomos/29413?changeLanguage=en (accessed 15 Dec. 2023).
84. Royal Decree 840/2002 of 2 August, Modifying and Developing the Basic Organic Structure of the Ministry of Health and Consumer Affairs, published by BOE No. 185 of 3 Aug. 2002.
85. This standard has been modified by Royal Decree 1434/2008, to update the composition of the General Council of this management entity (BOE No. 211 of 1 Sep. 2008).

78. The functions assumed by the IMSERSO are the management of non-contributory disability and retirement pensions and the complementary services of the Social Security System benefits, both for the elderly and dependants.[86] Nevertheless, the management of the non-contributory benefits for disability and retirement, and those related to the dependency, have been transferred to the CCAA. Therefore, nowadays, only the benefits corresponding to the autonomous cities of Ceuta and Melilla remain under the responsibility of IMSERSO.

79. In conjunction with the above competences, IMSERSO is responsible for monitoring the management of economic benefits for people with disabilities. It also carries out the proposal, management and monitoring of social service plans at a State level in the areas of the elderly and dependent persons, guaranteeing a universal, integrated and uniform service system. Finally, it maintains relations with foreign and international organizations and technical assistance for international cooperation programmes regarding its field of action.

IV. National Public Employment Service

80. The SPEE is the only Managing Body with a special legal nature since it is considered as an autonomous body. Its internal regulation is contained in Act 56/2003 and its implementing regulations.[87]

81. This management entity assumes functions regarding:

- the management of passive employment policies: the recognition, payment, suspension and termination of unemployment benefits;[88]
- ensuring compliance with current legislation and inspection in order to detect fraudulent situations;[89]
- managing the programmes and measures of employment policies and training for employment. Nevertheless, the CCAA also participate in the execution of measures on employment, through their own public services. The SPEE, together with the Public Employment Services of the CCAA, forms the National Employment System. The National Employment System promotes, designs and develops measures and actions for employment, whose execution is decentralized, in order to adapt to the different interests and needs of the users.

86. Article 66(1)b) of the GSSA and Art. 1 of the RD 1226/2005 (BOE No. 246 of 14 Oct. 2005).
87. Royal Legislative Decree 3/2015 and RD 1383/2008 of 1 August. After the entry into force of the Royal Decree 787/2020, of 1 September (BOE No. 235 of 2 Sep. 2020), changed its name to National Public Employment Service O.A.
88. Title III of the GSSA.
89. Article 297 of the GSSA.

V. The Social Marine Institute

82. The ISM is a sectorial Managing Body in charge of the Special Social Security Scheme for Sea Workers. It is a public organization, with its own legal personality, whose aim is the assistance of sea workers in Spain and abroad.[90] Within its specific competences, assumes, among others:[91] the managing, administering and recognizing entitlement to benefits in the Special Social Security Scheme for Sea Workers; the promotion of the actions in processing their unemployment benefits and in finding them employment, with the cooperation of the SPEE. The ISM attends the healthcare for sea workers and recipients of this form of healthcare nationally and abroad;[92] performs the sea workers' welfare on board and in port; carry out the evacuation and repatriation of sick or injured workers in foreign ports and the social assistance to sea workers and their beneficiaries, especially in case of abandonment by insolvent companies, apprehensions or shipwrecks, in Spanish or foreign ports.

VI. Managing Entities of Civil Servants

83. Traditionally, public officials had a special Social Security System, which is currently being integrated within the framework of the General Regime. However, at present, three special regimes are provisionally maintained: the Special Regime of Civil Servants of the State, the Special Regime of the Civil Servants at the service of the Administration of Justice, and the Special Regime of the Armed Forces.

84. Each regime is managed by a specific body, with legal personality, its own assets and treasury and management autonomy. As a result, civil servants of the State have the General Mutual Society of Civil Servants of the State (MUFACE), the personnel at the service of the Administration of Justice has the MUGEJU and the Armed Forces with the ISFAS. All of them are responsible for managing the benefits corresponding to the Special Regime, such as:

- healthcare;
- temporarily disabled based on common and professional contingencies;
- permanent disability pensions;
- family member benefits, social benefits and social welfare.

85. However, despite the progressive disappearance of the Special Regimes, the aforementioned management bodies will continue providing healthcare and health benefits through the administrative mutual benefit societies.

---

90. RD 504/2011 of 8 April, on the organizational structure and functions of the Social Institute of the Marine Social Institute (BOE No. 113 of 12 May 2011).
91. Articles 42–48 of Law 47/2015 of 21 October and Art. 3.1 of the RD 504/2011 of 8 April.
92. Additionally, gives health information for sea workers, educate and distribute the On-Board Health Guide, carrying out medical examinations prior to embarkation, inspecting and controlling health on board.

§2. THE COMMON SOCIAL SECURITY SERVICES

I. The General Treasury of the Social Security

86. Its function is to unify all the economic resources and the financial administration of the Social Security System, by applying the principles of financial solidarity and general fund.[93]

87. To summarize, the TGSS assumes functions of economic-financial management and other instrumental functions regarding the precedents. As established in their list of services, some of its competences are:[94] the management and control of contributions and the collection of payments and all other sources of financing for the Social Security System; organizing the means and the design and management of the processes needed to receive payments and other sources of financing for the Social Security System; authorizing the opening of accounts at financial institutions to hold Social Security funds; deferment and instalment plans for social security contributions; ordering the payment of the obligations of social security and the distribution over time and space of the money available to satisfy these obligations on time; owning, managing and administering the goods and rights that are the sole patrimony of social security, without prejudice to the powers given to other entities; creating, managing and applying a single financial stabilization fund for the Social Security System; carrying out any other duties of a similar type that are assigned to it by the MISSM.[95]

88. Furthermore, the TGSS identifies the individuals regarding contribution, by assuming the Registration of companies, and registration, affiliation and termination of workers.

II. The Information Technology Management of the Social Security

89. The Social Security IT Department is a common service for managing information and communication technologies in the Social Security System. As the rest of the common services, it has its own legal personality and full capacity.[96]

90. It was created to direct, coordinate and control the computer and data services of the managing entities and common services. Its role is increasingly prominent as a side effect of the technological revolution. Accordingly, the Department

93. Its regulation is set out in Art. 74 of the GSSA and RD 1314/1984 of 20 June.
94. A complete information about the TGSS competences: http://www.seg-social.es/wps/portal/wss/internet/Conocenos/QuienesSomos/29408 (accessed 15 Dec. 2023).
95. Among others, carrying out credit operations and cash advances that may at times be necessary; drawing up the budget; acquiring the buildings needed to carry out its objectives and organizing and managing the financial circuit that channels the monies available and the movements of money for the system's resources.
96. Its regulation is set out in Art. 74bis of the GSSA and RD 508/2000 of 14 April, through the Social Security Computer Accounting Centre (BOE No. 99 of 25 Apr. 2000).

provides auxiliary services to the coordination and inspection purposes of the Social Security Administration. The Social Security IT Department Manager will adapt its action to the guidelines established by the Social Security General Council for Information and Communication Technologies, notwithstanding the duties attributed by current regulations to the Ministry of Employment and Social Security's Ministerial Committee for the Digital Agenda.[97]

III. Legal Service of the Social Security Administration

91. This service exercises the functions and competencies related to representation and defence in court proceedings of the management bodies and Common Services of the social security.[98]

97. Its competences are included in the additional provision No. 1 of Royal Decree 497/2020 of 28 April.
98. Under the terms established in the Regulations of the Legal Service of the Social Security, approved by Royal Decree 947/2001 of 3 August. Its competences are included in the additional provision No. 2 of Royal Decree 497/2020 of 28 April.

Chapter 3. Private Institutions

92. On the other hand, there is also a possibility of collaboration in the management of social security through the private initiative, through the 'MCSS', companies, associations, foundations and public and private entities duly registered, as provided in Article 79 of the GSSA. Likewise, within the framework of the National Health System, it is possible to formalize agreements with public or private entities regarding certain benefits, such as to provide administrative or health services, or professional recovery, in accordance with Article 258 of the GSSA.

93. Notwithstanding, the collaboration in the management only involves cooperation to develop State services, but it does not signify in any means real management of them.

§1. Mutual Societies for Social Insurance

94. The MCSS plays the most prominent role within the collaborating private entities of social security. Its legal regulation is established in Articles 80–101 of the GSSA and the Regulation on collaboration of the Mutual Societies of Work Accidents and Occupational Diseases of Social Security.[99]

95. The MCSS are non-profit private associations of entrepreneurs, with their own statutes, constituted by authorization of the MISSM, and registered in a Special Registry. The MCSS' purpose is to collaborate in the management of social security. Its financing is made by the social security contributions of the member companies and the income derived from the financial investment of these resources and any other income regarding the collaboration. The MISSM exercises administrative controls related to its competences.

96. The companies, by registering in the TGSS Registry, can choose whether professional contingencies – work-related accidents and occupational diseases – are managed by the corresponding Managing Body or by an MCSS. In the latter case, they may also opt, if they wish, for the management of Temporary Disability.

97. Notwithstanding, self-employed workers must compulsorily arrange the management of professional contingencies, temporary disability and cessation of activity through an MCSS.[100]

98. Thus, the competences granted to the MCSS by the GSSA are the following:

- collaborate with the management of professional contingencies. It assumes all the competences related to its management, such as economic benefits, healthcare and recovery, its administration and services, etc.;

99. RD 1993/1995 of 7 December (BOE No. 296 of 12 Dec. 1995).
100. This obligation has been established since the entry into force of the RD-Law 28/2018.

- if the company has opted for the protection of professional contingencies through an MCSS, it may also arrange the following benefits;
- the management of the economic benefit of temporary disability derived from common contingencies;
- the management of benefits for risk during pregnancy and risk during breastfeeding;
- the management of the provision for the care of minors affected by cancer or another serious illness;
- the management of professional contingencies, temporary disability and economic benefits for cessation in the activity of self-employed workers.

99. In addition, the MCSS will assume any other competence set out by the Law.

§2. The Collaboration in the Management of the Social Security System of Enterprises

100. The private companies take part in the management of social security with respect to their own personnel.[101] In this case, collaboration can be established on a mandatory or voluntary basis.

101. On the one hand, the companies will compulsorily collaborate in the payment of benefits. This action consists in the advance payment of the worker's economic perceptions of temporary disability and partial unemployment, in order to speed the payment process. This payment will be offset in the monthly liquidation of the social contributions entered by the company. By no means, this is a transfer of the responsibility, which remains in the corresponding managing or mutual entity.

102. On the other hand, Article 102 of the GSSA establishes the voluntary collaboration of companies. They may collaborate, first, directly assuming the payment of temporary disability benefits arising from work-related injury and occupational disease, and the benefits of healthcare and professional recovery, including the payment of the social security allowance.

103. The requirements established to carry out this voluntary collaboration are: (1) the company has to have more than 250 permanent workers and sufficient medical facilities,[102] (2) request authorization from the MISSM, (3) and fulfil the obligations derived from the social legislation. In this case, the share of the quota corresponding to that contingency is withdrawn from the contribution and an amount is contributed to the maintenance of common services of the social security.[103]

101. Article 102(2) of the GSSA, and the MO 25 Nov. 1996.
102. Companies with more than hundred workers can be allowed if they have adequate medical facilities, if its purpose is health care.
103. This contribution is calculated after applying the rate set by the MISSM of Occupational Accident and Occupational Accident quotas collected for permanent disability, death and survival. In 2023,

104. Second, they may collaborate paying to their workers, under the responsibility of the Managing Body or mutual entity, the economic benefits for temporary incapacity, or other benefits that can be determined by regulation.

Article 25 of Order PCM/74/2023 of 30 January (BOE No. 26 of 31 January 2023), amended by Order PCM/313/2023 of 30 March (BOE No. 77 of 31 March 2023), sets the rate at 31%.

Part II. Contribution and Financing

María Isabel Ribes Moreno

105. Spanish social security relies on a mixed system of funding, as established in the GSSA. The economic resources for funding are constituted by different means and, at present, the most important are the contributions or payments to social security.[104] Therefore, the funding of the Spanish Social Security System is set up as a regime of a contributory nature, around the contributions of employers and workers, a contribution that is defined based on a percentage of the workers' remuneration. Notwithstanding, incomes are also obtained through public contributions, emanated from taxes or tax rates, which are provided through the General State Budgets.

106. The contribution to social security is based on several basic elements: the CB, the contribution rate and the quota. In this sense, in order to determine the amount of quota to be paid, the applicable regulations establish the amount of the CB to which the corresponding type of contribution has to be applied.[105] This quota may be minored by reductions and bonuses in contributions, as provided each year in the General State Budget Law (LPGE).

104. A total of 80% of the contributions come from an economic contribution from the employers and workers.
105. These operations are of special importance since the amount of benefits usually depends on the CB.

Chapter 1. Contribution Regulation for Employees

107. The Social Security Contribution System for workers is mandatory from their inclusion in the subjective scope of the Social Security General Scheme. The contribution to social security is determined from the total remuneration received by the worker. This amount is used as a CB to which different types of contributions – rates or percentages – are applied, depending on different contingencies and concepts, to obtain the quota to be paid. The payment periods will refer to full calendar months, according to the salary periodicity.

108. The TGSS is responsible for collecting the social security contributions and other resources, and unifying all, being the system's general fund. The TGSS is also responsible for levying and transferring the so-called 'other contributions', to the corresponding entities, organizations and administrations, since they are not part of the social security budget.

109. The regulation of the contribution is established in the GSSA and in the RD 2064/1995 of 22 December, which approves the General Regulation on Contribution and Liquidation of Other Social Security Rights, the LPGE and their implementing MOs.

§1. Field of Application

I. Territorial Field of Application

110. The obligated subjects included in the scope of the Social Security General Scheme are: the Spanish workers and foreign citizens with residence and work permits in Spain, who work as employees in industry or services, and carry out this work in Spain – whatever their sex, marital status and profession[106] – consequently, who render voluntarily their paid services on a dependent basis, in the different branches of economic activity.

111. On this basis, the factor of residence and performance of the activity in national territory has a crucial role regarding the application of social security regulations. Notwithstanding, Spanish workers who are not resident in Spain, are included in certain cases (civil servants or employees of international organizations, non-civil service employees of the Spanish Government abroad, etc.).

II. Personal Field of Application

112. Contribution to social security is compulsory for all natural or legal persons depending on what is provided in the regulations. Thus, as set up in the GSSA,

---

106. Including those who normally carry out their activity in national territory.

those who were obliged to contribute are the workers employed by another person in industry and services and their employers. In this sense, these shall be included in this scheme: permanent and temporary workers, seasonal or permanent, including discontinuous and remote workers, and independently of their professional group, regardless of the form and quantity of the remuneration, or whether the nature of their relationship.[107] Among others, the following will be covered by the general Scheme:[108] workers employed by another person and working partners of commercial capitalist companies or the worker-members of employee-owned companies,[109] even when they are members of its administration organ or the company management board; the board members and administrators of commercial capitalist companies who are remunerated for these posts and for their condition of workers company, in all cases as they do not have the control of the company and the post does mean carrying out the functions of company direction and management;[110] personnel hired to provide services to Notary Offices, Land Registries and other similar offices and centres; workers involved in the handling, packing, packaging and marketing of bananas; persons who provide paid services in bodies or institutions of a charitable nature; laypersons or secular staff who provide paid services for ecclesiastical institutions; drivers of private vehicles at the service of individuals; non-civil servant employees, who are subordinate to State organizations, services or bodies; training civil servants aspiring to be incorporated into Civil Servant Corps or Scales who are not subject to the Passive Classes Scheme and top-level officials in the public administration who are not civil service employees, as well as newly incorporated civil servants in the CCAA; civil servants transferred to the CCAA, who voluntarily enrol in the Civil Servant Corps or Scales of Autonomous Community they are transferred to; interim personnel at the service of the justice administration; representative management positions of trade union and those assimilated as such, as included in the field of application of the Social Security General Scheme.

113. Nevertheless, although the workers and their employers are obliged to contribute, the individual responsible for the payment or compliance with the obligation to make contributions is the employer, who must pay in the full amount of his or her own contributions plus those of the workers, to simplify the system.

---

107. Common or special relationship. Article 7 of the GSSA.
108. Article 136(2) of the GSSA.
109. Whatever their participation in the share capital within the limits provided for in Art. 1(2)b) of the Act 44/2015 on Employee-Owned Companies (BOE No. 247 of 15 Oct. 2015).
110. It is presumed, unless there is proof to the contrary, that the worker has the effective control of the company when any of the following circumstances exists: At least half the company capital for which they render their services is distributed among the partners in the company with whom they live and with whom they are linked by marriage or by blood, affinity or adoption family ties of up to a second degree. Their participation in the company capital is equal to or greater than one-third. Their participation in the company capital is equal to or greater than one-fourth, if they have been attributed with functions of direction and management of the company. Article 305.2 of the GSSA.

§2. CALCULATION OF CONTRIBUTIONS

114. The LPGE sets out, annually, the rules governing social security contributions. The calculation of the quota to be collected is made from differentiated contingencies and concepts. Thus, there are the common contingencies quotas – regarding temporary incapacity for work due to a common illness or non-work-related injury, benefits for retirement, disability and death and survival and healthcare – the occupational contingencies quotas – including the premiums for work-related injuries and occupational diseases – and the 'other contributions' quota – including unemployment, Wage Guarantee Fund (FOGASA) and occupational training contributions. Additionally, the LPGE 2023 includes a new contribution corresponding to the so-called intergenerational equity mechanism to strengthen the pension system in the long term, as a new contribution rate to be implemented between 2023 and 2050.[111]

115. Both, the FOGASA and occupational training contributions, are not related to social security although they are collected together with the other contributions. The regulations also establish the contributions for overtime which, without affecting benefits, are intended to increase the general resources of the Social Security System. It should be highlighted that each of these concepts has its own rules in determining both the CB and the rate, and will be paid and reported by those obligated, as stated, together with their social security payments, in the same way, with the same deadlines and in the same place.

I. Calculation Base

116. Therefore, the basis of contribution is not a concept with a single calculation, but, depending on the protection they cover, we can differentiate three basic types: first, that corresponding to common contingencies and to intergenerational equity mechanism; second, that of professional contingencies and 'other contributions'; and, finally, the overtime base.

117. First, the common contingencies base – and the intergenerational equity mechanism base – is calculated by the total remuneration that the worker receives, or is entitled to receive, on a monthly basis. In addition, the base should be set within minimum and maximum limits – according to the professional category – set up annually in the LPGE.[112] The CB calculation, starting from the monthly remuneration (in cash and in kind), requires the sum and subtraction of some concepts, proceeding as follows.

---

111. Article 122(14) LPGE 2023, by application of the provisions of the fourth final provision of Act 21/2021, on the guarantee and purchasing power of pensions, after the amendment introduced by the Royal Decree-Law 2/2023, of 16 March.

112. For 2023, the LPGE 2023, the Government through Act 31/2022 of 23 December established certain measures, including the bases, rates and contribution ceilings for 2023.

118. In particular, must be added all perceptions accrued for periods of more than one month. These concepts include extraordinary payments, profit-sharing or commissions, and will be distributed proportionally among the monthly payments integrating the monthly CB. The same process shall be applied regarding payments that cannot be fully or partially quantified in advance. Therefore, estimation will be made and assessed on a monthly basis for proportional distribution.

119. Moreover, the remuneration in kind has specific rules for its quantification. Hence, perceptions in kind include the use or consumption of goods or services free of charge or at a lower market price, without exceeding 30% of salary perceptions. We may consider as such: the use of housing or vehicle, food vouchers, etc.

120. As regards the valuation of payment in kind, it is carried out as follows: if the employer gives an amount to the worker for the purchase of the good or service, this financial amount is considered salary, as having a monetary value, and shall form part of the CB. It may also be quantified by the average cost for the employer and by dividing the total cost between the numbers of potential beneficiaries. Notwithstanding, when the remuneration in kind is not valued, the amount shall be determined in accordance with the following rules:

- The amounts in cash, vouchers or cheques of any kind for the purchase of a service, and the insurance premiums for the coverage of the worker, with the exception of civil liability or work accident insurance, are valued by its total amount, including taxes if applicable.
- The shares delivered to employees and the use of a car or housing provided to the worker are assessed in accordance with the provisions of tax regulations.
- The provision free of charge or at a lower market price of the nursery or education service – child, primary, secondary, high school or vocational training – will be assessed by the marginal cost for the company or employer.
- Contributions to pension schemes and improvements to social security benefits at their total cost.
- Loans with lower legal interest rate are quantified in the difference between the interest paid and the interest rate prevailing at the corresponding financial year.

121. Progressively, the number of items excluded from the CB has been reduced. Currently, they are limited to the following:

- Travel costs, living and accommodation expenses to perform services away from his normal place of work. The exclusion requires that the amount be within the limits laid down in the Personal Income Tax Regulation (hereinafter 'IRPF'). The excess over the limits is counted as the CB.
- Death and leave benefits, removal allowances, severance and termination payments. The legislation provides that in cases of death, removal or suspension, the payment shall be exempt if they do not exceed the maximum amount provided for in the sectorial rule or collective agreement applicable in such situations. Regarding dismissals or terminations, the exemption from inclusion in the Regulatory Base (RB) is limited to the amount compulsorily established by Law. In

the cases of collective dismissals based on economic, technical, organizational, production or force majeure reasons, the severance payment shall be exempt if it does not exceed the amount set forth in the Workers' Statute for unfair dismissal. Notwithstanding, anything in excess of this amount, even if established by collective agreement, agreement or contract, must be included in the CB proportionally, on a pro rata basis, in the preceding twelve months.
- Social security benefits and improvements to temporary disability benefits provided by the employer.
- Educational expenditures paid by the employer, when necessary to update or recycle the worker, and is essential to his work post or to develop the activity.
- Overtime worked.

122. Finally, the resulting amount according to these rules must be between the maximum and minimum CBs acting as limits. Consequently, the CB will be limited to the said maximum or minimum amount, even if the salary received is greater or less. The maximum limit is unique for all schemes and professional categories; on the opposite, the minimum limit presents differences according to the professional categories. For 2023, the minimum contribution bases, according to professional categories and contribution groups, are included in the Order PCM/74/2023, of 30 January, which develop the legal rules on Social Security contributions, unemployment, protection due to cessation of activity, the FOGASA and vocational training for the financial year 2023, modified after the Order PCM/313/2023, of 30 March. Thus, the provisional limits for 2023 are the following:

	Calculation Base for Common Contingencies		
Contribution Group	*Professional Categories*	*Minimum Bases EUR/Month*	*Maximum Bases EUR/Month*
1	Engineers and university graduates and managers	1,759.50	4,495.50
2	Technical engineers, experts and qualified assistants	1,459.20	4,495.50
3	Administrative and workshop managers	1,269.30	4,495.50
4	Non-qualified assistants	1,260.00	4,495.50
5	Administrative officers	1,260.00	4,495.50
6	Subordinates	1,260.00	4,495.50
7	Administrative assistants	1,260.00	4,495.50
		Minimum Bases EUR/Day	*Maximum Bases EUR/Day*
8	First- and second-class officials	42.00	149.85

Calculation Base for Common Contingencies			
Contribution Group	*Professional Categories*	*Minimum Bases EUR/Month*	*Maximum Bases EUR/Month*
9	Third-class officials and specialists	42.00	149.85
10	Pawns	42.00	149.85
11	Under 18	42.00	149.85

123. Second, the contribution basis for occupational contingencies and for 'other contributions' is calculated in the same way. To summarize, the remuneration received by workers for overtime needs to be included in the Contribution Base for common contingencies (CBCC) to calculate CB for occupational contingencies. This CB is also subject to maximum and minimum limits. The maximum limit is the same as indicated for the CBCC. Nevertheless, the minimum limit is different, being equal to the current minimum professional wage in force, increased with the proportionally distribution of the extraordinary payments. For 2023, as established in the Order PCM/74/2023, the limits will be the following:

Limits for Work-Related Injuries and Occupational Diseases CB	
Maximum	*Minimum*
EUR 4,495.50	EUR 1,260.00

124. A special regulation is established for part-time work contracts, where overtime wages are computed for both the CB, but the overtime wages for force majeure only will be included in the CB for occupational contingencies.

125. Lastly, regarding overtime, regardless of their contribution to occupational contingencies, unemployment, FOGASA and occupational training shall be subject to an additional contribution, as mentioned before. The overtime retribution constitutes itself a different CB,[113] estimated with the remuneration received by workers for overtime, without considering the reason that justifies the overtime.

II. Contribution Amount

126. As with the CBs and the limits, the LPGE and the MOs that implement their provisions set forth each tax year the rules that determine the social security contributions.[114]

113. Article 147(4) of the GSSA.
114. Article 122(2) of the LPGE 2023. PCM/74/2023, of 30 January, that implements the regulation for social security contributions, unemployment, protection for cessation of activity, Salary Guarantee Fund and professional training for 2023, amended by the Order PCM/313/2023, of 30 March.

127. The contributions consist of a total quota formed by the result of applying the contribution rates to the different CBs, which correspond to the different protected contingencies, to the so-called 'other contributions' and to overtime.

128. Regarding the rates of contribution, there is a general rate – by common contingencies – and special rates. The latter are those relating to the intergenerational equity mechanism, occupational contingencies, 'other contributions' and overtime due to force majeure.[115] In relation to the subjects responsible for the contribution, the obligation is funded by both employers and workers, except for the occupational contingencies contribution and to FOGASA, which is exclusively paid by employers.

129. The general rate for the calculation of the quota for common contingencies consists in the application to the CB at a rate of 28.3%, made up of two parts: 23.6% corresponds to the employer and 4.7% to the worker. There is a speciality in fixed-term contracts of duration to or less than thirty days. These contracts shall be subject to an additional contribution at the employer's expense at the end of the contract.[116]

130. With regard the Intergenerational equity mechanism, from 2023 to 2050 a progressive contribution will be made on the CB for common contingencies in all situations of registration or assimilated to registration in the Social Security system in which there is an obligation to contribute to cover the retirement pension, and in 2023 the rate is 0.6%.[117] Where the contribution is to be shared between employer and employee, a rate of 0.5% shall be borne by the employer and a rate of 0.1% by the employee.

131. The contribution for accidents at work and occupational disease is exclusively paid by the employer; the calculation of the quota is set up by applying to the CB a rate from a premium rate based on the corresponding economic activity or occupation. The premium rate is included in the Additional Provision No. 4 of Law 42/2006 of 28 December on LPGE 2007, updated by RD-Law 28/2018 of 28 December, on the revaluation of public pensions and urgent measures in social,

115. The general rate is applicable to overtime contribution.
116. This additional contribution shall be calculated by multiplying by three the contribution resulting from applying the minimum daily contribution base of group 8 for common contingencies, the general contribution rate payable by the company to cover common contingencies, as stated in Art. 151 of the GSSA. From 1 Jan. 2023, the additional contribution will be EUR 27.53, Art. 26(1) Order PCM/74/2023. This increase is not applicable to the Special System of Agricultural Workers, the special scheme for coal mining, the special employment relationship of arts, domestic employees, or standby contracts. Additionally, Art. 249bis of the GSSA establishes that, in these short-term contracts, to prove the minimum contribution periods necessary to cause entitlement to benefits each working day will be considered 1.4 contribution days.
117. The Royal Decree-Law 2/2023 established the progressive scale in its forty-third Transitional Provision.

labour and employment matters.[118] The rate is formed for two types of contributions: one to temporary incapacity and, the other, to permanent disability, death and survival, both depending on the economic activity carried out by the worker. The percentages vary according to the risk of the activity, for example, to the extraction of ornamental stone and for construction or mining work is applied the maximum rate, and the minimum, to office work.[119]

132. As for 'other contributions', it comprises three different concepts corresponding to unemployment, FOGASA and occupational training. First, the unemployment rate varies depending on the type of the worker's employment contract. The rate is lower if the contract is indefinite in any modality and higher if it is fixed-term, full-time or part-time contract. Second, the contribution to FOGASA is set up by 0.20% on the CB and is paid exclusively for the employer. Finally, regarding occupational training, the applicable rate is 0.70%: 0.60% corresponding to the employer and 0.10% of the worker.

133. Lastly, regarding overtime, regardless of their contribution to occupational contingencies, unemployment, FOGASA and occupational training shall be subject to an additional contribution, as mentioned before.[120] This additional contribution shall not be taken into account in determining the regulatory basis of the benefits. Although the general contribution rate is applied for overtime, when they are carried out due to force majeure, the rate is lower, consisting of 23.6% and 14%, respectively.

134. The following table differentiates the bases and rates applied by the different concepts, specifying to whom is responsible to contribute. It must be taken into account that, regardless of the subject responsible for the obligation to make contributions, it is the employer who deducts and pays the full amount of the contribution to simplify the system:

Contribution Base (CB)	*Contribution Rate*			
	Contingencies	*Employers*	*Workers*	*Total*
Common Contingencies	Common	23.60%	4.70%	28.30%
	Intergenerational equity mechanism	0.50%	0.10%	0.60%

118. The Act 35/2014 of 26 December, modifying the GSSA regarding the legal regime of Mutual Accidents at Work and Occupational Diseases of Social Security, provided, in its 4th Additional Provision, that the Government would address within one year an update of the regulation of the contribution for professional contingencies by updating the contribution rate for professional contingencies, reviewing the rates and reducing the number of situations contemplated in the following table. The update shall be based on the risk for the different activities, industries and tasks. Nowadays the update is still pending.
119. A complete list of rates can be found at: http://www.seg-social.es/wps/wcm/connect/wss/c02a30b4-b770-4b70-bca6-603d39c8e9bd/Tarifa+primas+RDley+28_2018.pdf?MOD=AJPERES&CVID= (accessed 15 Dec. 2023).
120. Article 149 of the GSSA.

Contribution Base (CB)	*Contribution Rate*			
	Contingencies	*Employers*	*Workers*	*Total*
Professional Contingencies	Occupational	Additional Provision No. 4, Act 42/2006 of 28 December (PGE 2007)	–	
	Other contributions			
	Unemployment	5.50%	1.55%	7.05%
	Unemployment (fixed-term contracts)	6.70%	1.60%	8.30%
	FOGASA	0.20%	–	0.20%
	Occupational training	0.60%	0.10%	0.70%
Overtime	Additional contribution for overtime			
	Common	23.60%	4.70%	28.30%
	Force majeure	12.00%	2.00%	14.00%

135. Finally, the contribution to training contracts has a remarkable speciality. Thereby, the social security contribution, when the CB for common contingencies, in accordance with the rules of the corresponding social security scheme, does not exceed the minimum monthly CB of that Scheme, shall be calculated through fixed monthly quotas for common contingencies, occupational contingencies, unemployment and FOGASA. Thus, in 2023, the social security contribution for training contracts will consist of a single monthly contribution distributed as follows:

Contingencies	*Employers*	*Workers*	*Total*
Common contingencies	EUR 51.06	EUR 7.03	*EUR 61.24*
Occupational contingencies	EUR 6.51 TD (Temporary Disability) EUR 3.93 DDS (Disability, Death and Survival) EUR 3.10 (euros)		*EUR 7.03*
FOGASA	EUR 3.88	–	*EUR 3.88*
Occupational training	EUR 1.90	EUR 0.25	*EUR 2.15*

136. In the above-mentioned cases, the contribution rate and distribution regarding unemployment are the same applied in non-fixed term contract.[121]

137. Notwithstanding, as stated in the GSSA,[122] if the monthly CBCC exceeds the minimum monthly CB of said Scheme, the contribution to be paid shall be made up of the result of adding the single contributions referred above and the contributions resulting from applying the contribution rates corresponding to the amount exceeding the CB.

138. At the same time, training contracts also need to contribute for the intergenerational equity mechanism, applying a contribution rate of 0.6% to the minimum CB of the General Scheme, funded by both employers and workers (0.5% and 0.1%, respectively).[123]

139. Additionally, some reductions or bonuses in contributions can be applied for some groups or certain situations, as will be seen in the next paragraph.

§3. Reductions and Exemptions

140. The quota resulting from the application of the rate or premium to the CB may be decreased by applying reductions and exemptions. The reasons that justify these measures are diverse, can be set up for boosting indefinite hiring, temporary hiring and/or for the maintenance of employment. In general terms, there are measures to promote employment of groups with difficulties in accessing the labour market, to prolong working life and/or to maintain employment in situations of crisis.

141. The different regulations established bonuses to reduce the contribution to be paid for a limited time or indefinitely, depending on the collective to whom they are directed. In this sense, the bonus can affect, among others, the total amount of the employer contribution, or only the contributions for common contingencies, or to a percentage of the quota. Other measures consist in establishing the exemption of paying a specific amount of the quotas per year, or per month with annual limits. Some measures are definitive and others for a period of time. The measures are modified to maximize the temporary access to employment for certain groups.

142. As an example, we can highlight the measures to reinforce the indefinite employment contract to the following groups: victims of gender-based violence or domestic violence, victims of terrorism, victims of the traffic in human beings, those

121. As stated in Art. 31(2) a.1 Order PCM74/2023, 3, amended by the Order PCM/313/2023, of 30 March.
122. Additional provision No. 43, s. 1.2 of the forty-third additional provision GSSA. Article 44 O. PCM/74/2023 of 1 January.
123. Article 44(1)c O. PCM/74/2023 of 1 January.

in a situation of social exclusion, temporary workers recruited by the user enterprise, fixed-term workers converted to open-ended, people with disabilities. Other groups are workers with old age, unemployed people over 52 years, people with disabilities, self-employed workers' family members, the unemployed who join cooperative societies as workers, prisoners in penitentiary institutions, minors in youth detention centres, household employees and certain workers in Ceuta and Melilla. Additionally, to the aforementioned groups, some working contracts as the training contract for unemployed youth, or contracts to substitute employees regarding reconciliation issues and the research personnel contracts, may receive bonuses.

143. Regarding the maintenance of employment, the measures ensure to continuing the jobs for those over 65 years of age, for those reinstated in their jobs for improvement after permanent disability, and for permanent seasonal contract workers in the tourism, commerce and hospitality sector. Moreover, to reduce the disadvantages caused to move the worker concerned to another job in situations of risk in pregnancy or breastfeeding, the employer, during the change, may apply a 50% reduction in its contribution for common contingencies. The same reduction will be applied to the employer that, due to occupational disease, changes the worker to another position compatible with his or her status, even when hired by another company to perform a compatible position, in cases that the said occupational disease has been verified.

144. On the other hand, it is possible to establish the total exemption of quotas for force majeure reasons in suspension or reduction of working hours in accordance with the provisions of Law 17/2015 of 9 July, of the National Civil Protection System,[124] when an area has been severely affected by a civil protection emergency. The TGSS can exempt the payment of social security contributions, in a specific temporal and territorial scope, to the companies that suspend the contracts or reduce the working day for that reason, during the maintenance of these measures.[125]

§4. Contributions on Benefits

145. Workers are also obliged to contribute, while in certain situations where they receive benefits. The obligation to make contributions remains during situations of temporary disability, risk during pregnancy, risk during breastfeeding, birth and childcare,[126] with special rules regarding the calculation of the CB.

146. Furthermore, the contribution for common contingencies is compulsory during contributory unemployment, having special rules for the determination of the CB. Nevertheless, when unemployment is due to the suspension of the employment

124. BOE No. 164 of 10 Jul. 2015.
125. The period will be considered as effectively quoted for the worker.
126. Birth and childcare benefits have recently replaced maternity and paternity benefits, owing to the entry into force of the RD-Law 6/2019 of 1 March (BOE No. 57 of 7 Mar. 2019).

relationship or temporary reduction of the ordinary working day due to economic, technical, organizational production or force majeure reasons shall also be quoted for occupational contingencies.

147. In the case of non-contributory unemployment, specific rules are also laid down for determining the CBs. In these cases, the contribution is only established for certain contingencies.

§5. Special Rules

148. Notwithstanding, there are special rules for the contribution of certain groups located in the General Social Security Scheme, such as the clergy of the Catholic Church and ministers of other religious confessions, for artists, professional football players and other professional athletes, professional bullfighters, trade representatives, research personnel in training or participants in training programmes, firemen and local police, inmates and sentenced to community service work.

149. Additionally, there are also Special Collective Systems, within the General Scheme of the Social Security, with peculiarities in matters of affiliation and contributions, being the most common for domestic employees or agricultural workers.[127]

§6. Administration

150. The management of all issues related to the collection of contribution quotas is attributed to the TGSS. The TGSS assumes both the collection and liquidation management, during voluntary or executive period.

151. The collection periods of employed workers are monthly since this is the usual pay period for salaries. In fact, as mentioned before, the corresponding CB is formed based on the worker's salary payments.

127. There is some Special Collective Systems as Special System of fruit, vegetables and the vegetable preserve industry; Special System for Resin Industry; Special System for extraordinary hostelry services; Special System for handling and packaging fresh tomato, carried out by harvester/exporters; Special System of intermittent permanent employees in cinema, dance halls, nightclubs and discotheques; Special System of intermittent permanent employees in market research and public opinion; Special Agricultural System; Special System for Domestic Employees.

Chapter 2. Contributions for Public Sector Workers

152. Traditionally, the regime of public servant was based on three special regimes, external to the General Scheme, which were provided in Articles 7 and 10 of the GSSA. Thus, there was the Regime of civil servants of the State, of the officials at the service of the Administration of Justice and of the Armed Forces, all of them governed by their own regulations.[128]

153. The different regimes include three areas with their own management, financing and protection rules, based on the following:

(1) The civil service pensions fund or passive classes (*Régimen de Clases Pasivas del Estado*) for the recognition and payment of retirement, disability, death and survival pensions, managed by the INSS.[129]
(2) The system of administrative mutualism, complementary to the above-mentioned, managed by its own management entities – mutualities of civil servants – that attend to the benefits of accident or illness, temporary disability and others.
(3) Assistance or family assistance benefits.[130]

154. At present, public administration personnel (state, autonomous, local and institutional) and regardless of whether they have labour, administrative or civil relationship are subject to the General Social Security Scheme. Actually, since 1 January 2011, all civil servants who join the civil service must be included in the General Social Security Scheme, only excluding former Presidents, Vice Presidents and Cabinet Ministers of Spain and all included in Article 51 of the Passive Classes Law. Notwithstanding, some civil services still retain the aforementioned special regimes and the regime of passive classes, on a transitional basis.[131]

155. The general social security regulations are applied to civil servants excluded from the special regimes and integrated into the General Scheme and the social security statutory personnel. Nevertheless, the integration into the General Scheme is not complete, is limited to retirement, death and survival pensions, that is the set of benefits that were assumed through the passive classes system. The rest of the contingencies are covered by their own mutual societies, or administrative mutualism, which will continue providing the benefits they are currently offering.

156. Consequently, the current regime is completed with administrative mutualism. This requires the affiliation of the civil servant to the corresponding

128. Royal Legislative Decree 4/2000 of 23 June, Royal Legislative Decree 1/2000 of 9 June and Royal Legislative Decree 3/2000 of 23 June, respectively.
129. Royal Legislative Decree 670/1987 of 30 April, consolidated text of the Passive Classes Law of the State (BOE No. 126, 27 May 1987).
130. Article 29 of the Royal Legislative Decree 4/2000.
131. Additional Provision No. 3 of the GSSA and Transitional Provision No. 4 RLD 13/2010.

mutuality: of civil servants of the State (MUFACE), of the personnel at the service of the Administration of Justice (MUGEJU) and of the Armed Forces (ISFAS).

157. Regarding the contribution scheme to their own mutual societies, it is determined by applying a rate set out annually in the LPGE to the CB. The CB is determined by a 'base pay', which is set for each civil service class by the Government in its LPGE for the purposes of contribution to Mutual Societies and the Passive Classes System. The monthly quota is obtained by multiplying the annual CB by the type and dividing the result by 14. A double quota will be paid in the months of June and December.[132]

158. The civil servants – of the State, the Administration of Justice or Armed Forces – still included in the Passive Classes System are regulated by other contribution standards.[133] This group must pay the quota to the contribution to the pension fund, determined by applying the percentage rate to the 'base pay',[134] established for each civil service class and included in the LGPE.[135] A double quota will be paid in the months of June and December.

159. Furthermore, the civil servants are integrated with the General Social Security Scheme, and are excluded from certain contingencies, such as temporary disability, suspension by birth, paternity, risk during pregnancy and risk during breastfeeding. The latter contingencies are assumed by the administrative mutualism. Consequently, its contribution, equal to the General Scheme, is reduced by applying a coefficient, which is currently 0.065%: 0.054% corresponding to the employer and 0.011% to the worker.[136]

132. For 2023, the monthly quota, regarding the service class, ranged from EUR 51.68 to EUR 21.07.
133. This regime will be maintained temporarily for those who were incorporated before 2011, and for the subjects set forth in Art. 2 of the RD Legislative 670/1987.
134. The contribution rate is 3.86% in general, although it is reduced to 1.93% for professional non-career military personnel and for military personnel of the Scales of Complement or Naval Reserve that has not completed – in both cases – fifteen years of services.
135. Currently, are included in the passive classes system, as stated in Art. 2 of the Royal Legislative Decree 670/1987.
136. Article 20 b) Order PCM/74/2023.

Chapter 3. Contributions for Self-Employed Workers

160. Self-employed workers have traditionally maintained substantial differences from employed workers regarding the Social Security System. Actually, their protection was not included in the General Social Security Scheme, but in the RETA. Nonetheless, although differences are maintained today, and the collective is still protected through the aforementioned Special Social Security Scheme, there is a clear trend to unify the schemes.[137] In this vain, after the publication of RD-Law 28/2018, the Royal Decree 504/2022, of 27 June and the RD-Law 13/2022 there are minimal differences. Thus, on 1 January 2023, they changed their system of paying contributions and from now on they will contribute on the basis of their income. Notwithstanding, there are several transitional rules for a progressive and gradual implementation of the new contribution system.[138]

§1. Field of Application

I. Territorial Field of Application

161. The territorial scope of the RETA is limited to Spaniards residing in Spain and foreigners legally residing in Spain. All of them are included in the field of application of the Social Security System when they exercise their activity in the national territory.

162. Therefore, foreigners fall within the scope of the RETA when they accomplish the requirements established in the Law. The Spanish OL on Foreigners provides that foreigners who have the legal authorizations to reside and work have the right to perform a paid activity on their own and to access the Social Security System.[139]

II. Personal Field of Application

163. The GSSA established the personal scope of RETA to 'Workers over 18 years of age who perform a for-profit economic activity in a regular, personal, and direct manner, without being subject to an employment contract, and may use, or not, the paid service of other people, according to the terms set forth in the Law.'[140] Within this field, as stated in Article 305 of the GSSA, numerous professional groups can be included, some of them having special rules, such as the following:

137. Title IV of the GSSA, together with the Decree 2530/1970 of 20 August, regulating the Special Social Security Scheme for Self-Employed Persons (BOE No. 221 of 15 Sep. 1970).
138. Transitional provisions No. 1, RD-Law 13/2022.
139. Organic Law 4/2000 of 11 January, on the rights, freedoms and social integration of foreigners in Spain, Art. 10.
140. Article 305(1) of the GSSA.

(a) Self-employed agricultural workers.
(b) Those who perform management or administration functions arising from the position of member of the Board of Directors or administrator, or who perform other services for a capitalist trading company, for profit and in a regular, personal, and direct manner, provided that they have effective, direct or indirect, control of the company.
(c) Associates of regular joint companies and collective associates of limited partnership companies.[141]
(d) Communal partners or partners of communities of property and irregular civil companies.
(e) Associate workers of worker-owned companies, when their share in the share capital, together with that of their spouse and relatives by consanguinity, affinity, or adoption up to the second degree, with whom they live, is at least 50%, unless they can prove that effective control of the company requires the participation of persons other than family relations.
(f) Self-employed workers who are economically dependent (*Trabajadores autónomos económicamente dependientes* (TRADE)).[142]
(g) Professionals who conduct, on their own behalf, an activity which requires membership of a Professional Association.
(h) Notary public members or Property, Mercantile and Real Estate Registers' members and applicants to membership.
(i) The personnel included in the application scope of Law 55/2003 of 16 December, Statute for Statutory Workers in the Health Service, who provide full-time services in the health services of the different CCAA or in the dependent centres on INGESA, for their complementary private activities carried out, determining their inclusion in the Social Security System, taking into account the provisions of Additional Provision No. 18.
(j) The spouse and relatives up to the second degree, inclusive (for workers in the RETA), up to the third degree by consanguinity, affinity, and adoption who work with the self-employed worker in a regular, personal, and direct manner and are not wage earners.
(k) Associate workers of Associated Work Cooperatives to street selling who receive income directly from buyers.
(l) Thus, any person included by regulation due to the activity performed.

164. This implies that Spaniards and foreign self-employed workers who reside and legally conduct their activity in Spanish territory are included in the RETA Scheme.

§2. Basis for Calculation of Contributions

165. The CB for RETA workers is configured differently from general regime. The regime is based on the premise that due to the activity they perform., they do

141. Article 1(2) a) of Law 20/2007 of 11 July, on the Self-Employed Work Statute (BOE No. 166 of 12 Jul. 2007).
142. As referred to in Ch. III of Title II of Law 20/2007 of 11 July.

not receive regular remuneration. Therefore, as they contribute on the basis of their income, these are calculated provisionally and regularised annually, after checking the data on their real net income. Thus, their CB are calculated provisionally, between a minimum base and a maximum base established annually by the corresponding LPGE for each of the net income brackets obtained in each calendar year, which the LPGE also set up.

166. From 1 January 2023, self-employed workers must choose their monthly CB within the general (or a reduced) table of bases established in the LPGE,[143] depending on their forecast average monthly average net monthly income. For 2023, there are two tables, a reduced table with three income brackets and a general table with twelve income brackets. All income brackets have a minimum and a maximum CB. The limits set up in the reduced table ranges from EUR 751.63 (minimum CB) to EUR 1,166.70 (maximum CB). The limits stated in the general scale ranges from EUR 950.98 to EUR 4,495.50.[144]

167. Consequently, the monthly Social Security contribution must be made provisionally, until the tax authorities determine the amount of the net income obtained by each self-employed worker. The amount of the monthly CB is determined on each self-employed worker's forecast of the monthly average net income obtained during that calendar year for the totality of their economic or professional activities. Therefore, in order to adjust their CB, self-employed workers must apply to the TGSS to change their monthly CB so that the annual computation of these CBs be between the minimum and maximum established in the LPGE for their net income bracket.

168. The possibility of modifying the provisional CB may be made six times during the year, always within the aforementioned minimum and maximum limits. The variation must be communicated to the TGSS and will have the following effective dates:

Date of Application	*Effective Date*
From 1 January to last calendar day of February	1 March
From 1 March to 30 April	1 May
From 1 May to 30 June	1 July
From 1 July to 31 August	1 September
From 1 September to 31 October	1 November
From 1 November to 31 December	1 January

143. Article 122(6) LPGE and Art. 16(1) Order PCM/74/2023.

144. In 2023 the contribution bases and the rate of contributions are stated in Arts 308 to 313 GSSA and Arts 44 to 46 RD 2064/1995, modified by the RD-Law 13/2022 and the Art. 16 of the Order PCM/74/2023.

169. The provisional monthly contribution made based on the forecast of the net income obtained by the self-employed workers will be compared with the data on this net income provided by the tax authorities after deducting a percentage of 7%, taking into account the following rules:[145]

- If the monthly average of the CBs for which provisional contributions have been paid is between the minimum and maximum bases established for the net income bracket in which the net income obtained is found, the provisional CBs become definitive. Consequently, no adjustment is necessary.
- If the monthly average of the CBs for which provisional contributions have been paid is lower than the minimum base established for the net income bracket in which the net income obtained is found, this minimum CB becomes the definitive base. Therefore, the corresponding differences between the CBs must be paid.
- If the monthly average of the CBs for which provisional contributions have been paid is higher than the maximum base established for the net income bracket in which the net income obtained is found, this maximum CB becomes the definitive base. In this case, the corresponding differences will be refunded. However, workers registered in December 2022 remain entitled to pay contributions on that CB, even if their net income results in a lower maximum base than December 2022.

170. Other special CBs and rules are established to some self-employed workers as:

- the partners or workers who perform management or administration functions arising from the position of member of the Board of Directors or administrator, or who perform other services for a capitalist trading company, when they have direct or indirect effective control of the company;[146]
- workers partners of worked-owned companies ascribed to this scheme due to their family participation in the social capital of the company;
- the self-employed workers in a situation of multi-jobbing, with reduced CBs, as a result of their simultaneous contribution in another contribution scheme, such as the General Scheme;[147]
- self-employed workers performing street or home selling, which also have a lower CB, established in the LPGE;
- self-employed Agricultural Workers.[148]

171. There are other specific rules for the determination of the CB for special situations such as Court-ordered affiliation, when the self-employed are unemployed, or during the perception of benefits for cessation of activity.[149]

145. Article 308 GSSA.
146. Article 16(4) of the Order PCM/74/2023.
147. Article 313 of the GSSA.
148. Set forth in Art. 16 of the Order PCM/74/2023.
149. Article 308 of the GSSA and Art. 35 of the O.PCM/74/2023.

§3. Amount of Contribution

172. The contribution of the self-employed maintains peculiarities regarding the General Regime. On the one hand, they are not obliged to contribute for all the concepts that the employed person does in the General Scheme, despite the increase in the contingencies to compulsorily contribute to the RETA and, on the other hand, by the very nature of its activity, without an employer.

173. The self-employed worker pays a quota formed by five different sub-quotas such as: the contribution for common contingencies, the professionals, the intergenerational equity mechanism, the training and the cessation of activity. The latter have the same function as the unemployment contribution for workers in the General Scheme.

174. Thus, the GSSA establishes that 'workers within the scope of the Special Regime of Social Security for Self-Employed or Self-Employed Workers must formalize the coverage of the protective action for professional contingencies, temporary disability and cessation of activity with a mutual partner, having to opt for the same mutual partner for the mentioned protective action. Similarly, the workers who change entities must formalize said protective action with a mutual partner. To implement the management by cessation of activity, they will subscribe the annex to the adhesion document, in the terms established by the rules that regulate collaboration'.[150]

175. The contribution is formed of several quotes, whose CB will be the amount chosen by the autonomous as mentioned before. The contribution for professional contingencies has a unique rate, currently set up at 1.3% (being the result of the sum of the rate for temporary incapacity protection and the rate for disability, death and survival),[151] established annually by the LPGE that is applied on the basis of the chosen CB.

176. In summary, the contribution rates are as follows:

Self-Employed Workers' Contribution

Concept	*Rate*
Common contingencies	28.3%
Occupational contingencies	1.30%
Cessation of trading	0.90%
Vocational training and guidance and entrepreneurship promotion	0.10%
Intergenerational equity mechanism	0.6%

150. Article 83(1) b) of the GSSA.
151. Article 308(3) of the GSSA. Article 7 RD 28/2018 and 16.2b) Order PCM/74/2023.

177. There are particular rules in contribution. When the worker has covered the temporary disability under another scheme, a reduction of contribution in common contingencies may apply. Additionally, when they do not have the protection of professional contingencies, shall pay an additional contribution of 0.10% to finance risk contingencies related to pregnancy and breastfeeding.

178. Nevertheless, the self-employed worker who compatibilists the retirement pension with the autonomous activity should only contribute for professional contingencies and temporary disability, being obliged to make a special contribution for solidarity of 9% on the basis of common contingencies, not taken into account for benefits.[152]

§4. ADMINISTRATION

179. The self-employed workers personally comply with the obligation to contribute to all contingencies. It is a single subject obligated and responsible for payment. All of its procedures must be carried out with the TGSS, through the Electronic Data Remission System.

180. In this Special Scheme, the quotas must be paid for complete monthly periods that coincide with calendar months, except when the registration or cancellation is made in the scheme, which will only include its effective contribution days. Thus, the quota is divided by thirty days and multiplied by the effective days. The amount of the quota is paid debit in a bank account or financial institution authorized as a social security collection office. The termination in the scheme shall be submitted at any time, paying only quotas until the effective day of ending.

181. As a result of the Government's great interest in encouraging the autonomous work, numerous regulations set forth reductions, bonuses and/or quota minorities. One of the most popular measures was the so-called 'flat rate' (*tarifa plana*).[153] This measure, implemented in 2013 and modified on numerous occasions, consists nowadays of the payment of a symbolic amount of quota for twelve months for the new self-employed. At the end of this period, if their expected net yield is equal to or less than the Minimum Interprofessional Wage, a significant reduction of the quota is established and may be extended for thirty-six months.

182. On the other hand, bonuses and reductions are also set up for some groups such as people with disabilities, victims of gender-based violence or terrorism, young people, mothers returning to work or people residing in small municipalities. Other benefits are applied in cases of multi-jobbing, labour cooperatives for street vendors, and in cases of damages due to natural or force majeure.

152. Articles 214 and 310(1) of the GSSA.
153. One of the most important regulations was Law No. 20/2007, Art. 38(ter) and Transitional Provision No. 3 of the RD-Law 28/2018. Nowadays, the regulation is established in the Royal Decree-Law 13/2022.

Chapter 4. Other Contributions: The Special Regime for Sea Workers

183. The importance and long tradition of the Special Social Security Scheme for Seafarers (*Régimen Especial de Trabajadores del Mar* hereinafter 'RETM') in Spain requires to be examined in this chapter. The RETM is set forth in Title I of Law 47/2015 of 21 October, regulating the social protection of people working in the maritime-fisheries sector.

184. One of the main characteristics of this regime is its mixed nature, since it integrates within its scope of self-employed and employed persons resident in Spain, within its scope of subjective application. This scope includes numerous people who carry out maritime-fishing activities and are connected with the previous ones, such as ship security personnel. Thus, as Article 3 of Law 47/2015 stated, are included in this regime as workers employed by another person:

- workers who perform sea fishing activity on board the following ships, vessels or platforms of merchant navy, sea fishing in any form, interior port traffic, sports and recreational, fixed platforms or artefacts or installations which may carry out operations to explore or exploit marine resources, on the sea bed, anchored to or supported by it.[154] They have to be included in the crew list as technicians or crew members;
- workers who work on board merchant navy or sea fishing ships or vessels, on the crew list as research staff, fisheries observers and safety staff;
- workers dedicated to extracting resources from the sea;
- workers dedicated to aquaculture in the maritime and maritime-land area, including aquaculture in sand and in sheets of water, such as cultivated banks, cultivation parks, rafts and cages;[155]
- marine resource extraction divers, and divers with professional qualifications in industrial activities, including teaching activity for obtaining these qualifications;[156]
- net makers;
- port stevedores and port pilots;
- and workers who carry out administrative, technical and subordinate activities in these above-mentioned companies, as long as they carry out their activity exclusively in ports, irrespective of the State-owned or regional nature of the port. This also includes workers who carry out such activities at the service of fishing guilds and their federations, of maritime cooperatives and trade unions from the marine

154. Oil pipelines, gas pipelines, undersea cables, marine outfalls and any other type of pipelines or installations of an industrial or sanitation nature will not be included in these installations.
155. Expressly excludes workers employed by other people who work on land for aquaculture companies, such as breeding centres, marine farms and marine culture research centres. Also excludes workers dedicated to fresh water aquaculture.
156. Excludes divers with sporting-recreational qualifications.

and fishing sector and shipowners' associations, and any other group of workers that carries out maritime-fishing activity and whose inclusion in this scheme is determined by the Ministry.

185. Additionally, the workers who carry out one of the following activities, on a habitual, personal and direct basis, without relying on the management and organization of another person and for gain have to be included in this scheme. These groups will be included in the RETM, as self-employed workers, as Article 4 of Law 47/2015 set up:

- maritime-fishing activity on board the ships or vessels of merchant navy, sea fishing in any form, interior port traffic or sports and recreational, such workers or operators being included in their crew lists as technicians or crew members;
- aquaculture carried out in maritime or maritime-land areas;
- shellfish and barnacle fishermen, seaweed collectors and their equivalents;
- marine resource extraction divers and divers with professional qualifications in industrial activities, including teaching activity for obtaining these qualifications, excluding such with sporting-recreational qualifications;
- net makers;
- port pilots.

186. The Special Scheme also includes self-employed workers, as set forth in Article 4(2) of Law 47/2015:

> The spouse and family members by blood and affinity up to and including the second degree, of any of the self-employed workers referred before, who work with them in their operations on a habitual basis, live with the head of household and depend economically on them, unless they can show that they are wage earners. Notwithstanding the foregoing, in order to be considered as a collaborating family member within the second and third contribution groups, it will be necessary for the person to carry out the exact same activity as the owner of the operation.

187. Furthermore, some people are assimilated as employed workers, as Article 5 of Law 47/2015 stated:

> The board members and administrators of commercial capitalist companies who are remunerated for these posts and for their condition of workers of such, as long as they do not have the control of the company, and the post involves carrying out the functions of company direction and management. In the same way, has to be considered workers, the port pilots who establish companies that hold port service licences for port pilotage, in order to carry out their pilotage duties.[157]

157. In both cases, excluding the right to unemployment protection and that of the Wage Guarantee Fund.

188. Regarding the system of contribution, the same rules apply as in the general social security regime or in the Self-Employed Workers Regime, depending on whether they are workers or self-employed. Thus, the subjects required to make contributions are, on one hand, the employer and the worker in the scheme for employees and, on the other hand, the self-employed worker in the scheme for self-employed workers. Notwithstanding the above, there are certain peculiarities in the contribution, especially of those employees who are paid by 'share of profits'.[158]

189. It is a priority to refer to the different groups in which the workers included in the scheme are classified, which will be of enormous importance for the contribution purposes. Thus, they are classified into three groups as established in Article 10 of Law 47/2015:[159]

(a) The first group includes:
   - Employees or similar remunerated with a salary and who conduct any of the activities listed before.
   - Self-employed workers who conduct any of the activities listed before, unless they should be included in another group.
   - Employees or similar, and self-employed workers or ship-owners, remunerated with a share of profits, who conduct their fishing activity on board vessels of over 150 gross registered tonnage (GRT).

(b) Group two, in turn subdivided into two, includes:
   (1) Group two A: Employees and self-employed workers or ship-owners, remunerated with a share of profits, who conduct their fishing activity on board vessels between 50.01 and 150 GRT, enrolled as technicians or crew.
   (2) Group two B: Employees and self-employed workers or ship-owners, remunerated with a share of profits, who conduct their fishing activity on board vessels between 10.01 and 50 GRT, enrolled as technicians or crew.

(c) Group three includes:
   - Employees, remunerated with a share of profits, who conduct their fishing activity on board vessels not exceeding 10 GRT, enrolled as technicians or crew.
   - Self-employed workers such as shellfish gatherers, seaweed gatherers and similar, divers who extract marine resources, net makers and ship-owners who conduct their fishing activity on board vessels up to 10 GRT, enrolled as technicians or crew.

158. Article 10 of Act No. 47/2015. The share of profits, called in Spain remuneration '*a la parte*', is the traditional system of remuneration in the fishing industry. This special salary system is based on the earning of a percentage of the gross revenue. To be more specific, the system consists in calculating the gross amount of the fishery and deducting the business profits and some operating expenses (such as the contribution for occupational contingencies). The net proceeds are then divided among the members of the crew according to an agreed formula. The contribution for common contingencies of the worker has to be deducted at the time of distribution of net proceeds.

159. Similarly, Art. 54 RD 2064/1995.

190. To be included in Group II or III as a self-employed worker, the income of these activities must be the main source of income even if, temporarily or permanently, they conduct other work that is not specifically related to fishing, whether it determines inclusion in social security system schemes or not. And the remuneration system adopted, salary or share of profits, will apply equally to all crew members, including the shipowner.

191. The contribution in the RETM is determined by a rate applied to the CBs. There are differences whether the subjects included in the Special Scheme are self-employed workers or not. Generally speaking, the CB is composed of the remunerations effectively received, but laying down some special rules for its calculation, depending on the group the self-employed workers or the workers are included.

192. In Group I, the same conditions as the General Scheme are applied to workers and same conditions of the RETA are applied to self-employed workers.

193. In Groups II and III, the contributions shall be made on the basis of the remuneration which is annually determined by Order of the MISSM, following the proposal of the ISM based on the organizations representing the sector. This calculation will be made by province, fishing methods and occupational classification, on the basis of the average values of the remuneration received in the preceding year.

194. Regarding the CB determined in this way for Groups II and III, it shall be unique. Notwithstanding, these CBs may not be less than the minimum bases specified for the various occupational classifications stated for the General Scheme.

195. Additionally, some correction coefficients shall be applied to the CBCC and to the CB for unemployment and out-of-work protection for Groups II and III, as set forth in Article 11 of Law 47/2015:

Group	*Correction Coefficient*
Group II A	2/3
Group II B	1/2
Group III	1/3

196. The rules laid down in the regulations applicable to RETA set up the contribution rates to the self-employed workers and their equivalent. Similarly, the contribution rates are the same as applied in the General Scheme if they are workers or their equivalent.

Chapter 5. Government Funding

197. The social security funding in Spain is a hybrid system, since the income does not come exclusively from the contribution quotas of the obligated persons, but it has to be completed through other income. Thus, according to the provisions of Article 109(1) of the GSSA, the social security will be financed through its general resources such as:

(a) the progressive contributions of the State, which will be consigned on a permanent basis in its General Budgets, and those that are agreed upon for special attention or are required by the demand of the conjuncture;
(b) the quotas of the obligated persons;
(c) the amounts collected as surcharges, penalties or others of an analogous nature;
(d) the rewards, rents or interests and any other product of their patrimonial resources;
(e) any other income, notwithstanding the stated of Additional Provision No. 10.

198. The social security patrimony is configured, therefore, by the income mentioned above, the goods and resources belonging to the social security. The regulation of the patrimony of the social security is set up by the specific provisions of the GSSA, its rules of application and development and Law No. 33/2003 of 3 November, of the Patrimony of the public administrations.[160]

199. Various instruments are configured as adjustment elements to the economic regime of social security. The Social Security Reserve Fund has the aim to review the future requirements of the system relating to contributory benefits. It is funded by the surplus of income regarding the contributory benefits and its expenses, resulting from the budgetary allocation or liquidation of each fiscal year, if the financial situation of the Social Security System permits it. Additionally, the surplus resulting after allocation of the Reserve with Stabilization of Common Contingencies of MCSS shall be deposited in the Reserve Fund.[161] Another instrument that supports the financial system of the whole Social Security System is the Stabilization Fund to stabilize the differences or deficits between incomes and expenditures.

200. The GSSA consolidates the principle of separation of sources of resources and funding. Consequently, on the one hand, as regards the contributory level of protection, Article 109(2) of the GSSA set up that 'the expenses arising from their management and those of operation for the services corresponding to affiliation, collection and economic-financial and patrimonial management shall be basically funded by the resources stated in the Article 109(1) b) c) d) and e)'. The latter means to be financed by the quotas and the rest of incomes above-mentioned referred. If necessary, it shall be complemented with the State contributions established specifically.

160. Articles 103 and following of the GSSA.
161. Articles 117 and following of the GSSA.

201. On the other hand, the non-contributory or welfare level of protection will be paid by the State, setting its funding in the respective Budget Laws for each year.

202. Lastly, the healthcare services and the social services transferred to the CCAA will be financed according to the regional financing system in force.

Part III. Health Care

María Teresa Velasco Portero

203. The right to health protection of citizens is recognized in Article 43(1) of the SC; paragraph (2) states, 'It is incumbent upon the public authorities to organise and safeguard public health by means of preventive measures and the necessary benefits and services.' Competences in health matters have been gradually assumed by all the CCAA under the constitutional provisions and the respective autonomy statutes, completing this process with a stable financing model.

204. In the Social Security System, relating to persons affected by its subjective scope, the GSSA provides that protective action comprises the healthcare in cases of maternity, common or occupational disease and accident, whether at work or not.[162] Then, the purpose of social security healthcare is to provide the medical and pharmaceutical services necessary to maintain or restore the health of the beneficiaries of the system, as well as their capacity for work.

205. As healthcare is considered a universal right of citizens, it will be developed through generic but not social security-specific rules.

206. The right to health protection of citizens is implemented by the General Health Act (Law 14/1986 of 25 April), which contains the organizational structure of the National Health System, and by Law 16/2003 of 28 May, on the Cohesion and Quality of the National Health System, which is the legal frame to the coordination and cooperation among the health public administrations from the State and the CCAA according to their respective competences. The latter states, among its general principles, the following: the universal and public insurance of the State; the provision of comprehensive healthcare, and the public financing of the National Health System.

162. Article 42(1) a) of the GSSA.

Chapter 1. Field of Application

§1. Personal Field of Application

207. Healthcare in Spain, financed with public funds through the National Health System, is guaranteed to Spaniards and foreigners who have established their residence in Spanish territory.[163] In general, the MSCBS is responsible for the recognition and supervision of this right.

208. However, persons entitled to healthcare in Spain in application of EU Regulations on coordination of social security systems or bilateral agreements that include the provision of healthcare will have access to it, as long as they reside in Spanish territory or during their temporary trips to Spain, in the form, extension and conditions established in the EU or in indicated bilateral provisions. In this situation, the INSS is the competent body to recognize and supervise the right to health protection and healthcare.

209. Persons entitled to health protection and healthcare may exercise this right if they are in any of the following circumstances:

- Have Spanish nationality and habitual residence in Spanish territory.
- Have their right to healthcare in Spain recognized by any other legal title, even if they do not have their habitual residence in Spanish territory, as long as there is no third party obliged to pay for said care.
- Be a foreigner with legal and habitual residence in Spanish territory and not have the obligation to accredit the compulsory coverage of healthcare by any other means.

210. Persons who are not entitled to healthcare from public funds may obtain this benefit by signing a special agreement (*convenio especial*), therefore paying the corresponding fee.

211. In the case of irregular migrants, that is not registered or authorized to reside in Spanish territory, they have the right to health protection and healthcare under the same conditions as Spaniards and financed with public funds from the competent administrations, provided that they meet all of the following requirements:

(a) Not be required to provide proof of compulsory healthcare coverage by any other means, such as the provisions of EU law, bilateral agreements and other applicable legislation.
(b) Not being able to export the right to health coverage from their country of origin or provenance.
(c) There is no third party obliged to pay.

163. Article 3 of Law 16/2003.

212. Once the right has been recognized in charge to public funds, it will be implemented by the competent health administrations, which will facilitate citizens' access to healthcare benefits by issuing them with an individual health card.

213. In addition to these general rules, there are specific cases of people entitled to healthcare:[164]

(a) Returned Spaniards and Spanish employees, self-employed workers and pensioners resident abroad (not in the EU/EEA (European Economic Area)/ Switzerland) and temporarily in Spain, and relatives of the above living with or accompanying them: They are entitled to healthcare paid for with public funds through the National Health System when they do not obtain this coverage by other means, specifically, through the Spanish social security, the home State or international social security regulations and agreements set for this purpose. The recognition of this entitlement lies with the INSS in any case, which shall issue a document accrediting the right. This one shall be maintained until the beneficiary meets the requirements established to obtain such right according to one of the aforementioned means.
(b) Medical care in application of EU Regulations and international agreements: The access to such assistance is possible when they reside in Spanish territory or when travelling temporarily to Spain.
(c) Medical assistance for people with disabilities: In this case, the CCAA or the IMSERSO has power to recognize the right to healthcare.
(d) Special schemes for civil servants: They have obligatory cover for healthcare provision, in accordance with the special regulations governing each Mutual Society (MUFACE, MUGEJU or ISFAS).
(e) Applicants for international protection and victims of human trafficking in a period of recovery and reflection: They can receive medical assistance to the extent provided for in the basic common portfolio of the National Health System. The necessary assistance will be given to applicants with special needs. The CCAA are responsible for recognizing this right.

214. Relating to the Social Security System, there are some specialities with regard to sea workers included in its Special Scheme.[165] The ISM will provide healthcare for common diseases, birth and non-work-related injuries, under the same scope and conditions as in the General Scheme. People entitled to receive healthcare are employed workers and assimilated employees in this Special Scheme, pensioners and non-pensioners who are receiving periodic benefits, and any dependent family members or assimilated family members of the aforementioned persons fulfilling the requirements. The healthcare differs regarding the location where it is received. The ISM has the power on the board ships based in Spain, corresponding to the competent autonomous entity if the power has been transferred to the

164. RD 1192/2012 of 3 August, which regulates the status of insured and beneficiary for the purposes of healthcare in Spain, with charge to public funds, through the National Health System (BOE No. 186 of 4 Aug. 2012).
165. Article 21 of the Law 47/2015.

CCAA.[166] Special rules are applied when the board ship is at sea, depending on the location: the Spanish territory, in EU countries or abroad.

§2. Territorial Field of Application

215. In principle, healthcare, financed with public funds through the National Health System, is provided in Spanish territory, being mandatory the residence in Spain.

216. Access to the health services of the National Health System (detailed in the portfolio of common services, *see* 'Benefits' *infra*) will be guaranteed regardless of where in the national territory users of the system are at all times. To this end, the health services of the CCAA are coordinated among themselves, so that in cases where a Community does not provide a particular service from the common portfolio, it will dispose of the necessary means to transfer the user to another centre in another Community where the service is provided.

217. In particular and for the purpose of maintaining the right to health benefits in which residence in Spanish territory is required, it shall be understood that the beneficiary of said benefits has his habitual residence in Spain even when he has had stays abroad, provided that these do not exceed ninety days during each calendar year.[167]

166. Coordinated and supplemented by healthcare from the INGESA or the corresponding Health Service of the Autonomous Communities.
167. Article 51 of the GSSA.

Chapter 2. Benefits

§1. Care Provided

218. The catalogue of benefits of the National Health System includes the benefits corresponding to public health, primary healthcare, specialized care, emergency care, pharmaceutical benefits, orthotics and prosthetics benefits, dietary supplements and health transport.

219. Health services are provided through the National Health System's 'common portfolio of services', which is structured around the following modalities:[168]

(a) The common portfolio of basic care services: It includes all prevention, diagnosis, treatment and rehabilitation activities carried out at health and social health centres, as well as emergency health transport. It is fully financed by public funds. These services are provided so as to guarantee the continuity of care, through a multidisciplinary, patient-centred approach, thereby guaranteeing the highest quality and safety of provision, as well as providing accessibility and equal treatment to the entire population.
(b) The supplementary common portfolio: It includes all benefits provided to outpatients and subject to a user contribution, such as provision of pharmaceuticals, ortho-prosthetics, dietary products and non-urgent medical transport, subject to a doctor's prescription, for clinical reasons and with a level of user contribution in accordance with that set for the pharmacy benefit.
(c) The common portfolio of ancillary services: It includes all activities, services and techniques, which are not considered as a benefit, nor to be essential and/or help or support the improvement of a chronic pathology. These are subject to a contribution and/or repayment by the user.
(d) The additional portfolio of services of the CCAA: Within the scope of their competences, the CCAA are able to approve their respective portfolios of services, providing the necessary additional resources and assuming their costs, payable by their own budgets. The CCAA must include at least the portfolio of common services of the National Health System, which must be guaranteed to all their users. Under no circumstances will these additional services be included in the general funding of the National Health System benefits.

§2. Benefits

I. Public Health

220. The public health benefit is a set of initiatives organized by the Government to preserve, protect and promote the health of the population. It is provided by means of the National Health Service primary care infrastructure. The public health

168. Articles 8-8 quinquies of Law 16/2003.

benefit includes activities such as preventing illnesses, disabilities and injuries; protecting and promoting environmental health; evaluating the impact on health; early prevention and detection of rare diseases, as well as support for people who contract these illnesses and their families; etc.

II. Primary Healthcare

221. Primary care is the initial and basic level of care, which includes health promotion, health education, disease prevention, healthcare, maintenance and recovery, as well as physical rehabilitation and social work. This level tackles health problems, risk factors and risk behaviour. Services included are on-demand healthcare, both through consultations and at the patient's home; prevention, health promotion, family support and community care activities; basic rehabilitation; specific support and services for women, children, teenagers, adults, the elderly, risk groups and the chronically ill; etc.

III. Specialized Care

222. Specialized care ensures continuity of care for the patient as a whole, once primary care options are exhausted and until the patient is able to return to that level. It includes specialized care through consultations; specialized care provided through nurseries, medical and surgical hospitals; hospital admission; support for primary healthcare for early discharge from hospital and, where appropriate, home hospitalization; mental healthcare, etc.

IV. Emergency Care

223. Emergency care is provided when the patient's medical condition is such that immediate medical attention is required. It is provided both in health centres and elsewhere, including the patient's home address and on-site, twenty-four hours a day, through medical care and nursing care, in collaboration with other professionals. The portfolio of common services for the provision of emergency care includes: the provision of telephone support through emergency care coordination centres; the initial and immediate assessment of patients to determine the risks to their health and life and, where appropriate, the classification of these patients to prioritise the medical care they need; the provision of land, air and sea medical transport services where it is necessary to adequately transfer them to the health centre; etc.

V. Pharmaceutical Benefits

224. An ambulatory pharmacy benefit consists of dispensing prescriptions through pharmacies. This benefit is subject to a user contribution, which is paid at the time of purchase of the drug or healthcare product, is proportional to the level of income, and is updated at least once a year. The pharmaceutical delivery excludes some products such as those of cosmetic use or Homeopathic medicines, among others. In any case, it is not possible to get medicines without a prescription, as well as medicines not used for the treatment of a clearly determined pathology.

VI. Orthotics and Prosthetics Benefit

225. The orthotic and prosthetic benefits consist of the use of implantable and non-implantable medical devices, with the purpose of totally or partially replacing a part of the body, or modifying, correcting or helping its function. It will include the elements necessary to improve the patient's quality of life and autonomy. This benefit is provided by the SPS or will give rise to economic aid. These benefits include surgical implants, external prostheses, wheelchairs and orthopaedic and special prostheses.

VII. Dietary Supplements

226. The benefit of dietary supplements includes the administration of dietary-therapeutic treatments to people suffering from certain congenital metabolic disorders and domiciliary enteral nutrition for patients who, as a consequence of their state of health, are not able to satisfy their nutritional needs with normal consumption of food. This provision will be provided by the health services, which may give rise to economic aid.

VIII. Health Transport

227. Medical transport of patients is carried out for exclusive medical reasons when their state of health prevents them from being transported by ordinary means of transport. In particular, it must be accessible to people with disabilities. The portfolio of common services includes transport without medical care on board, which is designed for the special transport of patients or accident victims requiring technical healthcare en route.

Chapter 3. Finance

228. The competence for healthcare has been transferred to the CCAA, which determines that they have assumed financial responsibility for the healthcare benefits provided by Law 16/2003. Then, if a new benefit is included in the catalogue of benefits of the National Health System, the CCAA must attach a financial report containing an assessment of the positive or negative impact it may have. This report shall be submitted to the Fiscal and Financial Policy Council for analysis in the context of the principle of institutional loyalty.[169]

§1. Common Portfolio of Basic Care Services

229. It should be noted that the portfolio of common services will only be provided by centres, establishments and services of the National Health System, either owned or contracted. However, there is an exception in situations of vital risk, when it is justified that those means cannot be used. In this matter, there is abundant case law on what should be understood by urgent, immediate and vital healthcare, to approve the reimbursement of medical expenses incurred as a result of having been treated outside the National Health System. In principle, expenses will be reimbursed when it has been demonstrated that these services cannot be used in time and that they do not constitute a diverted or abusive use of this exception.[170]

§2. Supplementary Common Portfolio

230. The benefits of the supplementary common portfolio are provided on an outpatient basis and are subject to the user's contribution. Such benefits include: (a) pharmaceuticals provisions; (b) ortho-prosthetics provision; (c) dietary products and (d) non-urgent medical transport, in the following terms.

I. Pharmaceuticals Benefits

231. The user's contribution will be made at the time of dispensing the medicine product and is proportional to the level of income. In general, the user's contribution percentage will be as follows: [171]

(a) 60% of the price for users and their beneficiaries, whose income is greater than or equal to EUR 100,000 as entered in the general tax base amount for IRPF.

169. Article 10 of Law 16/2003.
170. Article 4(3) of the RD 1030/2006 of 15 September, establishing the portfolio of common services of the National Health System and the procedure for updating it (BOE No. 222 of 16 Sep. 2006).
171. Article 102 of the Royal Legislative Decree 1/2015 of 24 July, approving the revised text of the Law on Guarantees and Rational Use of Medicines and Health Products (BOE No. 177 of 25 Jul. 2015).

(b) 50% of the price for working people with insured status and their beneficiaries, whose income is greater than or equal to EUR 18,000 and less than EUR 100,000, as entered in the general tax base amount for IRPF.
(c) 40% of the price for working people who have insured status and their beneficiaries, who are not included in the foregoing section (a) or (b).
(d) 10% of the price for working people who have insured status as social security pensioners, except for people included in section (a).
(e) 40% of the price for irregular foreigners (not registered or authorized as residents in Spain).

232. Notwithstanding, users and their beneficiaries belonging to one of the following categories shall be exempt from making contributions:

(a) People affected by toxic shock syndrome and people with disabilities in the cases provided for in their specific regulations.
(b) People receiving social integration income.
(c) People receiving non-contributory benefits.
(d) Unemployed people who are no longer entitled to receive unemployment benefits, for as long as their situation continues.
(e) Financial benefits for work-related injuries and occupational diseases.
(f) Beneficiaries of the minimum vital income.
(g) Minors affected by a disability of at least 33%.
(h) Beneficiaries of economic allowance for dependent child or minor in permanent foster care or under pre-adoption guardianship.
(i) Social Security pensioners whose declared annual income is less than EUR 5,635. Also, those who are not obliged to present the IRPF declaration and receive an annual income of less than EUR 11,200.

233. Lastly, the contribution level for members of mutual societies and the passive classes of MUFACE, ISFAS and MUGEJU will be 30%.

II. Ortho-Prosthetics Provision

234. In general, the supplementary ortho-prosthetic provision portfolio is subject to the user's contribution, with a scheme similar to that of pharmaceutical provision, taking the product price as the basis for calculation.

235. However, the following are exempt from making the contribution:

- Persons affected by toxic syndrome.
- People with disabilities according to their specific regulations.
- Persons receiving social integration income.
- Persons receiving non-contributory pensions.
- Unemployed who have lost the right to receive unemployment benefit as long as their situation persists.

– People who require treatment as a result of an accident at work or occupational disease, although the corresponding MCSS, the INSS or the ISM will pay for its financing.

236. Lastly, the contribution level for members of MUFACE, ISFAS and MUGEJU will be 30%, except for the treatments derived from an accident in the act of service or professional illness, which will be exempt from contribution.

III. Dietary Supplements

237. As mentioned before, certain dietary-therapeutic treatments to persons suffering from certain congenital metabolic disorders and home enteral nutrition can be provided by health services or generate financial assistance, as set up in RD 1205/2010 of 24 September, on laying down the basis for the inclusion of dietary foods for special medical uses in the provision with dietary products of the National Health System and for the establishment of their maximum financing amounts.[172]

IV. Non-urgent Health Transport

238. The urgent health transport shall be totally covered by public funds.[173] Notwithstanding, when it is not urgent, for clinical reasons and due to doctor's orders, it is considered part of the supplementary common portfolio and the user has to contribute economically. The percentage of a user's contribution is regulated by the same rules of pharmaceutical benefit, considering the final price of the service as the calculation basis and not applying limits to the contribution.

§3. Common Portfolio of Ancillary Services

239. In this case, the user's contribution or, as the case may be, reimbursement shall be governed by the same rules as those governing pharmaceutical provision.

§4. Additional Portfolio of Services of the CCAA

240. See supra Chapter 2, §1.

172. BOE No. 233 of 25 Sep. 2010.
173. Article 8 (ter) (3) of Law 16/2003.

Part IV. Family Allowances

Cristina Sánchez-Rodas Navarro

Chapter 1. The Constitutional Basis of the Family Benefits and Its Legal Development

241. According to Article 39(1) of the SC, 'the public authorities shall ensure the social, economic and legal protection of the family'. However, family protection is not a fundamental right binding for all public authorities but a right that may only be invoked in the ordinary courts in the context of the legal provisions by which they are developed.[174]

242. In the field of social protection, this constitutional right is regulated by the GSSA and developed by the RD 1335/2005 with respect to family benefits. The latter are legally classified as contributory and non-contributory family benefits. With regard to the dependents, the family circle is rather restricted in both cases.

243. Contributory family benefit in Spain is always non-economic benefit. All economic family allowances are legally qualified as non-contributory benefits and there are three types:

(1) Financial allowance for each child under 18 years of age with a disability of 33% or more, or over 18 years of age with a disability of 65% or more.
(2) Economic benefit for the birth or adoption of a child, in cases of large families, single-parent families and in the case of disabled mothers.
(3) Benefits for multiple births or adoptions.

244. A peculiarity of the Spanish legislation is that economic family allowances have little practical relevance in general for family economies since their amount is modest but the requirements for granting them and the incompatibility regime are very strict.

174. Article 53(3) of the SC.

Chapter 2. Family Protection

§1. Contributory Family Benefit

245. Under the heading 'Protection of the Family', the GSSA regulates, among other non-economic benefits, the contributory family benefit. Although it is legally qualified as a contributory benefit, it is neither financed by social contributions paid by employees and/or employers nor is its recognition subordinated to the accreditation of any previous contribution period. According to Article 237 of the GSSA, it is a non-economic benefit for childcare, of a minor fostered or from other family members. The right to get this non-economic benefit does not expire.

I. Territorial Field of Application

246. To get contributory family benefits, no residence requirement is established in fact. The cornerstone is that these family benefits are granted only to workers and civil servants included in the personal scope of the Social Security System. Therefore, not only nationals but also EU citizens and third-country nationals could be entitled to these family benefits when they accomplish the requisites to work legally in Spain. In the case of third-country nationals, they will require a work authorization that as a general rule is recognized simultaneously with the residence authorization in Spain if they fulfil the requirements established in the domestic law.

II. Personal Field of Application

247. Beneficiaries of contributory family benefits are those workers and civil servants who have taken periods of leave to take care of:

- each child (biological or adopted);
- dependent minor in permanent foster care or under pre-adoption guardianship;
- relatives up to the second degree needing long-term care as far as they are not in paid employment.

248. To take periods of leave is a *sine qua non* previous requisite to get contributory family benefits. During the period of leave the obligation of the employer and the worker to pay contributions ceases.

249. In any case, self-employed workers included in the personal scope of the Special Scheme for Sea Workers and Self-employed Workers cannot be beneficiaries of these family benefits because they have not recognized the right to take periods of leave to take care of their relatives under domestic law.

III. A Non-economic Benefit

250. Contributory family benefits are not economic benefits. The benefits consist of 'fictional' contribution periods recognized to beneficiaries in order to calculate their future pensions with a maximum contribution (three or one year) depending on the type of leave:

(1) Workers and civil servants who take periods of leave to take care of each child (biological or adopted), or dependent minor in permanent foster care or under pre-adoption guardianship are guaranteed up to a maximum of three years of 'fictional' contribution periods.
(2) The first year of the period of leave that the workers and civil servants enjoy to care relatives needing long-term care. These relatives must accomplish cumulatively these three requisites:
   (a) To be a relative up to the second degree of consanguinity or affinity (or adoption although the legislator has forgotten this situation).
   (b) To be unable to take care of himself/herself for reasons of age, accident, illness or incapacity. Because of age not only the elderly but also children are included.
   (c) Not performing a paid work.

251. That means that these years devoted to attending family responsibilities during which they have not worked or paid social contributions will be considered to be effective contribution periods in order to get retirement, permanent disability, death and survival pensions and maternity and paternity benefits.

252. Moreover, in both cases, the leave period is considered as a situation of assimilated contribution in order to get unemployment benefits and the beneficiaries will maintain the right to healthcare benefits in the Spanish Social Security System.

253. Under the heading of 'contributory family benefit', the following situations are also legally regulated by the GSSA:

- Social contributions made during the first two years of the period of reduced working hours in order to care for a child aged under 12 are going to be calculated with an increase up to 100% of the amount that would have applied if there had been no reduction in working hours in order to get retirement, permanent disability, death and survival pensions and maternity and paternity benefits.
- When the reduction of time worked is related to disabled persons aged over 12 and relatives up to the second degree, as far as the dependents do not perform a paid employment, the quoted increase up to 100% will apply only during the first year.
- When de reduction in working hours is due to the care of minors affected by cancer or another serious illness, the contributions made during these periods of reduction will be computed increased to 100% of the amount that would have

been maintained without this reduction, for the purposes of benefits for retirement, permanent disability, death and survival, maternity, paternity, risk during pregnancy, risk during breastfeeding and temporary disability.

254. The sum of all 'fictional contributions periods' cannot exceed five years per beneficiary.

§2. Other Non-economic Family Benefits

255. The GSSA regulates under the heading of 'Family Protection' other set of facts that must be considered as 'effective contribution periods' to access to social security pensions in the future. In this way, the legislator tries to avoid that the exercise of rights derived from work and family conciliation entails a reduction in the amount of future social security benefits.

I. Computable 'Fictional Periods of Contributions' for Childbirth

256. In order to get contributory old-age pensions and permanent disability, the non-economic family benefit consists of taking into account a total of 112 full days of contribution for each delivery of a single child (and fourteen more days for each child from the second, this included, if the delivery was multiple). This rule is not applicable when social contributions have been paid during the entire sixteen weeks (or the correspondent period in case of multiple delivery).

II. Periods Considered Effective Social Contribution by Birth, Adoption and Foster Care

257. It will be computed as a contribution period for all purposes, except for compliance of the minimum contribution period required, the time in which the contribution has been interrupted due to the end of the employment relationship or the end of the collection of unemployment benefits a far as such circumstances have occurred between the nine months prior to birth, or the three months prior to the adoption or permanent foster of a minor, and the end of the sixth year following that situation.

258. The time computable as 'fictional contribution periods' will be a maximum of 270 days per child or minor adopted or hosted, without in any case being greater than the actual interruption of the contribution. The family benefit will be granted only to one of the parents. In case of controversy among them, the mother's right will prevail.

Chapter 3. Non-contributory Family Allowances

259. All family allowances regulated in Chapter I of Title VI of the GSSA are qualified as non-contributory.[175] They are financed by taxes. Non-contributory family allowances consist of an economic allowance. These benefits try to cover situations of need related to the existence of family responsibilities: birth and adoption of children, or fostering of children.

260. Beneficiaries can be not only Spaniards but also citizens of States where EU law is applicable and even third-country nationals as far as they reside legally in Spain. They are not required to prove any previous period of contributions.

§1. Territorial Field of Application

261. The residence requirement traditionally has been considered as one of the typical features of non-contributory social security benefits. As a general rule, both beneficiaries of non-contributory family allowances and children or minors in charge must reside legally in Spanish territory. Nevertheless, regarding non-contributory family allowances, it is not required to accomplish a minimum previous period of residence in Spain. To prove the residence requirement is only necessary at the time of the request and shall be made as follows:

(a) Spanish beneficiaries can prove their legal residence by presenting the valid national identity document that will prove the address.[176]
(b) The right of residence of EU citizens, citizens of the EEA and Switzerland is currently governed by Directive 2004/38/EC on the right of citizens of the Union and their family members to move and reside freely within the territory of the Member States, transposed to Spanish legislation by RD 240/2007.[177] Nationals of States in which the EU law applies may reside legally in Spain if they:[178]
   - are workers or self-employed persons in the host Member State;
   - have sufficient resources for themselves and their family members not to become a burden on the social assistance system of the host Member State during their period of residence and have comprehensive sickness insurance cover in the host Member State;
   - are enrolled at a private or public establishment, accredited or financed by the host Member State on the basis of its legislation or administrative practice, for the principal purpose of following a course of study, including

175. Article 109(3) b) of the GSSA.
176. Article 1 of the RD 1553/2005.
177. RD 240/2007 of 16 February, on the entry, free movement and residence in Spain of citizens of the Member States of the European Union and of other States party to the Agreement on the European Economic Area (BOE No. 51 of 28 Feb. 2007).
178. Nationals of States in which the European Union law applies will prove their residence in Spain through the certificate of registration in the Central Registry of Foreigners.

vocational training; and have comprehensive sickness insurance cover in the host Member State and assure the relevant national authority, by means of a declaration or by such equivalent means as they may choose, that they have sufficient resources for themselves and their family members not to become a burden on the social assistance system of the host Member State during their period of residence;
- are family members accompanying or joining a Union citizen who satisfies the above-mentioned conditions, whether as a worker, inactive person or student.

(c) Third-country nationals: they can also get Spanish family benefits in equal conditions if they have authorization of residence in Spain.[179]

262. It is important to highlight that legally 'residence' and 'stay' are not synonymous under our domestic law. Precisely, the lack of residence authorization is what prevents access to non-contributory allowances to people who can legally work in Spain but reside in another country: this is the case of cross-border workers. According to Article 182 of the RD 557/2011,[180] cross-border workers are workers who have been authorized to develop lucrative, labour or professional activities on their own account or on behalf of another in the border areas of Spanish territory, residing in the border area of a bordering State to which they return daily.

263. There may also be people who being legally in Spain will not be entitled to non-contributory family allowances, such as third-country nationals who are in Spain with a study permit, doing non-work practices or volunteering services. These groups – and their families – are granted authorization to stay, but not residence permits.

264. Due to the fact that legal residence is legally required to get non-contributory family allowances, it implies that irregular migrants are excluded from the personal scope of Spanish family allowances. This conclusion is corroborated by *a contrario sensu* interpretation of Article 14(1) of the OL 4/2000.

265. It must also take into account that the Multilateral Ibero-American Social Security Agreement – in force in Spain since 2011 – does not affect this residence requisite established by the domestic law applicable to non-contributory family allowances. The reason is evident: its material scope includes exclusively 'the branches of social security relating to invalidity benefit; old-age cash benefits; economic survivors' benefits; and economic benefits of workplace accidents and occupational diseases'.[181] Therefore, all non-contributory social security benefits – including family allowances – are excluded.

179. Article 14(1) of the Organic Law 4/2000 of 11 January, on the Rights and Freedoms of Foreigners in Spain and Their Social Integration.
180. RD 557/2011 of 20 April, approving the Regulations to Organic Law 4/2000, following its reform by Organic Law 2/2009 (BOE No. 103 of 30 Apr. 2011).
181. Article (3)1 of the OL 4/2000.

I. Exceptions to the Residency Requirement

A. *By Application of the National Law*

266. With regard to non-contributory family allowances, the requirement of residency in Spain will be considered fulfilled even when there is a cessation of cohabitation due to the work of the subject beneficiary: this is just the case of workers transferred by their company outside of Spain, who are legally in a similar contributory situation and pay social contributions in the corresponding Spanish Social Security Scheme according to Article 10(1)a) of RD 1335/2005.

267. Concerning the children or foster children, the requirement of residence will be considered fulfilled when they accompany the workers transferred by their company outside the national territory on their journeys.[182]

268. The residence will not be considered interrupted by the absences of the Spanish territory inferior to ninety days throughout each natural year, nor when the absence is motivated by cause of duly justified illness.

B. *By Application of the EU Law: Family Benefits and Regulation No. 883/2004 – Waiving of Residence Rules*

269. As the Spanish Supreme Court claimed in its judgment of 11 April 2000, the lack of family cohabitation is just another adverse consequence that migrants face.[183] Since migrant workers are not always accompanied by members of their families, Regulation No. 883/2004 contains specific provisions to avoid not only that the migrant worker may be dissuaded from exercising the right to free movement for fear of losing social security benefits but also that he/she may be subject to direct or indirect discrimination with respect to national workers whose family members reside in the country of employment.

270. Chapter 8 of Regulation No. 883/2004,[184] further developed in Articles 58–61 of Regulation No. 987/2009,[185] is devoted to family benefits. According to Article 1(z) of Regulation No. 883/2004, 'family benefit' means all benefits in kind or in cash intended to meet family expenses, excluding advances of maintenance payments and special childbirth and adoption allowances mentioned in Annex I.

182. Article 10(2) of the RD 1335/2005.
183. Regulation (EC) No. 883/2004 of the European Parliament and of the Council of 29 Apr. 2004 on the Coordination of Social Security Systems.
184. Articles 67–69.
185. Regulation (EC) No. 987/2009 of the European Parliament and of the Council of 16 Sep. 2009 laying down the procedure for implementing Regulation (EC) No. 883/2004.

271. Spain has notified under Annex I that 'single payment birth and adoption grants'. That means that among the Spanish non-contributory family benefits only the allowances for dependent children or foster children are coordinated by EU Regulation No. 883/2004.

272. Although States may list in said Annex I the family benefits they wish to exclude from the EU coordination rules, this does not mean that the European Court of Justice (ECJ) is bound by such notifications. That is to say, as the highest authority on the interpretation of EU law, the European Court should the case arise may accept or reject the inclusion of a given benefit in the Annex.

273. With regard to non-economic family benefits (family protection) as far as they are neither cash benefits nor benefits in kind, Article 7 of Regulation No. 883/2004 is not applicable.

274. In accordance with Article 67 of Regulation No. 883/2004, 'a person shall be entitled to family benefits in accordance with the legislation of the competent Member State, including for his/her family members residing in another Member State, as if they were residing in the former Member State. However, a pensioner shall be entitled to family benefits in accordance with the legislation of the Member State competent for his/her pension'.

275. According to Article 7 EU of Regulation No. 883/2004, 'unless otherwise provided for by this Regulation, cash benefits payable under the legislation of one or more Member States or under this Regulation shall not be subject to any reduction, amendment, suspension, withdrawal or confiscation on account of the fact that the beneficiary or the members of his/her family reside in a Member State other than that in which the institution responsible for providing benefits is situated'.

276. However, EU Regulations have never declared family benefits to be exportable, because in the case of the payment of family allowances for children who do not reside in the competent State which makes the payment, it is not so much a question of exportability, given that the worker is in the territory of the competent State, but of not discriminating on the grounds of the place of residence of the family members.

277. That is, although the competent State must pay family benefits for children resident in other Member States when appropriate, this is not strictly a case of the export of benefits as contemplated for cases in which the beneficiary of the benefit transfers his residence to another Member State, with the competent State continuing to pay – in a foreign country – the benefit to which the worker is entitled under national legislation.

278. For this reason, the current Article 67 of Regulation No. 883/2004 provides that 'a person shall be entitled to family benefits, including for his/her family members residing in another Member State, as if they were residing in the former Member State'.

279. It can be said, therefore, that the purpose of Chapter 8 of Regulation No. 883/2004 is, basically, to prevent a Member State from making the award or the amount of family benefits depending on residence requirements applied to the worker's family members in the awarding State, in order to guarantee the migrant worker's right to freedom of movement.

280. That is, when, according to the legislation applicable to the beneficiary he/she is entitled to family benefits, the competent paying authority cannot deny or reduce these family benefits by claiming residence clauses provided for in their domestic legislation.

281. In conclusion, in the case of beneficiaries to whom Regulation No. 883/2004 applies, Spain will pay allowances for a dependent child or minor in permanent foster care or under pre-adoption guardianship even when the children or minors do not reside in Spain as long as they do so in another State in which EU law is applicable.

282. The obligation to reside in Spain will continue to be required for the rest of the family benefits notified in Annex I because they are excluded from EU coordination rules.

C. *By Application of International Social Security Agreements*

283. Even when the children do not reside in Spain, non-contributory family allowances can be granted if this possibility has been foreseen by international agreements. The Circular 4/2006 on Instructions for the application of the rules on family protection of social security lists the bilateral agreements signed by Spain that include family benefits within its scope. In application of these agreements, with the exception of Australia, the residence of the child or foster minor in the other signatory State will be considered as residence in national territory. These international standards only refer to the residence of the children or foster minors, not the beneficiaries.

284. In other words, in spite of the requirement of residence in Spain of the children or foster children established by Article 352 of the GSSA, workers included in the personal scope of application of international agreements that provide for this may be beneficiaries of Spanish non-contributory family allowances with respect to the children or foster children under their care when the latter reside in: Brazil, Canada, Chile, the Dominican Republic, Morocco, Paraguay, Peru, Russia, Tunisia, Ukraine and Uruguay.

§2. Personal Field of Application

285.

(a) Spaniards residing in Spain may be beneficiaries of non-contributory family benefits. In order to prove the residence requirement, it is necessary to be domiciled in Spanish territory and hold resident status.

(b) EU citizens, citizens of the EEA and Switzerland may also be beneficiaries of non-contributory family benefits if they reside legally in Spain. Their right of residence in EU States is governed by EU law.
(c) Third-country nationals can get Spanish family benefits as far as they and their dependents have authorization of residence in Spain.

§3. Financial Allowance for Each Child under 18 Years of Age with a Disability of 33% or More, or over 18 Years of Age with a Disability of 65% or More

I. Beneficiaries

286. Beneficiaries can be biological or adoptive parents, foster parents and even applicants for adoption in charge of minors. The legislator avoids in particular the allusions to the beneficiaries' gender (the reference to father or mother). In case of judicial separation or divorce, the parent, or foster parent, who is in charge of the children or minors will receive the allowance. In exceptional situations, beneficiary and dependent may coincide.

II. Dependent

287. The economic allowance is for each one of the dependents who meet the legal requirements.

A. Handicapped Minors under 18 Years Old

288. In this case, a 'dependent child' is a handicapped child in charge under 18 years old, irrespective of his/her filiation. Regarding this situation, the family allowance is not means-tested and the economic family allowance will be granted regardless of the beneficiaries' income.

B. Handicapped Child over 18 Years Old

289. A 'dependent child' is considered a child in charge over 18 years old affected by a degree of disability greater than or equal to 65%, regardless of his/her filiation. In order to be entitled to this economic family allowance, the incomes are not taken into account because it is not means-tested.

C. Common Rules

290. Dependent children or minors shall maintain their status even if they developed a lucrative activity as worker or self-employed provided that they cumulatively meet two requirements:

(1) The annual income earned from their jobs must not exceed 100% of the current interprofessional minimum wage. For this purpose, only income from work will be computed. In other words, incomes from movable or real estate capital are excluded. It is also irrelevant that as a result of his/her job the dependent must be affiliated into a social security scheme different from that in which is affiliated the beneficiary of the economic family allowance.
(2) The beneficiary and dependent must continue living together.

291. According to Article 9(1) of the RD 1335/2005, it is compulsory that children and minors live with the beneficiary and depend economically on him/her. This situation will not be altered in the cases of temporary separation motivated by reason of studies, work of parents or foster parents, medical treatment, rehabilitation or other similar causes.[186]

292. Moreover, when the beneficiary lives with the minors or dependents, the requirement of economic dependence is presumed *iuris tantum.* This presumption favours the applicants of these family allowances because once it is proved the requirement of living together it would correspond to the Social Security Administration to prove the absence of economic dependence.[187]

293. The Social Security Administration has even admitted that the permanent residence of disabled children in special centres will not be a cause of non-compliance with the requirement of living together if the parents, or foster parents, prove that they pay in whole or in part, the centre's expenses. In such cases, the minors and dependents are considered still in charge of the family allowance beneficiaries. In other words, in such extreme situations, the economic dependence prevails over the fact or living together in order to maintain the right to get this non-contributory family allowance.

294. Children and minors will not satisfy the requirement of being 'dependent' on the beneficiary if:

(a) their annual job's incomes exceed 100% of the current interprofessional minimum wage;
(b) they get a contributory pension from a public Social Security System, different from the orphanage pension or pension for family members of grandchildren and siblings;[188]
(c) they are over 18 years of age but have a disability of less than 65% regardless they still live with the beneficiary and depend economically on him/her.

295. It is possible that beneficiary and dependent will be the same person when he/she is in charge of himself/herself. In such case, the economic family allowance has the purpose to mitigate his/her own state of need.

---

186. Article 9(2) RD 1335/2005.
187. Article 9(2) of the RD 1335/2005.
188. Article 9(4) of the RD 1335/2005.

III. Non-Means-Tested Economic Family Allowances

296. When the child or minor has a disability of 33% or more, or s(he) is over 18 years of age with a disability of 65% or more, the level of income is not taken into account. In other words, in such cases, the family allowance is not means-tested.

297. The assessment and determination of the degree of disability for the recognition of the allowances for the dependent child or disabled foster child shall be determined through the application of the scale approved by the Government. Currently, the scales of assessment of the degrees and levels of dependency for over three years and the scale of specific assessment of dependence for people under three years are contained in the annexes of RD 174/2011 of 11 February.[189]

IV. Amount

298. The Spanish legislator has established different amounts related to the dependent's age and/or degree of the disability:

(a) Dependent child or minor with a disability of 33% or more: EUR 1,000 per year.
(b) Dependent child over 18 years of age and is affected by a disability in a degree of 65% or more: EUR 4,790.40 per year.
(c) When the dependent child is over 18 years old, is affected by a disability in a degree of 75% or more and, as a consequence of anatomical or functional losses, needs the assistance of another person to perform the most essential acts of life: EUR 7,185.60 per year.

299. The marriage of the beneficiary, as far as s(he) has a disability of 65% or more, is compatible with the family allowance. The non-contributory family allowance is not a pension and therefore is compatible with the SOVI-pension (*see* 'Historical Background', *supra*) as the Supreme Court has established. However, when the child gets a non-contributory pension, he cannot perceive economic family allowances for handicapped child over 18 years old simultaneously.

V. Payment

300. The management and recognition of this benefit corresponds to the INSS, but the payment is the responsibility of the TGSS. In the case of persons under 18

---

189. RD 174/2011 of 11 February, approving the scale of assessment of the situation of dependency established by Law 39/2006 of 14 December, on the Promotion of Personal Autonomy and Care for dependent persons (BOE No. 42 of 18 Feb. 2011).

years old, disabled or not, the payment will be half-yearly and must be made by the expired semester. In cases of disabled people over 18 years old, it will be monthly and will be paid monthly.

301. The right to recognition of benefits shall expire after five years, counted from the day on which the triggering event occurred. All beneficiaries are obliged to send to the INSS, within thirty days from the day they are produced, a communication of all variations that would affect the beneficiary's situation that may provoke modification or the end of the right to the economic family allowance. Never will be necessary to accredit the facts or circumstances that the Social Security Administration should know for itself directly. Before 1 April of each year, all the beneficiaries are obliged to submit a statement of their incomes during the previous year.

302. The right to get the economic allowance ends:

- due to the dependents' deaths;
- when dependents reach the age of 18 years, except when they are affected by a disability equal or greater than 65%;
- by disappearance or improvements of the dependents' disability that provokes that he/she does not accomplish the degree of disability legally required to get this family allowance;
- when finished the economic dependence of the dependent on the beneficiary.

§4. Economic Benefit for the Birth or Adoption of a Child, in Cases of Large Families, Single-Parent Families and in the Case of Disabled Mothers

I. Beneficiaries

303. They will be biological and adoptive parents.

A. *Large Families*

304. In this case, the right to get the benefit will only be recognized to one of the couples. If both parents or adopters live together, any of them can be the beneficiary as far as they agree. However, in case of absence of agreement, the mother will be the beneficiary. When parents or adopters do not live together, the beneficiary will be who has the dependents' custody.

B. *Single-Parent Family*

305. The beneficiary is the parent with whom the child or adopted child lives and takes care of their livelihood.

C. Handicapped Mothers

306. Beneficiaries can be also mothers with a disability of 65% or more. With such measure, the legislator tries to protect persons who might be close to social exclusion for their double quality of being a woman and disabled. It has been criticized from the perspective of gender equality that protection is not extended when it is the father who is disabled.

D. Double Orphans and Abandoned Children

307. In such a situation, the beneficiary will be the person who legally takes charge of the dependents. In this case, legal residence of the beneficiary in Spain is required. Even Spanish nationals are subject to the residence requirement that is also applicable to EU Nationals and third-country nationals. Due to the lack of legal residence in Spain, illegal migrants are excluded as well as those who work legally or stay legally in national territory without a residence authorization.

308. Moreover, the law requires that the birth or adoption must have taken place in Spanish territory. It will be considered that this requirement is met when it is proven that the child has been immediately integrated into a family nucleus with residence in Spain.

309. Beneficiaries will be excluded from this economic family allowance if they are entitled to benefits of this same nature in any other public social protection scheme.

II. Dependent

310. The law recognizes family allowances for the birth or adoption of a child in Spain when it happens:

- in large families, or family that becomes large due to this birth or adoption;
- into single-parent families: this one is formed by a single parent with whom the child lives and this parent is the only breadwinner of the family;
- when the mother suffers a disability of 65% or more.

311. According to the Civil Code, the personality is acquired at the time of birth with life, once the entire detachment of the mother's womb has taken place. For the purposes of considering large families, Law 40/2003 of 18 November, on the Protection of Large Families, will be applicable.[190]

190. BOE No. 277 of 19 Nov. 2003.

III. Means-Tested Economic Benefit

312. It is a means-tested allowance. Beneficiaries' incomes, of any kind, must be equal or under the poverty-line. If parents and adopters live together, the incomes of both of them are going to take into account. When the sum of their incomes is over the poverty-line legally established, none of them will be entitled to the family allowance.

313. With regard to the economic benefit for the birth or adoption of a child, the poverty-line is calculated by applying the same rules for access to economic benefits for a dependent child or minor in permanent foster care or under pre-adoption guardianship.

IV. Amount

314. It is not a periodic payment but a lump-sum economic benefit (EUR 1,000) for the birth or adoption of a child in Spain that is only recognized in the cases of large families, single-parent families and when the mothers have a disability at or above 65%. Exceptionally, the amount of the family allowance can be less than EUR 1,000 when the beneficiary's income exceeds the poverty-line, but is lower than the amount resulting from adding to that limit the amount of the benefit. If the resulting amount is less than EUR 10.00, no economic family allowance will be recognized at all. This family allowance is not liable to income tax in accordance with current legislation.

V. Payment

315. Beneficiaries must not be entitled to benefits of this kind in any other public system of social protection. The management and recognition of the right corresponds to the National Institute of Social Security. The right to access to this family allowance expired five years after the day following the one in which the birth takes place or the adoption is formalized. The benefit is compatible with the economic benefit for multiple births or adoptions and also with the family allowances for a dependent child or minor in permanent foster care or under pre-adoption guardianship.

§5. Economic Benefit for Multiple Births or Adoptions

I. Beneficiaries

316. Beneficiaries will be the parents or adopters as long as they do not have the right to benefits of this same nature in any other public social protection scheme. If both parents or adopters live together and there is no agreement between them, the mother will be the beneficiary. If they do not live together the family allowance will be paid to who has the guardianship and custody of the children.

317. Legal residence of the beneficiary in Spain is required in any case. Even Spanish nationals are subject to the residence requirement that is also applicable to EU Nationals and third-country nationals. Due to the lack of legal residence in Spain, illegal migrants are excluded, as well as those who work legally or stay legally in national territory without residence authorization.

318. When the dependents are double orphans or have been abandoned, the beneficiary will be the person who legally takes care of the dependent.

II. Dependent

319. The protected contingency is a multiple birth or multiple adoption that has occurred in Spain as far as the number of births or children adopted is equal to or greater than two. However, children born or adopted affected by a disability of 33% or more will compute the double.

320. When the birth or adoption has taken place abroad, it will be considered as happened in Spain provided that the child has been immediately integrated into a family residing in Spain.

III. Non-Means-Tested Economic Benefit

321. Although this family allowance is legally classified as non-contributory, it is not a means-tested benefit.

IV. Amount

322. It is a single-payment economic benefit as well as a flat-rate allowance:

- For two children: a single payment of EUR 3,800.
- For three children: a single payment of EUR 7,600.
- For four or more children: a single payment of EUR 11,400.

323. It must be remembered that if one of the dependents has a disability of at least 33%, the allowance will be increased as the beneficiary has an additional child. These benefits are considered rents exempt for the purposes of the tax legislation.

V. Payment

324. This family benefit allowance is compatible with the special maternity allowance for multiple births or adoptions and with the orphan's pension and the pension for grandchildren and siblings that may correspond. It is also compatible with the economic benefit for the birth or adoption of a child, in cases of large families, single-parent families and in the case of disabled mothers and with the economic benefits for a dependent child or minor in permanent foster care or under pre-adoption guardianship. On the contrary, the benefit is incompatible with the perception by the parents or adopters of any other similar allowance established in the other public social protection schemes.

325. The right to recognition of this benefit is prescribed at five years. The management entity is the INSS, which is the one competent to recognize the right.

Part V. Incapacity to Work

Olga Fotinopoulou Basurko & María Gorrochategui Polo

Chapter 1. Field of Application

326. The incapacity to work, in the contributory level, is regulated in the GSSA distinguishing between temporary disablement and permanent disablement. According to Article 169 of the GSSA, the temporary disablement aims to cover the loss of earnings that occurs when the worker, due to an illness or accident, is temporarily unable to work and requires medical care from the social security. On the other hand, the permanent disablement regulated in Articles 193 et seq. seeks to cover the loss of wages suffered by an individual whose ability to work is determined to be permanently reduced or impaired, after being affected by a pathological or traumatic process as a consequence of an illness or accident. In both cases, the disablement can be caused by professional contingencies, but in this chapter, we will only refer to these situations when they are a result of common contingencies since the others will be described in Part VI related to industrial accidents and occupational diseases.

§1. Territorial Field of Application

327. Article 7 of the GSSA states that the contributory level of the Social Security System is provided to Spanish citizens residing in Spain and foreign citizens residing legally in Spain. In both cases, a professional activity in national territory and are included in the different paragraphs of the same Article. Such categories are: employed workers who provide their services under the terms provided for in Article 1(1) of the Workers' Statute in the various branches of economic activity; self-employed workers over the age of 18; worker-members of associated work cooperatives; students and civil servants or military personnel.

§2. Personal Field of Application

328. According to Article 41 of the SC and Article 1 of the GSSA, the Spanish system is based on the principle of universality, meaning that all citizens are included in the Spanish Social Security System. However, the State guarantees their protection in the contributory level when the citizens carry out a professional activity, which would imply the duty to pay contributions and, in return, the entitlement to 'contributory' benefits as temporary or permanent disability ones.

Chapter 2. Benefits

§1. Incapacity to Work

I. Wage Earners

329. The following are considered determining situations for temporary disability: common or occupational diseases (and accidents), whether they are work-related or not if the worker is unable to work and is receiving social security healthcare, with a maximum duration of 365 days, extendable automatically for another 180 days when presuming that during them the worker can be discharged by medical healing.[191] From 1 June 2023, two special situations of temporary disability due to common contingencies have been considered: those in which women may find herself in case of incapacitating menstruation as well as that due to the interruption of pregnancy, voluntary or not, while she receives health care from the Public Health Service and is unable to work, without prejudice to those cases in which the interruption of pregnancy is due to an accident at work or occupational disease, in which case it will be considered to be a situation of temporary disability due to occupational contingencies; and those from pregnant women from the first day to the thirty-ninth week.[192]

330. In relation to the extension of the subsidy of temporary disablement, the responsibility for granting an extension is exclusively of the INSS or, where, applicable, the ISM in the case of sea workers. This extension will be exclusively granted for the time that the Medical Inspectorate from the INSS considers is needed for recovery, up to a maximum of 180 days. If the estimated recovery time exceeds 180 days, then the extension will not be granted, and instead, a Permanent disablement file will be opened, even where the debilitating sequelae are not permanent.

331. During the extension period, the worker will undergo medical check-ups from the INSS. As a result of such monitoring, medical discharge certificate or continuation of the extension of the benefit may be made. In the first case, after a new medical examination, if the worker can be given a medical discharge at the proposal of the Medical Inspectorate, the INSS will issue a decision declaring the medical discharge of the worker. The medical discharger issued by the INSS, from the temporary disablement extension, entails the termination of this benefit without suspending its effectiveness due to the submission of a previous claim. In the second case, the INSS can declare the continuation of the benefit extension to a maximum of 180 days, launching the process of a permanent disability ex Article 169 of the GSSA.

332. As part of the contributory system, workers who after having undergone the prescribed treatments still present serious anatomical or functional reductions,

191. Article 169(1) a) of the GSSA.

192. Organic Law 1/2023 of 28 February, amending Organic Law 2/2010 of 3 Mar. 2010, on sexual and reproductive health and the voluntary interruption of pregnancy.

which can be determined objectively and are expected to be permanent, and which diminish or impair their capacity to work, are considered to be permanently disabled. The possibility that the disabled person will recover his/her capacity to work shall not prevent him/her being classed as permanently disabled, provided that said possibility is deemed medically uncertain or a long-term prospect.[193]

333. Anatomical or functional reductions that exist on the date of the workers' affiliation with the social security shall not prevent them being classed as permanently disabled, provided that he/she is a disabled person whose conditions have worsened after their affiliation causing, either independently or due to the occurrence of new injuries or diseases, a decrease or total impairment in the interested party's capacity to work at the time of their affiliation.[194]

334. As part of the non-contributory system, foreseeably permanent physical or psychological deficiencies, whether congenital in nature or not, that annul or change the physical, psychological or sensorial capacity of the sufferer may be considered a disability.[195]

335. The permanent disability must derive from a temporary disability, except when it affects persons who do not have protection for said temporary disablement, whether they have a status assimilated to affiliation that does not cover it, or they are assimilated to employees to whom the same circumstance applies, or in cases in which persons contract a permanent disablement when not affiliated.[196]

336. Article 194 of the GSSA regulates the permanent disability levels which in Spanish regulation are four:

(1) *Partial permanent disability for the usual profession:* A disability that, without being total, causes the worker's ability to perform his or her usual profession to be reduced a 33% or more, without keeping the worker from performing the basic tasks of the profession.
(2) *Total permanent disability for the usual profession:* A disability that keeps the worker from performing all main tasks in his or her profession, if the worker can take up a different profession.
(3) *Absolute permanent disability for all types of work:* That which absolutely disables a worker to perform any work or trade.
(4) *Serious disability:* A situation suffered by a permanently disabled worker that, because of anatomical or functional losses, needs the care of a third person for the most basic acts of life, such as getting dressed, moving about, eating, etc.

193. Article 193 of the GSSA.
194. Article 193 of the GSSA.
195. Article 193 of the GSSA.
196. Article 193 of the GSSA.

337. Each of these degrees that classify permanent disability will give rise to entitlement, where appropriate, to the corresponding financial permanent disability benefit.

II. Self-Employed Workers

338. The temporary disablement benefit is recognized in the same terms and conditions as in the General Scheme of Social Security, with the following features in relation to the option and formalization of coverage.

339. The workers included in the scope of application of the RETA must formalize the coverage of the protective action due to professional contingencies, temporary disability, cessation of activity and professional training with an MCSS, having to opt for the same MCSS for all the indicated protective action.

340. The coverage of the temporary disablement financial benefit derived from common contingencies will be mandatory and must be formalized with an MCSS, which will be obliged to accept any accession proposal that must be formulated to that effect. The self-employed workers (except for TRADE – or those who carry out activities in which the coverage of professional contingencies is mandatory due to their higher risk of accidents) covered by the temporary disablement benefit in another system of the Social Security System in which, if they are in high status, they may, as long as their pluri-activity situation is maintained, voluntarily accept coverage of said benefit in the RETA as well as, if necessary, renounce it.

341. In the case of permanent disability benefit for self-employed workers, it is recognized under the same terms and conditions as in the General Social Security Scheme, with the following characteristics:

(a) RB. If the disability derives from common contingencies (common illness or non-occupational accident), there is no gap integration, so if during the period taken into account to perform the calculation, months would appear during which there was no obligation to contribute, these will not be completed with the current minimum bases, corresponding to workers over 18 years of age.
(b) In the case of partial permanent disability, if it derives from common contingencies, there is no protection.
(c) In the case of total permanent disability, the percentage will be increased by 20% of the RB that is considered to determine the amount of the pension, provided that the beneficiary:
   - is aged 55 years or over. If the initial recognition of the pension is made at a lower age, the increase will be applied, at the request of the interested party, from the 1st day of the month following that in which the worker reaches the age of 55, provided that on that date he meets the requirements

required in the following two points. If the right to increase is born in a calendar year subsequent to the initial recognition of the pension, to it, increased with 20%, the revaluations that have taken place since the date will be applied;
- do not engage in a paid activity, as an employed or self-employed person, that results in their inclusion in any of the social security schemes. The increase of the pension will be suspended during the period in which the worker obtains a job or performs a gainful activity on his/her own account that is compatible with the total permanent disability pension that he/she received;
- do not hold the ownership of an agrarian or maritime-fishing operation, or of a commercial or industrial establishment as owner, lessee, usufructuary or any other analogous concept.

(d) Compensation. The total permanent disability pension may be replaced by a lump sum, if it derives from common contingencies, equivalent to forty monthly payments of the RB for these contingencies, provided that the interested party exercises this option within thirty days following the declaration of incapacity. The option in favour of life annuity will be understood to have taken place, when the worker has reached the age of 60 years on the date on which the benefit is deemed to have occurred.

Chapter 3. Certification of Incapacity to Work

342. The recognition of the temporary disablement subsidy corresponds to the INSS, the ISM for sea workers' cases or the MCSS that covers common contingencies.

343. *From day 1 to 365*, the following entities are responsible for controlling temporary disability situations:

(a) The SPS, for issuing certificates of the start of sick leave, confirmation and medical discharge.
(b) The INSS, for issuing medical discharges, for all effects and purposes, and for commencing permanent disability procedures. The INSS is also competent to issue a sick leave report in the case of a relapse in a process of under 365 days, which ended with a medical discharge issued by the INSS doctor.
(c) The ISM, for issuing leave and discharge certificates (non-devolved healthcare), medical discharge certificates for all effects and purposes and for commencing permanent disablement procedures for workers falling within the scope of application of the RETM.
(d) MCSS, to issue sick leave, confirmation and discharge certificates for ordinary contingencies.

344. *Once the 365-day term has expired*, the INSS or the ISM will be the only bodies authorized in their respective spheres, to:

- decide the subsidy extension;
- decide to start with the permanent disablement procedures;
- issue the medical discharge certificate;
- issue a new sick leave certificate when this occurs within a period of 180 *calendar* days after the medical discharge for the same or a similar pathology.

345. There are different types of temporary disablement processes depending on the estimated duration:[197]

(a) Process with a very short-estimated duration: under five calendar days.
(b) Process with a short-estimated duration: five to thirty calendar days.
(c) Process with a medium estimated duration: thirty-one to sixty calendar days.
(d) Process with a long-estimated duration: sixty-one or more calendar days.

346. The medical personnel who issue the sick leave and confirmation reports must determine, at the time of issue, the estimated duration of the process. The medical personnel may alter the estimated duration later, due to changes or updates in the worker's diagnosis or the evolution of their health problem. For this purpose,

197. Article 2(3) of Royal Decree 625/2014.

as set out in Article 2(4) of RD 625/2014, they will issue a confirmation report stating the new estimated duration, and if applicable, framing the process as a different type to those stated in the previous section.

347. The medical report beginning the period of temporary disability, whatever the determining contingency may be, will be issued immediately after the worker's medical examination, by the same medical personnel, using the form shown in Annex I of Order ESS/1187/2015 of 15 June.

348. With respect to the permanent disablement recognition, classification and review, the INSS, through its corresponding management organs, is responsible for assessing, qualifying and reviewing eligibility for contributory social security benefits for permanent disability in all steps of the procedure, as well as of determining the contingencies that caused this condition.[198] The review of the previous classification in one of any degree can be made in the following situations: worsening, improvement, misdiagnosis and in the case in which the pensioner works as an employee or self-employed worker.

Review Periods

349. All initial or revised decisions that lead to the granting of benefits for permanent disability of any degree, or that *confirm the previously recognized degree of disability*, must state the time period following which a review may be requested due to a worsening or improvement in the individual's condition while the person with the disability is below the age established in Article 205 of the GSSA for accessing the retirement pension.

350. Notwithstanding the foregoing, the degree of permanent disability and the benefit initially awarded may be reviewed, even if the beneficiary has reached retirement age, if the disability is caused by occupational illness.

351. When a period of time equal to or less than two years is specified in the initial resolution establishing the permanent disability, in order to conduct a review due to a foreseeable improvement in the disabling condition, the worker has the right to reserve his or her job, for two years from the date of the resolution that establishes the permanent disability.

352. This review period is binding on all individuals and it may not be requested prior to the completion of the period, except in the following cases:

– the permanently disabled pensioner carrying out any job as an employee or a self-employed worker: The INSS may, by its own initiative or upon request by the beneficiary, instigate the review regardless of whether or not the period indicated in the resolution has elapsed;

198. Article 200(1) of the GSSA.

- misdiagnosis: The review may be carried out at any time while the individual is below the age established for receiving the retirement pension;
- in the event of new aliments.

353. The remaining resolutions, especially those rejecting the review requests, cannot have a fixed time period since a new review may be initiated at any time.

354. The review results can be the confirmation of the degree of disability, modification of the degree of disability and, as a result, of the benefit or termination of the disability and, as a result, of the pension.

Chapter 4. Amount of Benefits

355. The temporary disablement benefit is a subsidy and the amount of which depends on the RB and the percentages applicable to it.[199] In accordance with Article 13 of the Decree 1646/1972,[200] the RB is, in the general rule, the result of dividing the amount of the worker's contribution basis in the month prior to the one in which the disability commences by the number of days said contribution refers to (this divisor will specifically be: 30, if the worker has a monthly salary; 30, 31 or 28 or 29 if the salary is daily). However, if the worker joins the company in the same month as his disability begins, the RB taken will be the contribution basis of said month, divided by the number of days for which contributions have been made. When the worker has not been employed for the whole of the previous month, the divisor will also be the number of days for which contributions have been made. There are special rules for cases of pluri-employment, part-time workers, in the case of contracts for training and apprenticeship/research staff under training or, among others, for cases of workers performing their work in special sectors.

356. The percentage applicable to the RB is, in case of common diseases and non-work-related injury, 60% from the fourth day to the 20th inclusive and 75% from the 21st day on.[201] As it is visible, the right to access to the benefit of temporary disablement arises from common disease or non-work-related injury, starts from the fourth day the worker is on sick leave from work.[202] The benefit will be paid during the time the beneficiary is considered temporarily disabled and this will last for, in the event of an injury or disease, due to whatever cause, 365 days extendible for a further 180 days when it is presumed that, in that period, the worker may be cured and medically discharged. For the purposes of determining the maximum duration period and a possible extension, relapses will also compute.[203] It will be considered a relapse of the same process when there is new sick leave for the same or similar pathology within 180 calendar days following the effective date of the previous medical discharge.

357. The permanent disablement benefit award is different in function of the different levels:[204]

- in the case of *partial permanent disability*, the benefit consists of a lump-sum compensation;

199. Article 171 of the GSSA.
200. Decree 1646/1972 of 23 Jun. 1972, implementing Law 24/1972 of 21 Jun. 1972, on benefits under the General Social Security Scheme (BOE No. 154 of 28 Jun. 1972).
201. Article 2(1), first paragraph of the Decree 3158/1966, approving the General Regulations determining the amount of economic benefits under the General Social Security System and the conditions for entitlement thereto (BOE No. 312 of 30 Dec. 1966).
202. Article 173 of the GSSA.
203. Article 174(1) of the GSSA.
204. Article 196 of the GSSA.

- in the case of *total permanent disability*, the amount consists of a lifetime monthly pension that, under exceptional circumstances, may be substituted for a lump-sum payment, when the beneficiary is under the age of 60;
- in the cases of *absolute permanent disability* and *serious disability*, the amount consists of a lifetime monthly pension;
- the permanent disablement benefit amount depends also on mentioned levels.[205]

§1. Partial Permanent Disability

358. In the case of *partial permanent disability*, the compensation amount is equal to twenty-four months of the base pension used to calculate the subsidy for the temporary disability from which the permanent disability is derived. In cases in which there was no previous temporary disability because the beneficiary did not have coverage, the base pension that would have corresponded to a temporary disability, had the beneficiary acquired that right, is used.

§2. Total Permanent Disability

359. In the case of *total permanent disability*, the amount consists of a lifetime monthly pension that, under exceptional circumstances, may be substituted for a lump-sum payment, when the beneficiary is under the age of 60. The amount of this pension is calculated by applying the corresponding percentage to the RB, in accordance with the cause of the disability. If it is result of a common disease, the amount of the pension cannot be less than the minimum amount fixed annually in the General Budget Law for the pension of total permanent disability resulting from common disease of holders under 60 years with spouse not in charge. In general rule, the percentage applicable to the RB is 55%. This percentage may be increased by 20% for beneficiaries over the age of 55 when it is difficult to gain employment in an activity different from the habitual one, due to a lack of general or specialized training and the social and employment conditions at their place of residence. In cases in which a worker, who has reached or is above the ordinary retirement age, accesses the pension for total permanent disability arising from common contingencies, due to failing to meet the requirements for accessing the retirement pension: the applicable percentage corresponds to the minimum contributory period established at any given moment to be eligible for the retirement pension. The percentage that will be applied to the corresponding RB is currently 50%.

360. The calculation of the base pension will change depending on the cause of the permanent disability. If the disability is the result of common contingencies, we must make differences between workers in relation to the age that they have on the date of the causal event:[206]

205. Article 197 of the GSSA.
206. *See* RD 1646/1972.

(1) Workers aged over 52 and under 65 on the date of the causal event	The RB is the result obtained from dividing the interested party's CBs during the 96 months immediately before the month prior to the causal event by 112. These bases will be calculated according to the following rules: the bases for the 24 months prior to the causal event are calculated at their nominal value. The remaining bases are updated in accordance with the evolution of the CPI, from the month to which they correspond ending the month immediately prior to the month when the period of non-updatable bases described in the foregoing paragraph begins. To this result, the corresponding percentage is applied, depending on the years of contributions, in accordance with the scale provided for retirement pensions, with the years that remain for the worker, on the date of the causal event, to reach the standard retirement age applicable at all times being considered to this end. If the contributory period is less than 15 years, 50% will be applied. The resulting amount of the foregoing rules will give the RB to which, in order to obtain the amount of the corresponding pension, the percentage provided for the recognized degree of disability must be applied.
(2) Workers aged under 52 on the date of the causal event (for which a contribution period of less than eight years is required)	The RB will be calculated in the same way as above; however, the ratio will be obtained by dividing the sum of the monthly CBs by a number equal to the number of months of the minimum contribution period required, not counting partial months, by the number of months to which said bases correspond, multiplying this ratio by the coefficient of 1.1666, and excluding, in all instances, the updated bases corresponding to the twenty-four months immediately prior to the month before the causal event.
(3) Workers aged 65 or over on the date of the causal event who do not meet the requirements for retirement	The RB will be the ratio obtained from dividing the interested parties CBs during the 96 months immediately before the month prior to the causal event by 12, according to the provisions of rule 1.
(4) Part-time workers	When the permanent disability is a result of a common illness, the same rules applied to retirement pensions will be employed.

361. If the disability is a result of a non-work-related injury, the RB will be the ratio obtained from dividing the sum of the interested parties CBs during an uninterrupted period of twenty-four months by 28. Said period must be chosen by the beneficiary from within the seven years immediately prior to the date of the causal event of the allowance. If, on the date of the causal event, the interested party had not completed an uninterrupted period of twenty-four months of contributions, the RB will be determined using the most beneficial formula of the following two bases: the basis provided for in the previous paragraph or by dividing the sum of the minimum contribution basis in force in the twenty-four months immediately before the causal event of the disability by 28, including these in the amount corresponding to the last contracted working day completed by the originator.

§3. Absolute Permanent Disability

362. In the case of *absolute permanent disability*, the pension amount is 100% of the RB, which is different if the disability stems from common illness or non-work-related injury. In the first case and if the beneficiary has active contributor, assimilated contributor status or 'non-contributor' status, it is calculated by applying all the rules specified for total permanent disability arising from common diseases. If the disability is caused by a non-work-related injury, we must make difference between the cases in which the beneficiary is on active or assimilated contributor status or has 'non-contributor status'. In the first case, the pension is calculated by applying the rules specified for total permanent disability arising from non-work-related injuries, while in the second case, the RB is the result obtained from dividing the interested parties CBs during the 96 months immediately prior to the month before the triggering event by 112. The calculation of these bases will be performed in accordance with the rules explained (*see* 'Total Permanent Disability' *supra*).

§4. Serious Disability

363. The amount of the *serious disability* pension shall be made up by the corresponding pension amount for (total or absolute) permanent disability, increased by a supplement to remunerate the person caring for the beneficiary. The amount of the supplement will be the result of adding together 45% of the minimum CB in force in the General Scheme at the time of the causal event, irrespective of the scheme that grants the pension, and 30% of the worker's last CB corresponding to the contingency from which the permanent disability arises. Under no circumstances may this supplement have a value of less than 45% of the pension – not including the supplement – received by the worker.

Minimum pension

364. Pensions under the General Regime are recognized and awarded on the basis of the amount of the person's regular contributions, which generates a certain benefit. However, the 'minimum' amount to be received by the beneficiary is set annually. Therefore, if the mathematical amount of his/her pension is lower, it is automatically supplemented up to the limit set as a 'minimum' pension or benefit, taking into account a combination of several factors, such as age, family responsibilities, degree of disability of those affected, contingency and others. The cost of this supplement is borne by the general state budget. The supplement is revalued annually in accordance with the general rules for their economic updating.

365. For 2023, the minimum amount of the contributory permanent disability pensions are as follows:[207]

Permanent Disability. Yearly Amount (EUR)	
Serious disability	
Does not need to take care of a spouse	15,610.00
Single (single-person family unit)	16,445.80
Needs to take care of a spouse	20,290.20
Absolute Permanent Disability.	
Does not need to take care of a spouse	10,406.20
Single (single-person family unit)	10,963.40
Needs to take care of a spouse	13,526.80
Total Permanent Disability: Right holder aged 65	
Does not need to take care of a spouse	10,406.20
Single (single-person family unit)	10,963.40
Needs to take care of a spouse	13,526.80
Total Permanent Disability: Right holder aged between 60 and 64	
Does not need to take care of a spouse	9,695.00
Single (single-person family unit)	10,256.40
Needs to take care of a spouse	12,682.60
Total Permanent Disability due to illness, aged under 60	
Does not need to take care of a spouse	8,012.20
Single (single-person family unit)	8,082.00
Needs to take care of a spouse	8,082.00
Right holder aged 65	
Does not need to take care of a spouse	10,406.20
Single (single-person family unit)	10,963.40
Needs to take care of a spouse	13,526.80

207. The minimum quantity of old-age pensions and pension caused by death and survival is set up on Part VIII dedicated to pensions.

Chapter 5. Conditions

366. The persons belonging to the General System must accomplish the foll ing requirements to be beneficiaries of temporary disability:[208] (1) be affiliated registered as in employment or in an equivalent situation on the date the ca event occurred,[209] while they receive medical care from the social security anc unfit for work; (2) also, when the temporary disability is caused by a commo ness or disease, the beneficiaries have fulfilled a previous contribution of 180 in the five years immediately preceding the causal event.[210] The temporary dis ment benefit may be denied, cancelled or suspended due to different reasons r lated in Article 175 of the GSSA:

(a) fraudulent conduct on the part of the beneficiary to obtain or conserve the efit;
(b) when the beneficiary works as salaried or as self-employed;
(c) rejection or abandonment of the treatment for no reasonable cause;
(d) the beneficiary failing to attend a summons from the doctors attached tc INSS and the MCSS for an examination and medical check-up will lead tc right being provisionally suspended pending verification of whether this justified.

367. The procedure for suspending the right and its effects will be determ by the regulations.

368. The temporary disablement benefit will terminate in different cases r lated in Article 174 of the GSSA:

(a) on expiry of the maximum 545-day period from the date sick leave c mences;
(b) when the worker is medically discharged because she/he is cured or impr ment that allows the worker to perform his/her usual work;
(c) when the worker is discharged with or without being declared as suffering a permanent disability;
(d) when a retirement pension is granted;
(e) due to the beneficiary failing to appear at any of the official examin appointments established by the medical practitioners who are members o INSS, or the MCSS;
(f) due to death.

369. The temporary disablement subsidy payment corresponds to the INSS, or the MCSS. In the cases of temporary disablement subsidies which arise common disease/illness or non-work accident, the subsidy payment between da

208. Article 172 of the GSSA.
209. Article 165(1) of the GSSA.
210. Article 172 a) of the GSSA.

and 15 of work leave, both inclusive, corresponds to the employer. As of the 16th of discharge, the responsibility for payment is attributed to the INSS, ISM or MCSS, if applicable, even if the materiality of the payment is still carried out as a payment delegated by the same employer.

370. The payment of the economic benefit is made by the company with the same periodicity as salaries, by virtue of the compulsory collaboration of the companies in the management of the General Social Security Scheme, discounting from the amount of the subsidy the withholding by IRPF and the social security fees. The obligatory collaboration of the companies in the payment of the temporary disablement benefit will cease on the last day of the month in which the competent Managing Body has issued the resolution in which the extension of said situation or the initiation of a permanent disability file is expressly declared.

371. Notwithstanding the provisions of the preceding paragraph, the companies authorized to collaborate in the management will continue to pay for said benefit in the cases indicated therein, either until the temporary disablement situation is extinguished or until the rating of the permanent disability. These apply to the local corporations with respect to the personnel they were recognizing and paying the temporary disablement benefit, in accordance with the transitory provision of RD 480/1993.[211]

372. When the worker is receiving contributory benefits for unemployment and goes to the temporary disablement situation, the SPEE will pay the subsidy in a delegated payment scheme until the duration of the unemployment benefit is exhausted, as well as such contributions to social security. In some cases, regulated in Articles 283, 284 and 285 of the GSSA, the SPEE will only continue to pay the benefit when the Management Entity declares the express extension of said situation, with the maximum limit of the duration of the unemployment benefit. From that moment, the benefit will be paid by the INSS. There are special rules for domestic employees and agrarian workers.

373. The INSS, ISM or the MCSS, in its case, are responsible for the direct payment of the subsidy in the following cases:

(a) in the case of entities and organizations excluded from the delegated payment;
(b) due to non-compliance with the employer's obligation of delegated payment;
(c) companies with less than ten workers and more than six consecutive months of payment of the subsidy, who request it by regulation;
(d) termination of the employment relationship while the worker is in temporary disablement situation;
(e) continuation of the temporary disablement situation after the voluntary termination of the employment relationship in the company;

211. RD 480/1993 of 2 April, integrating into the General Social Security System the Special Social Security System for Local Government Officials (BOE No. 80 of 3 Apr. 1993).

(f) continuation of the temporary disablement situation once extinguished the unemployment subsidy;
(g) medical discharge for proposed report of recipients of unemployment benefit;
(h) when it comes to trade representatives, bullfighting professionals and artists. In the case of the latter, when the duration of the contract does not exceed thirty days;
(i) in the cases of exhaustion of the temporary disablement due to the expiration of the maximum term, during the extension of the effects of the benefit up to the rating of the permanent disablement;
(j) by moving to the extension of temporary disablement after twelve months, following the resolution of the Managing Body, unless the worker at the beginning of the temporary disablement was receiving a contributory unemployment benefit, in which case, the benefit is paid by the SPEE on a payment basis delegated until unemployment is exhausted;
(k) to initiate the permanent disability file, following the resolution of the managing entity;
(l) in the event that the INSS issues a resolution ordering the medical discharge, in accordance with the provisions of Article 170(1) of the GSSA, the obligatory collaboration of the companies in the payment of the benefit will cease on the day in which said resolution is issued, the corresponding subsidy being paid directly by the MCSS during the period that elapses between the date of the aforementioned resolution and its notification to the interested party. The companies that collaborate in the management of the economic benefit for temporary disability in accordance with the provisions of Article 102(1) a) of the GSSA will also be obliged to pay directly the subsidy corresponding to the period.

374. With respect to permanent disablement benefit according to Article 195 of the GSSA, persons included in the General Scheme who have been declared as having any type of permanent disability are affiliated and registered or have a status assimilated to affiliation who have a previous contribution period when the disability is caused by a common illness. In this situation and for the case of *partial permanent disability*, 1,800 days of contributions over ten years immediately preceding the date of termination of the temporary disability from which the permanent disability arises is required. For the rest of disability levels, the previous contribution period varies depending on the age of the interested party:

(1) If he/she is aged under 31: *Generic contributory period*: A third of the time that has elapsed since the interested party turned 16 and the causal event. No specific contributory period is required.
(2) If he/she is aged 31 or over: *Generic contributory period:* A quarter of the time that has elapsed since the interested party turned 20 and the causal event, with a minimum of at least five years under all circumstances. *Specific contributory period:* a fifth of the required contributory period must be included:
   - in the ten years immediately prior to the causal event; or
   - in the ten years immediately prior to the date on which contributions were no longer required, if the pension is granted when the interested party was

affiliated or assimilated to affiliation, with no obligation to make contributions. Similarly, the above paragraph applies to those who, without having completed the required specific period, become eligible for the pension when affiliated, and are obliged to make contributions, when this originates from a situation with no obligation to make contributions immediately prior to the period in which the interested party was affiliated or assimilated to affiliation.

375. Age fractions of less than six months will not be considered; fractions of more than six months are considered equivalent to half a year. The resulting contributory periods will be rounded down, not counting any partial months, where applicable.

376. When the interested party is not considered to be affiliated, the contributory previous periods required access to the *absolute permanent disability for all types of work* or for *Serious disability*, required fifteen years of generic contribution period on three of the preceding ten years. For workers on part-time contracts, to certify the contribution period required, effective 4 August 2013, the regulations set out in RD-Law 11/2013 shall be applied.[212] Finally, the right to access to permanent disability benefits will be not recognized when they arise from common contingencies when the beneficiary, in the date of causal event, has the age provided for in Article 205(1) a) and brings together the requirements to access the system's contributory retirement pension.

377. In relation to the management and payment of permanent disability benefit, it is carried out by the INSS in general and by the social Maritime institute in cases where workers are included under the Special Scheme for Sea Workers, the payment is made by the national social security system or, when appropriate, the social maritime institute when the permanent disability is the result of common sickness or non-occupational injury. In the case of *partial permanent disability*, a single payment is made and in the rest of cases, *pensions arising from common diseases and non-work-related injuries* are paid in fourteen instalments, one for each month of the year and two extra payments per year, which are paid together with the June and November monthly instalments, and are the same amount as the ordinary amounts for these months.

378. The permanent disability pension will be suspended in the following cases:

(a) When the beneficiary has committed fraud in obtaining or retaining benefit rights.
(b) When the permanent disability is due to or has been worsened by criminal negligence by the beneficiary.

212. RD-Law 11/2013 of 2 August, on the Protection of Part-time Workers and other Urgent Economic and Social Measures (BOE No. 185 of 3 Aug. 2013).

(c) When the permanent disability is due to or has been worsened by rejecting or abandoning the medical treatment prescribed during the temporary disability situation, without reasonable cause.
(d) When the beneficiary rejects or abandons the corresponding readjustment and rehabilitation treatments or processes, without reasonable cause.

379. The termination of permanent disablement benefits will occur:

- due to revision resulting in recovery;
- due to death of the beneficiary;
- due to eligibility for the retirement pension, when this pension is selected;
- due to official review ordered by the management entity in any of the cases in which this action is legally allowed and when it leads to the loss of eligibility for the pension.

Chapter 6. Accumulation Rules

380. According to Article 198 of the GSSA, the existing compatibilities and incompatibilities in the permanent disablement benefit are the following:

(a) In the case of *partial permanent disability*, the benefit is compatible with performing any working activity, both as an employee and as a self-employed worker. Also, it is compatible with keeping the job held.
(b) In the case of total permanent disability, the pension will be compatible with the salary the worker may receive in the same or another company, provided the duties are not the same as those that led to the total permanent disability. On the 20% increase with work and other benefits case, the increase is incompatible with working for another person or self-employed work. Also, it is incompatible with social security benefits that may arise from said work, such as temporary disability or maternity subsidy beyond the labour relationship or professional activity, or any possible unemployment benefit for the same.
(c) In the cases of *absolute permanent disability* and *serious disability*, the reception of the benefit does not prevent the individual from carrying out profit or non-profit activities that are compatible with his/her degree of disability and that do not represent a change in his/her ability to work for the purpose of reviews. If the job carried out results in inclusion in any social security scheme, the corresponding affiliation must be presented and contributions made, and the beneficiary must notify the Managing Body that the activity has begun, whether as an employee or working on a self-employed basis. Complying with these obligations does not affect the powers of permanent disability reviews of the Managing Body that approved the allowance. Effective as of 1 January 2014, entitlement to an absolute permanent disability and severe disability benefit once the individual has reached retirement age shall be incompatible with work carried out by the pensioner, as an employee or on a self-employed basis, that results in his/her inclusion in any of the Social Security System Schemes, under the same terms and conditions that regulate contributory retirement pensions under Article 213 of the GSSA.

Chapter 7. Guaranteed Income for the Disabled (Non-contributory Disability Pension)

381. The non-contributory disability pension provides all citizens who are disabled and in a state of need with a financial benefit, free medical and pharmaceutical assistance and complementary social services, even if they have not contributed or have not done so sufficiently to be entitled to a contributory pension.[213]

382. Beneficiaries of this pension may be Spanish citizens and nationals of other countries, with legal residence in Spain who meet specific requirements relating to age, residence, disability and lack of sufficient income.

383. In particular, to have the right to this specific pension it is necessary to fulfil the following requirements: first, applicants must be between the ages of 18 and 65. Second, they must reside in Spanish territory and having done so for a period of five years, two of which must be consecutive and immediately prior to the date of application. Third, applicants must have a degree of disability of 65% or more. Finally, they must lack sufficient income. However, if they are less than the amount indicated, and the applicant lives with family members, the requirement is only met when the sum of the annual income of all the members of the economic unit living is less than a certain amount prescribed by law.

384. The amount of the pension is fixed annually in the LPGE. The full annual amount established for non-contributory disability (and retirement) pensions in 2023 is EUR 6,784.54 per year. The amount of an individual's pension is set on the basis of his/her personal income and/or that of his/her economic unit living, which cannot be less than the minimum of 25% (EUR 1,696.14 per year). Non-tax paying disability pensioners whose degree of disability is 75% or more and who can prove that they need the assistance of another person to carry out the essential acts of life will also receive a supplement of 50% of the full annual pension (EUR 10,176.81 per year). When more than one beneficiary is present in the same family unit, special rules of concurrence apply.

385. In any case, the rule prevents, as compatible with non-contributory disability pension, the possibility of carrying out a work activity whether lucrative or not. In this case, the sum of the annual amount of the pension and the annual income resulting from the work activity must not exceed a certain amount (i.e., EUR 13,984.54 for 2023) which is equal to the sum of the annual amount of the Public Indicator of Multiple Effect Income (IPREM) and the annual amount of the non-contributory disability pension. If this amount is exceeded, the pension is reduced so as not to exceed the established limit.

386. Moreover, the pension in question is incompatible with the non-contributory retirement pension and the minimum vital income benefit.

---

213. Articles 363 and subsequent of the GSSA.

Chapter 8. Birth and Childcare Subsidy

387. The beneficiaries of the birth and childcare subsidy are all persons included in the General Scheme of Social Security, whatever their sexes, who have suspended their employment contracts due to the situations regulated in Article 48(4), 48(5) and 48(6) of the Spanish Workers' Statute, which regulate the childbirth, adoption, custody for purposes of adoption and fostering.[214]

388. The persons belonging to the General System must accomplish the following requirements to be beneficiaries of the Birth and childcare subsidy:[215] First, be affiliated and registered as in employment or in an equivalent situation on the date the causal event occurred,[216] and second, prove the following required contribution periods:

(a) For those who are younger than 21 years of age in the date of childbirth or in the date of the administrative decision of custody for purposes of adoption or fostering, as well as the judicial resolution for adoption, no contribution period is required.
(b) For those who are 26 and over on the date of childbirth or in the date of the administrative decision or judicial resolution mentioned above, 90 days of contributions within the 7 years immediately prior to said date are required. Alternatively, the aforementioned requirement shall be deemed fulfilled in cases of those who can prove 180 days of contributions throughout their working life, prior to the date in question.
(c) For those who are 26 and over on the date of childbirth or in the date of the administrative decision or judicial resolution mentioned in paragraph a), 180 days' contributions within the 7 years immediately prior to said date are required. Alternatively, the aforementioned requirement shall be deemed fulfilled in cases of those who can prove 360 days of contributions throughout their working life, prior to the date in question.

389. In the birth case, the age indicated in the previous section will be the one that the interested person has met at the time of the start of the suspension period, taking as reference the moment of the birth in order to verify the accomplishment of the minimum contribution period that, where appropriate, corresponds. In the cases of international adoption provided for in Article 48(5) of the Workers' Statute, the age indicated in the previous section will be the one that the interested person has met at the time of the start of the suspension period, taking as reference the moment of the resolution in order to verify the accomplishment of the minimum contribution period that, where appropriate, corresponds.[217]

214. Article 177 of the GSSA, modified by RD-Law 6/2019.
215. Article 178 of the GSSA.
216. Article 165(1) of the GSSA.
217. Article 178(2) and 178(3) of the GSSA, respectively.

390. The birth and childcare subsidy amount is equivalent to 100% of the corresponding RB, which will be equivalent to the base established for temporary disability benefit arising from common contingencies. However, the subsidy may be recognized by the INSS by provisional resolution taking into account the last CBCC recorded in the corporate bases of the Social Security System, as long as the CBCC related to the month immediately before the start of the employment contract suspension or of the child's birth and care leave are not incorporated to the system. If the CBCC of the month immediately prior to the start of the care leave is different with respect to the provisional resolution, the subsidy will be recalculated and the final resolution will be issued. If the bases do not change, the provisional resolution will become definitive within three months from its issuance.[218]

391. In case of self-employment workers, the protection is the same provided for wage earners excepting for the benefit amount calculation which consists, following Article 318 of the GSSA, in a subsidy equivalent to the 100% of an RB whose daily amount will be the result of dividing the sum of the CBs accredited to this special social security regime during the six months immediately before the causal event by 180. If they have not been registered in the Special Regime during the entire six-month referred period, the RB will be the result of dividing the CBs to the Special Regime accredited in the six months immediately prior to the causal event by the days in which the worker has been registered in said regime within that period.

218. Article 179 of the GSSA.

Chapter 9. Risk During Pregnancy and During Breastfeeding: Care of Minors Affected by Cancer or Another Serious Illness

392. The risk during pregnancy,[219] and the risk during breastfeeding,[220] protect situations in which the pregnant or the female worker during breastfeeding a child under nine months old have to suspend their employment contracts due to the risks or diseases that may have a negative impact on the health of female worker or her child due to agents, procedures or conditions of the job position or activity being carried out and is not possible to change her job position for one that is compatible with her condition, under the terms provided in Article 26 of Law 31/1995 of 8 November, about occupational risk prevention law.[221]

393. With respect to care of minors affected by cancer or another serious illness,[222] any reduction in working hours along with the proportional reduction of salary experienced by the parents, adoptive parents or foster parents in pre-adoptive and permanent foster care, in those cases where both parents work, in order to care for their dependent minors under 18 years of age suffering from cancer or another serious illness included in the list provided in the appendix of RD 1148/2011 – or up to 23 years of age when the disease persists – which requires long-term hospital admission in order to provide direct, continuous and permanent care, during the period of hospitalization and the ongoing treatment of the illness, shall be deemed a protect situation.

394. The female employees and female members of cooperative or employee-owned companies in a situation of contract suspension or authorized leave due to risk during pregnancy or risk during breastfeeding are beneficiaries of this benefit if they accomplish the following requirements: to be affiliated and have active contributor status in any scheme of the Social Security System on the starting date of the suspension and to be in possession of the incapacity to work certificate provided by the medical services of the INSS or the relevant MCSS. No minimum contribution period is required in such cases since it arises from occupational contingencies.

395. The beneficiaries of the benefit for care of minors affected by cancer or another serious illness are employed or self-employed, and equivalent workers, irrespective of their gender, provided that they meet the necessary requirements: (1) to reduce their working hours by at least 50%; (2) be affiliated and have active contributor status in a social security scheme; and (3) accomplish the required contribution period in each case:

(a) for those who are younger than 21 years of age on the date when the reduction in working hours begins: no contribution period is required;

219. Articles 186–187 of the GSSA.
220. Articles 188–189 of the GSSA.
221. BOE No. 269 of 10 Nov. 1995.
222. Articles 190–192 of the GSSA.

(b) for those who are older than 21 but less than 26 years of age on the date when the reduction of working hours begins: 90 days of contributions within the seven years immediately prior to said date. Alternatively, the aforementioned requirement shall be deemed fulfilled in cases of those who can prove 180 days of contributions throughout their working life, prior to the date in question; and
(c) for those who are 26 and over on the date when the reduction in working hours begins: 180 days of contributions within the seven years immediately prior to said date. Alternatively, the aforementioned requirement shall be deemed fulfilled in cases of those who can prove 360 days of contributions throughout their working life, prior to the date in question.

396. The financial benefit in cases of risk of pregnancy and risk during breastfeeding consists of a subsidy equivalent to 100% of the corresponding RB, which will be equivalent to the base established for temporary disability benefit arising from occupational contingencies, considering the starting date of leave as reference point. The benefit in case of care of minors affected by cancer or another serious illness is a daily accrual benefit, equivalent to 100% of the RB established for the benefit for temporary disablement arising from occupational contingencies or, where applicable, arising from common contingencies for those who have not opted for professional contingency coverage, and in proportion with the reduction of working hours.

Part VI. Industrial Accidents and Occupational Diseases

Cristina Aragón Gómez

Chapter 1. Field of Application

§1. Territorial Field of Application

397. Pursuant to Article 7 of the GSSA, for the purposes of contributory protection and irrespective of their gender, civil status and profession, all Spanish citizens who reside in Spain and foreign nationals who reside or are legally in Spain are included in the Social Security System, provided that, in both cases, they work within the national territory. Therefore, only foreign nationals who are in possession of an authorization to reside and work in Spain can legally engage in paid work as self-employed or employed workers and have full legal access to the Social Security System. However, without this, every foreign national who require prior administrative authorization to work and carry out business in Spain are not included in the Social Security System.[223] Consequently, they cannot have a social security number, be registered or pay contributions into said system.

398. Based on the above, a general rule can be drawn: foreign nationals who provide their labour services without authorization to reside and work in Spain will not be entitled to a contributory benefit from the Social Security System. However, this rule must immediately be clarified, as Article 36.5 of the OL 4/2000 provides a significant exception in this regard. By virtue of said law, not having authorization to reside and work in Spain will not invalidate an employment contract regarding the rights of foreign workers, nor will it be an obstacle to obtaining benefits arising from scenarios considered in international agreements on the protection of workers, or other benefits that they might be entitled to, provided that they are applicable to their situation.

399. Article 42.2 of the RD 84/1996, as restated in Article 1.10 of the RD 1041/2005,[224] considers the provisions of Article 36.5 of OL 4/2000, regarding the right of illegal foreign nationals to contributory benefits from the Social Security System. Specifically, it establishes that 'foreign employed workers from countries that

223. Article 42(2) of the RD 84/1996.
224. Royal Decree 1041/2005 of 5 September (BOE No. 222 of 16 Sep. 2005).

have ratified Convention 19 of the International Labour Organisation of 5 June 1925 who provide their services without legally residing in Spain and without authorisation to work or documents that accredit their exception to the obligation to obtain it, shall be considered as included in the Spanish Social Security System and registered in the appropriate regime for the sole purposes of protection against the risks of industrial accidents and occupational diseases. This is understood without prejudice to the application, for the same protective purposes, of the expressly or tacitly recognised principle of reciprocity'. It also clarifies that although foreign workers who provide services illegally are not included in the Social Security System, this is understood as 'without prejudice to the fact that they might be considered included for the purposes of obtaining certain benefits, in accordance with the terms established by law'.

400. Regarding work-related risks, Article 42.2 of the RD 84/1996 applies the principle of presumed registration or registration by operation of law to foreign nationals, as contained in Article 166.4 of the GSSA. Therefore, foreign workers who do not have the appropriate authorization to reside and work in Spain would be entitled to social security benefits arising from work-related risks, on the condition that those affected are natives of countries that have signed Convention 19 of the ILO or of countries with which Spain has signed social security agreements that establish a relevant system of reciprocity.

§2. Personal Field of Application

401. The Spanish legal system includes, in the contributory protection of the Social Security System, all employed workers, self-employed, workers that are members of workers' cooperatives, students and civil and military state employees.[225]

402. The fact is that protection for work-related risks is only aimed at those who have a job (whether self-employed or employed). We should also state that self-employed workers did not originally have the right to protection against work-related risks. Therefore, the treatment of situations of need was unknown, irrespective of its origin (ordinary or occupational). Through the reform made by Law 53/2002,[226] the protective system for risks was extended to the RETA, giving self-employed workers the chance to be included in the coverage against industrial accidents and occupational diseases. This Law was later implemented by RD 1273/2003.[227] Notwithstanding the above, this general rule of the voluntary nature of the

225. Article 7 of the GSSA.
226. The 53/2002 Act of 30 December, on Tax, Administrative and Social Order Measures (BOE No. 313 of 31 Dec. 2002).
227. RD 1273/2003 of 10 October, regulating the coverage of work-related risks of workers included in the Special Social Security System for self-employed workers, and the extension of benefits for temporary disabilities for self-employed workers (BOE No. 253 of 22 Oct. 2003).

coverage of work-related risks presented two exceptions: (1) regarding self-employed workers that carry out hazardous, difficult or toxic activities, and (2) regarding economically dependent self-employed workers.

403. Later, Law 27/2011 imposed the obligation to cover the work-related risks of all workers that were registered in any of the regimes of the Social Security System from 1 January 2013. The legislator thereby followed the trend set by Law 20/2007 to abandon the voluntary and optional principle in favour of the mandatory nature of all types of coverage. Therefore, self-employed workers registered in the RETA from 1 January 2013 were obliged, without exception, to extend their coverage to all work-related risks. Self-employed workers that were registered in the RETA before 1 January 2013 could, however, maintain the coverage regime that they had established until that date.

404. However, this legal provision did not enter into force on the initially established date, because the LPGE for 2013 postponed the mandatory coverage of work-related risks in the RETA until 1 January 2014 and this postponement was extended for another year in the LPGE for 2014. Moreover, before Additional Provision No. 58 of the GSSA was introduced, the LPGE for 2015 repealed it. Consequently, the coverage for work-related risks in the RETA retained its voluntary nature until 1 January 2019, the date of the entry into force of the reform implemented by RD-Law 28/2018.

405. Indeed, in accordance with Additional Provision No. 34 of the GSSA of 1994, self-employed workers included in the RETA can voluntarily improve the scope of the protective coverage, by adding the relevant coverage to their industrial accident and occupational disease risks, provided that the interested parties have chosen to include economic benefits due to temporary disability within said protective scope. In addition, Article 316(1) of the GSSA of 2015, with effects from 2 January 2016, establishes the same.

Chapter 2. Industrial Accidents

§1. Essential Elements of the Concept

I. The Concept of Industrial Accidents in the System for Employed Workers

406. The legislator defines industrial accidents as all injuries that workers suffer in the course of or as a consequence of the work they carry out as employees.[228]

407. Concerning the concept of industrial accidents, the first thing we need to clarify is that injuries must manifest themselves in the form of damage to the body of the accident victim, but present not only a physical manifestation but also a psychological one (stress, etc.)

408. In addition, for an accident to be considered industrial, there must be a connection between the injury suffered and the work carried out. This causal relationship can be direct or immediate ('as a consequence of work') or indirect or gradual ('during the course of work'). The causal relationship thereby includes both scenarios in which work is the sole cause of the injury and others in which work acts as a mere condition, without which said result would not have occurred.

409. Therefore, those accidents that are due to force majeure outside of work are not considered industrial accidents. And in this sense, the legislator has clarified that under no circumstances will sunstroke, lightning and other similar natural phenomena be considered cases of force majeure outside of work.

410. Neither are accidents that are due to the wilful misconduct or reckless disregard of the injured worker considered industrial accidents. Wilful misconduct represents the free and voluntary production of the injury and acceptance of the result, which has no relation to work, even if it has been carried out during working hours and in the workplace. Reckless disregard also causes a break in the causal relationship between accidents and work. Wilful disregard is defined as a subjective act attributable to the injured worker himself, which does not directly seek the production of the harmful event, but whose conduct voluntarily and consciously accepts unnecessary risks that include the likelihood that physical injuries will be caused, without grounds or reason that could justify or exonerate it. In other words, employees that assume serious, obvious and unnecessary risks not consistent with the normal behaviour of people and not befitting normal conduct are guilty of wilful disregard. Therefore, wilful disregard constitutes a patent and clear disregard for risk and of the most basic sense of caution.

228. Article 156.1 of the GSSA.

411. In contrast, negligence at work does not break the causal relationship between the injury and work, as this is a consequence of the normal course of work and of the trust that this inspires through the repetition of the same actions.

412. In addition, the legislator has granted the consideration of industrial accidents to:

- those suffered by workers when travelling to and from work;
- those suffered by workers in the course of or as a consequence of optional trade union duties, and those caused when travelling to or from the location where said duties are carried out;
- those that occur in the course of or as a consequence of tasks that, although not included in their professional group, workers carry out in the compliance of orders from an employer or spontaneously in the interest of the correct functioning of a company;
- those that occur in actions of rescue and similar acts, when these are connected with work;
- non-occupational diseases that workers catch due to the performance of their work, provided it is proven that the exclusive cause of the disease was said performance. Therefore, the concept of industrial accidents includes both sudden and violent actions by an external agent on the human body and injuries that come from certain diseases, and internal actions that are sudden or gradual, which have their origin in work. Taking into account the literal nature of the legislation, for a disease to be considered occupational it requires a direct causal relationship, which excludes diseases indirectly connected to work or those where several causal agents are involved;
- diseases or disabilities, suffered previously by workers, that are aggravated as a consequence of the injury caused by an accident;
- consequences of accidents that are changed in terms of their nature, duration, seriousness or termination, due to intercurrent diseases that constitute complications arising from the pathological process determined by the accident itself or that have their origin in conditions acquired in the new setting where patients are located for their recovery;
- during the health crisis caused by COVID-19, the emergency legislator has protected, through the temporary disability subsidy, both contagious situations and situations of home isolation for reasons of prevention. And, to this end, he had assimilated this situation of need to an accident at work.

II. The Concept of Industrial Accidents in the Self-Employed Workers' Scheme

413. Regarding self-employed workers, industrial accidents are defined as those that occur as a direct and immediate consequence of work.[229] However, in the case

229. Article 316.2 of the GSSA.

of economically dependent self-employed workers, industrial accidents are defined as all physical injuries that workers suffer in the course of or as a consequence of their work.[230]

414. Concerning ordinary self-employed workers, Article 3(2) of the RD 1273/2003 defines industrial accidents as those that occur 'as a direct and immediate consequence of the work that they carry out and that determines their inclusion in the scope of the application of the Special regime'. If we compare what is established in this provision with the legal system applicable to salaried workers, we can see the following differences.

415. First, that in the RETA the legislator requires a stricter connection between accidents and work carried out by the self-employed, as they must be a direct or immediate consequence of said work. However, the legal system for salaried workers defines industrial accidents as all injuries that workers suffer in the course of or as a consequence of employed work, and therefore admits not only an immediate causal relationship (as a consequence of) but also gradual (in the course of).

416. Second, in the RETA the burden of proof is shifted to self-employed workers, who are the ones that must prove the causal relationship between the injuries suffered and the work carried out. In the General regime, Article 156.3 of the GSSA includes a presumption of work-related injuries, in accordance with which injuries that workers suffer during working hours and in the workplace are considered as constituting industrial accidents (in the absence of proof to the contrary). However, in the RETA, Article 3(2) b) of RD 1273/2003 states that injuries that workers suffer during working hours and in the workplace will be considered industrial accidents 'when the connection to the self-employed work is proven'.

417. Third, in the RETA the possibility that workers can suffer industrial accidents as the consequence of carrying out optional trade union duties does not appear.

418. However, Article 26(3) of Law 20/2007 establishes, for economically dependent self-employed workers, a broader concept of industrial accidents. Said Article states:

> Industrial accidents shall be understood as all physical injuries to economically dependent self-employed workers that are suffered in the course of or as a consequence of work, with industrial accidents also being considered those that workers suffer when travelling to or from the location where they provide their work, caused by or as a consequence of said work. In the absence of proof to the contrary, it shall be presumed that accidents are not related to work when they have occurred outside of the performance of the work in question.

419. Therefore, the legislator broadens the situations to be considered as industrial accidents for economically dependent self-employed workers compared to

230. Article 317 of the GSSA.

ordinary self-employed workers: (a) a gradual causal relationship between work and injuries is accepted, and (b) the presumption included in Article 156(3) of the GSSA created for employed workers is established, although it is worded in reverse.

420. Indeed, Article 26(3) of Law 20/2007 does not state that it presumes the existence of a causal relationship between work and accidents when they take place during the performance of the work by economically dependent self-employed workers; it states that it presumes that accidents suffered by economically dependent self-employed workers outside of the performance of their work have no relationship to work. Although the wording is made in a reverse sense, the result cannot be anything other than that sought by Article 156(3) of the GSSA.

§2. Presumptions

421. In the absence of proof to the contrary, it is presumed that injuries suffered by workers during working hours or in the workplace are industrial accidents.[231] Therefore, if these two circumstances arise, it is not necessary to prove the causal relationship. The presumption covers not only accidents in the strictest sense (injuries caused by the sudden or violent actions by an external agent) but also diseases or conditions of vital processes that might arise at work, to the extent that work has been able to act as a triggering factor. To this end, the decisive factor is that the first symptoms must occur during work hours and in the workplace, although more serious consequences may manifest themselves later and away from the workplace.

422. It can therefore be deduced that this presumption cannot be extended to diseases that due to their very nature exclude work as the cause (such as epileptic attacks), as they are congenital diseases and manifest themselves without the influence of external factors.

423. This presumption exempts workers from proving the causal relationship, and therefore they only have to prove the fact that the accident took place during working hours and in the workplace. However, this presumption accepts proof to the contrary and therefore can be broken if a lack of a connection between the injury and work is proved, through convincing evidence.

§3. Accidents on the Way to Work

I. The Concept of Accidents When Travelling to and from Work in the Case of Salaried Workers

424. Pursuant to Article 156(2) a) of the GSSA, accidents that workers suffer when travelling to and from work are considered a work-related risk. To be considered a work-related risk, accidents need to occur on the way to or from work, and

231. Article 156.3 of the GSSA.

therefore predicate acts are not covered. Therefore, if accidents occur at the home of employees before they leave for work, they cannot be considered accidents *in itinere*.

425. For accidents to be defined as *in itinere* and therefore work-related, the following requirements must all be met simultaneously:

- The teleological element: The main and direct purpose of the journey must be determined by the obligation to go to work. Therefore, the motivation to work must be present during the journey.
- The topographic element: The accident must occur on the usual and normal route that workers take from their home to their workplace and vice versa. The route must not be altered by unusual temporary diversions that are the result of particular interests that break the causal relationship with travelling to and from work.
- The chronological element: The accident must occur within the time that is usually and reasonably spent travelling the route. A brief stop, therefore, would not break the causal relationship.
- The suitability element: The route must be travelled using a suitable mode of transport.

426. If an accident occurs *in itinere* outside of working hours and the workplace, there is no presumption that it is work-related. The onus is therefore on the worker or their successors to demonstrate that all the requirements or elements are met in order for it to be considered an industrial accident.

II. The Concept of Accidents When Travelling to and from Work in the Case of Self-Employed Workers

427. With legal effects from 26 October 2017 as the result of the reform made by Law 6/2017,[232] self-employed workers are also protected against accidents when travelling to and from work. To this end, Article 316(2) of the GSSA clarifies, ‘for these purposes, the workplace shall be understood as the establishment where the self-employed worker usually carries out their work, provided that this is not their home and are the premises, warehouse or office that have been declared as a workplace for tax purposes’.

232. Law 6/2017 of 24 October, on Urgent Reforms to Self-employed Work (BOE No. 257 of 25 Oct. 2017).

Chapter 3. Concept of 'Occupational Disease'

428. The concept of occupational disease is established in Article 157 of the GSSA, which defines it as 'a disease contracted as a consequence of the work carried out for another', provided that it is caused by the action of elements or substances and occurs in the activities that are specified in a table established in the implementing regulations. Occupational diseases are, therefore, the listed diseases. Other work-related diseases are technically industrial accidents and are subject to their system. The list of occupational diseases is included in RD 1299/2006.[233]

429. Regarding self-employed workers, Article 3 of RD 1273/2003 extends protection to them under terms that are identical to those established in Article 157 of the GSSA.

233. RD 1299/2006 of 10 November, approving the list of occupational diseases in the Social Security System and laying down criteria for the notification and registration thereof. (BOE No. 302 of 19 Dec. 2006).

Chapter 4. Medical Care

430. The extent and scope of the medical care to which an insured of the Public Health System is entitled do not vary according to the contingency that originates it. Modification introduced by RD 1192/2012, which develops the status of insured and beneficiary for the purposes of healthcare in Spain, charged to public funds, through the National Health System, repeals Article 11 of Decree 2766/1967, which regulated, among other issues, the content of healthcare due to work accidents or occupational diseases.

Chapter 5. Special Protection for Work-Related Risks

431. The Spanish legal system confers special protection to situations of need that have their origin in work-related risks. This special protection manifests itself as follows.

§1. A Special Financing System

432. First, work-related risks have a special financing system. Indeed, concerning pensions arising from an industrial accident or an occupational disease, these are not subject to a public distribution system, but to a private pension fund system. Therefore, in the event of permanent disability or death due to said causes, the MCSS that works with social security or the company declared responsible must constitute the relevant capital cost with the General Treasury of Social Security. Capital cost is understood as the current value of said benefit.

433. On the other hand, in the General Social Security System (which covers employed workers), the financing of work-related risks is assumed exclusively by the employer. In general, the people that have to pay contributions are, on one hand, the workers included in the scope of application, and on the other, the employers that they work for. Therefore, the amount of the contribution is broken down into two parts: (1) the employer's contribution payable by the company, and (2) the worker's contribution payable by the worker. The financing of work-related risks, however, is the exclusive responsibility of the company.

434. Also, the contribution rate for industrial accidents and occupational diseases varies depending on the accident rate of the line of business (Final Provision No. 5 of Law 42/2006 – LPGE for 2007).

435. Finally, the postponement of the payment of contributions is not permitted.

§2. The Collaboration of MCSS

436. The collaboration of industrial accident and occupational disease mutual societies is admitted to the management of benefits due to work-related risks. MCSS are private associations of non-profit entrepreneurs who work with social security under the supervision of the MISSM.

§3. Guarantee of Access to the System's Protection

437. If the situation of need derives from a professional risk, the Spanish legal system guarantees the individual access to the protection of the Social Security System.

438. First, the requirements for access to the system's protection are kept to a minimum. Indeed, in the General Social Security System, access to benefits is dependent upon the existence of a situation of need and that the employment status of the individual is accredited. Therefore, applicants for the benefit are required: (a) to be registered in the system, and (b) to demonstrate a certain period of contributions.

439. However, when the benefit arises from a work-related risk, it is sufficient to demonstrate the actual provision of services (even if the company has not complied with its obligation to process the registration of the worker with social security). Specifically, in accordance with the provisions of Article 166(4) of the GSSA:

> Workers included in the scope of application of this Special system shall be considered, by operation of law, as registered for the purposes of industrial accidents, occupational diseases and unemployment, even if their employer has not fulfilled its obligations. The same rule shall be applied for the sole purposes of healthcare due to ordinary diseases, maternity and non-industrial accidents.

440. Also, prior contribution periods are not required in order to have the right to benefits arising from industrial accidents and occupational diseases.[234] This is an exemption that is included in the regulation relating to the various benefits of the system that workers might receive due to industrial accidents or occupational diseases: temporary disability,[235] permanent disability,[236] and benefits due to death and for survivors.[237]

441. Second, the principle of automaticity governs the payment of benefits: Following the logic of private insurance, if there is no insurance policy or if the insurance contract has been terminated due to non-payment of the premium, the insuring entity does not accept a claim. However, in the Spanish Social Security System, the breach of obligations concerning registration or the payment of contributions does not stop protection; instead, this is passed to the company, although the principle of automaticity governs the payment of benefits.

442. By virtue of said principle, the MCSS pays the beneficiary the benefit, even when the employer is the party responsible for the benefit, being subrogated in the rights that the beneficiary would have against the breaching employer. This way, individuals are protected in the event of the insolvency of the employer and are exempted from suing the company.

443. However, having the principle of automaticity governing benefits presents some major problems:

234. Article 165(4) of the GSSA.
235. Article 172 of the GSSA.
236. Article 195 of the GSSA.
237. Article 219 of the GSSA.

(1) Its application is dependent upon the demonstration of the existence of the provision of services as an employee which was not formalized with the General Treasury of Social Security, which might not be easy.
(2) The principle of automaticity does not guarantee the right fully, as the advance cannot exceed the sum equivalent to 2.5 times the IPREM in force at the time of the triggering event.[238]

§4. Clear Special Protection

444. The special treatment that work-related risks receive in the Spanish Social Security System is also reflected in the strength of the protective coverage. There are specific benefits available that are not granted when the situation of need is caused by an ordinary risk. This is the case for permanent non-disabling injuries, mutilations and deformities, which are only considered situations of need worthy of protection if the risk that causes them is an industrial accident or an occupational disease.[239] And the same is true regarding special lump-sum compensation in the event of death, which is reserved for deaths due to industrial accidents or occupational diseases.[240]

445. In addition, advantageous criteria have been established for the calculation of benefits.

446. In general, the amount of benefits is obtained by applying a certain percentage to a base amount. This base expresses the connection between the individual's salary (replaced income) and the benefit (replacement income):

– Regarding temporary disability: The base amount for temporary disability is calculated on the basis of the contribution made in the month immediately prior to the triggering event, which includes the average of overtime.
– Regarding pensions: When a pension arises from an industrial accident or from an occupational disease, the base amount is calculated based on the actual salaries paid to the worker at the time immediately prior to the triggering event (instead of remote salaries).
– The applicable percentage: In the case of temporary disability, if the situation of need arises from a work-related risk, the percentage applicable to the base amount is higher.

238. Article 167.3 of the GSSA.
239. Article 201 of the GSSA and Art. 46 of the Order 15 Apr. 1969.
240. Articles 216(2) and 227(1) of the GSSA.

Chapter 6. Inability to Work

§1. TEMPORARY DISABILITY

447. As Part V of this monograph deals in detail with the legal regulation of temporary disability in the Spanish legal system, in the following lines we will highlight the peculiarities of the legal system for benefits, when they arise from work-related risks.

448. First, in order to have the right to benefits due to temporary disability in general it is necessary to fulfil two requirements: (1) applicants must be registered in an equivalent situation with social security, and (2) they must demonstrate a contribution period of 180 days in the five years immediately prior to their sick leave. However, when the temporary disability is due to an industrial accident or an occupational disease, we have seen that registration by operation of law enters into force and no contribution period is required whatsoever.[241]

449. Second, the amount of benefits is also higher when a disability is due to an industrial accident or an occupational disease. Indeed, if the temporary disability is due to an ordinary risk, the benefit is fixed at the following sums: (a) for the first three days of sick leave there is no right to any benefit from social security, (b) from the 4th to the 20th day the benefit amounts to 60% of the base amount, and (c) from the 21st day, the beneficiary will be entitled to receive 75% of the base amount. And, to calculate this, the base amount is the result of dividing the contribution amount for ordinary risks in the month prior to the starting date of the temporary disability by the number of days of said contribution. Consequently, this divisor will be: (a) 30 if a worker has a monthly salary, or (b) 28, 29, 30 or 31 if a worker has a daily wage.

450. However, if the temporary disability arises from a work-related risk, benefits are received from the day after leave from work and are established at 75% of the base amount. This base amount is calculated according to the above rule, although the contribution amount for work-related risks for the month prior to the sick leave is adjusted by adding the average received by the worker for overtime during the twelve months immediately prior to the sick leave.

451. If the company is associated with an MCSS, the management of temporary disabilities due to work-related risks is the MCSS responsibility and, in fact, it will be this entity that will process the sick leave through its own medical service.

452. If temporary disability arises from an ordinary risk, the company must assume the cost of the benefit until the 15th day of the sick leave. From the 16th day, the cost is assumed by the Social Security System or by the MCSS, depending on who manages this specific benefit in the company. In contrast, if the sick leave

241. Article 172 of the GSSA.

is due to an industrial accident or an occupational disease, the managing company assumes the payment of the benefit from the 1st day of sick leave irrespective of whether, in practice, delegated payment is applicable.

453. Finally, concerning the duration of benefits, there is no specific duration regarding ordinary risks.

§2. Permanent Disability

454. On the one hand, focusing on the particularities of the pension for permanent disability derived from professional contingencies, we must bear in mind that, in order to cause the right, registration by operation of law enters into force and no contribution period is required whatsoever.

455. On the other hand, regarding the size of pensions due to permanent disability arising from work-related risks, we should clarify that: the percentage applicable to the base amount is the same, irrespective of the event (ordinary or work-related) that caused the situation of need. However, there are differences regarding the calculation criteria of the base amount. If permanent disability is due to an ordinary risk, the base amount is calculated by taking remote salaries as a reference, as the average of contribution amounts from several previous years is taken. However, if permanent disability is due to an industrial accident or an occupational disease, the base amount is calculated based on the actual salaries received by the worker in the last twelve months of effective work.

§3. Permanent Non-disabling Injuries

456. The special protection that the Spanish legal system confers on work-related risks is expressed, among other things, in the recognition of a benefit in the event of permanent non-disabling injuries.

457. Situation of need: The existence of permanent injuries, mutilations or deformities that, without constituting a situation of permanent disability, alter the physical well-being of a worker. As they do not affect the ability to work, beneficiaries keep their right to continue being employed by the company.

458. Content of the right: The benefit for permanent non-disabling injuries consists of the payment of lump-sum compensation, the amount of which is determined by MO ESS/66/2013 of 28 January,[242] depending on the extent of the damages.

459. We should also remember that there is corporate liability due to a breach in health and safety measures when compensation would be increased by between 30% and 50% at the exclusive expense of the employer.

242. BOE No. 26 of 31 Jan. 2013.

460. Recipients: The workers included in the Social Security System who have their work-related risks protected and fulfil the requirements.

461. Requirements: To have the right to a benefit for permanent non-disabling injuries it is necessary to fulfil the following requirements:

(1) the injury, mutilation or deformity must arise from an industrial accident or occupational disease. If the damage is due to an ordinary risk, workers are not entitled to protection by the Social Security System;
(2) applicants for benefits must be registered in an equivalent situation at the time of the event. However, we should remember that a worker is presumed to be registered or is registered by operation of law, even if the employer has breached its legal obligations;
(3) applicants must be discharged, as this proves that the injury, mutilation or deformity is permanent;
(4) the specific damage must be expressly included in the scale contained in regulatory provisions.

462. Management: The recognition of the right to compensation for permanent non-disabling injuries is the responsibility of the National Institute of Social Security, through its disability evaluation team.

463. The payment of the benefit must be assumed by the National Institute of Social Security or by the MCSS, depending on which entity the company has work-related risks insured with.

Chapter 7. Death

§1. The Individual That Triggers a Benefit

464. In the event of death, the Spanish legal system recognizes some of the following benefits: (a) aid for funeral expenses, (b) a lifetime widow's or widower's pension, (c) a temporary widow's or widower's pension, (d) an orphan's pension, and (e) a lifetime pension or, if applicable, a temporary benefit to family members. And in the event of death due to an industrial accident or occupational disease, a lump-sum compensation is also recognized.[243]

465. Therefore, the person who triggers the benefits due to death and for survivors because of work-related risks is the person who dies due to an industrial accident or an occupational disease. We should also state that the legislator considers deaths as a consequence of industrial accidents or occupational diseases for those who are recognized as having a total permanent disability or a severe disability.[244] In addition, it is important to clarify that this is a presumption that does not admit evidence to the contrary.

466. If a triggering individual is the recipient of a benefit for partial or total permanent disability then the presumption is not applicable, meaning that the individual must demonstrate that the death was due to an industrial accident or an occupational disease. Therefore, regarding evidence, it is necessary to make a new distinction:

- If the origin of the benefit for permanent disability was an industrial accident, this evidence is only admitted when the event has occurred within five years of the date of the accident. Therefore, if the death of a triggering individual occurs after more than five years have passed since the accident, it is presumed that the pensioner has died due to an ordinary risk and evidence to the contrary is not admitted.
- If the origin of the permanent disability is an occupational disease, said evidence will be admitted no matter how much time has passed.

467. Finally, workers that have disappeared due to an industrial accident can also trigger benefits due to death and for survivors (except for aid for funeral expenses). In this specific situation, Article 217(3) of the GSSA requires the fulfilment of the following requirements: (a) the disappearance must have occurred in circumstances that make the death of the worker presumable, and (b) there must have been no news of the worker for ninety calendar days after the accident. If both requirements are fulfilled, then a preliminary legal declaration of death is not necessary and the financial effects of benefits are backdated to the date of the accident.

243. Article 216 of the GSSA.
244. Article 217(2) of the GSSA.

§2. Surviving Spouse

468. The Spanish legal system continues to preferably protect situations of need arising from work-related risks compared to those arising from ordinary risks. And, concerning benefits to surviving spouses, this special protection is expressed as follows.

469. First, if the death occurs due to work-related risks, then benefits are triggered by operation of law and no waiting period whatsoever is required.[245]

470. Second, when the event arises from an industrial accident or from an occupational disease, then the requirements for one year to have passed since the date of the wedding or the existence of children from the marriage are not necessary. However, this is a requirement that must be accredited when the death of the individual arises from an ordinary disease, not a sudden disease after the marriage.

471. Also, if the triggering individual was the recipient of a pension due to a permanent disability arising from a work-related risk, the base amount for the benefits due to death and for survivors will be the same as used to determine said pension, updated in accordance with legislation.

472. Finally, in the event of deaths due to an industrial accident or occupational disease, surviving spouses and survivors of civil partnerships that fulfil the conditions required to be recipients of widow's or widower's pensions are entitled to an additional benefit. Indeed, the legislator recognizes the right to a benefit in the form of a lump-sum compensation worth six monthly payments of the base amount of the widow's or widower's pension.[246]

§3. Orphans

473. If the orphan's pension has its origin in an occupational risk, the same characteristics as in the widow's pension apply: registration by operation of law enters into force and does not require a previous period of contribution to the system. Also, when the death of an individual is due to a work-related risk, orphans are entitled to an additional benefit in the form of lump-sum compensation worth one monthly payment of the base amount for the orphan's pension. In addition, if there is no beneficiary of the widow's or widower's pension, the six monthly payments will be divided between the orphans.

245. Article 219 of the GSSA.
246. Article 227 of the GSSA.

§4. Dependent Parents and Other Relatives

474. A special lump-sum compensation is granted to parents who were in charge of the deceased when the death derives from an accident at work or occupational disease, providing there are no other relatives of the deceased entitled to pension.

475. In this case, the mother or father will receive a special lump-sum compensation equivalent to nine monthly payments of the base amount of the widow's or widower's pension. These monthly payments will be raised to twelve if both parents are alive.

Chapter 8. Prevention

476. The protection of the physical integrity of the worker has given rise, from the first moments of state interventionism, to a profuse organization of guarantee of safety (prevention of work accidents) and hygiene (prevention of illness).

477. The SC guarantees a generic right to health[247] while establishing a specific commitment for public authorities to 'ensure occupational safety and health'.[248]

478. The worker's constitutional right to effective protection in matters of occupational safety and health correlates with the employer's duty to protect workers against occupational hazards, which implies the duty of the employer to guarantee safety and security, and the health of its workers, adopting as many measures as necessary for their protection. The generic duty of security is specified in a series of obligations:

(a) Duty of evaluation of the risks and planning of the preventive activity. The employer must plan its preventive activity based on an initial assessment of the risks to the safety and health of workers, which takes into account all relevant elements (work equipment, chemical substances or preparations, places of work, etc.), so that, after such evaluation, it can adopt preventive activities to guarantee the highest level of safety and health, either by totally eliminating the risks that are possible or by avoiding their consequences as much as possible.
(b) Duty of monitoring the health of workers. The employer must guarantee the workers at their service the periodic monitoring of their health status. In addition, it must organize the necessary means to comply with this obligation, as well as to defray the expenses, direct and indirect, that it causes, without it being able to entail any cost for the worker. Surveillance can only be carried out when the worker gives his consent, that is, it will be voluntary and not compulsory by the employer except in certain cases assessed by the law.
(c) Business information duty. The employer is obliged to take appropriate measures so that workers receive information relating, on the one hand, to the risks to the safety and health of workers at work, both those that affect the company as a whole, as to each type of job or function and, on the other to the measures and activities of prevention and protection applicable to risks above.
(d) Duties of training of workers. The employer must guarantee each worker the relevant training in safety and health at work. The training must be taught initially, both at the time of beginning the work, and in all those cases in which change of work or function, especially if it is work with risks. It must be repeated periodically, whenever technological changes occur, as well as in the work teams, and it is advisable to repeat it as often as possible. The training must be given within the day and will be counted as work time, without it being possible to transfer its cost to the worker.

247. Article 43(1) of the SC.
248. Article 40(2) of the SC.

(e) The business obligation of information and stoppage of the company's activity. When the workers are or may be exposed to a serious and imminent risk on the occasion of their work, the employer is obliged to:

- inform all the workers of the company as urgently as possible about the risks detected, about the seriousness and imminence thereof and the measures adopted;
- adopt the necessary measures and give precise instructions so that workers can interrupt and, if necessary, leave the workplace immediately;
- provide the necessary for the worker who could not contact his superior, in a situation of serious and imminent danger to his safety, that of other workers or of third parties, be in conditions, taking into account his knowledge and the means available to take the necessary measures to avoid the consequences of such danger.

Chapter 9. Supplementary Benefits

§1. Supplementary Benefits Due to Breach of Health and Safety Measures

I. The Channels for the Reparation of Damages in the Case of Work-Related Risks

479. In the event of damages caused by an industrial accident or by an occupational disease, the Spanish legal system provides a reparation system that is organized through three channels: (1) social security benefits, which cover the objective liability of the employer and take the form of a defined payment; (2) compensation for civil liability, which is based on liability due to fault; and (3) supplementary benefits, which provide additional reparation if an industrial accident or occupational disease occurs as a consequence of breach by an employer of its health and safety at work obligations.[249]

480. Indeed, in accordance with the provisions of Article 164.1 of the GSSA:

> All financial benefits that are due to an industrial accident or occupational disease shall be increased, according to the seriousness of the infringement, by between 30 and 50 per cent, when the injury occurs due to work equipment or at facilities, centres or workplaces that do not have regulatory safety resources, do not use them or have them in poor condition, or when general and specific health and safety at work measures have not been observed, or when personal training has not been given for each job, considering its characteristics and the age, gender and other characteristics of the worker.

481. We should clarify that this supplement is not a benefit, simply an increase that, because of its nature and purpose, exceeds the level of compensation normally established for social security benefits. Precisely because of this, it is not subject to revaluation and is not included in the calculation of the maximum amount of pensions, nor does the principle of automaticity govern in the payment and subsidiary liability of the National Institute of Social Security.

II. The Situations for the Application of Supplementary Benefits

482. For supplementary benefits to be applicable, the following requirements must be met:

(1) The company must have committed an infringement of health and safety measures that constitutes the cause of the industrial accident or occupational disease.

249. Article 164 of the GSSA.

(2) The cause of actual damages must be demonstrated. For supplementary benefits to be applicable, it is not sufficient to demonstrate a breach of the health and safety obligation, it must be demonstrated that actual damages have occurred to a worker as a result of this. Therefore, breach by an employer becomes a necessary but not sufficient condition for supplementary benefits.
(3) The damages must be covered by the protective system of social security. It is essential that the right to a social security benefit is recognized as a result of said damages, and the damages must be attributable to an industrial accident or occupational disease. In view of the above, its scope extends to temporary disability, to permanent disability in all its various scales and to benefits due to death and for survivors (widows and widowers, orphans and for family members).
(4) There must be a causal connection between the infringement and the resulting damages. Finally, there must be a causal relationship between the infringement committed and the damages caused, meaning that if the correct health and safety measures had been adopted, then the damages would not have occurred. Therefore, if the specific circumstances in which an industrial accident occurs are unknown, and if there is evidence of an infringement of health and safety measures, then a causal connection is presumed to exist. In short, the principle of the presumption of innocence is only applicable in the criminal/legal sphere but not in the civil/labour sphere of contractual breaches of the health and safety obligation assumed by employers.

483. Therefore, we need to remember that this causal connection could be broken in cases of force majeure, the actions of a third party outside of the company or when the infringement is solely and exclusively attributable to the interested party. In contrast, the causal connection remains when an infringement has been committed by a worker from the same company because, in that case, the liability is attributable to the employer based on Article 1903 of the Spanish Civil Code, according to which the obligation to make reparations for the damages caused is not only enforceable due to own acts or omissions but also enforceable for those acts or omissions by people that the employer is responsible for. And, in fact, this same provision states that the owners or managers of an establishment or company are liable 'for the damages caused by their employees in the line of business in which they are employed as part of their duties'.

484. The fact that a company has trained its employees in health and safety and has provided them with the necessary protective resources does not break the causal connection either, because a company's health and safety obligation does not end there. The company must also ensure that said orders are complied with and can even dismiss those who do not use protective resources correctly. Finally, we should state that if an injured worker has contributed to the occurrence of the resulting damage due to negligent or reckless behaviour, this is irrelevant because the obligation of the employer to anticipate possible non-negligent distractions or reckless actions of workers falls within the health and safety obligation of the employer. Also, although a right of resistance might be recognized in favour of a worker who refuses to carry out work in conditions that represent a threat to health and safety, the failure to exercise this right does not represent any consent whatsoever in the production of the damages or contributory negligence that might offset the negligence of the company. However, the behaviour of an employee is considered relevant in order to determine the amount of the supplement, as we will see.

III. Determination of the Amount of the Supplement

485. In accordance with the provisions of Article 164.1 of the GSSA, the supplement varies between 30% and 50% of the benefit, depending on the seriousness of the infringement. In view of the above, the amount will depend, on one hand, on the seriousness of the infringement (because the specific percentage is determined based on this) and on the other, on the size of the benefit (because this is the base amount that the percentage is applied to):

(a) The applicable percentage. The GSSA does not contain the criteria required for the determination of the percentage of supplements. Therefore, within the defined limits, their size is at the discretion of the National Institute of Social Security and the courts, when appropriate.
(b) The base amount the percentage is applied to. The percentage is applied to all financial benefits that are due to an industrial accident or occupational disease (benefits, pensions and lump-sum compensation payments).

IV. Compatibility of the Supplement with Other Liabilities

486. Taking into account the requirements that determine the right to the supplement, it is inevitable that this might coincide, in practice, with a claim for damages and with the imposition of sanctions. In this regard, Article 164.3 of the GSSA expressly states that this liability 'is independent and compatible with liabilities of all kinds, including criminal, that might arise from the infringement'.

§2. Planned Improvements in Collective Agreements

487. The protective system of the Social Security System represents basic coverage that can be improved. In the General Social Security System, voluntary improvements can be organized through two channels: (1) through the establishment of additional contributions, and (2) through the direct improvement of benefits.[250]

488. The establishment of additional contributions is regulated in Article 241 of the GSSA. This is an improvement option that could be approved by the MISSM at the proposal of the interested parties themselves, and its purpose is the regular

250. Article 238 of the GSSA.

revaluation of already paid benefits or an increase in the size of future benefits. However, this is a legal provision that has not yet been put into practice.

489. For its part, the direct improvement of benefits could consist of the payment of a lump sum, in a temporary benefit or in a lifetime pension.

490. In the Spanish legal system, voluntary improvements are characterized by the inclusion of the following notes:

- Voluntary nature. First, we should consider that voluntary social security improvements do not operate with the force of law, but are the result of private autonomy as the consequence of an agreement (individual or collective) or of the unilateral decision of a company.
- Complementary nature. Intrinsic to the concept itself of voluntary improvement is the prior existence of a social security benefit, with which it maintains an inverse dialectical relationship.
- Private financing. In the systems for employed workers, the general rule is that voluntary improvements are paid for by the companies themselves. Notwithstanding the above, a financial benefit could be provided at the expense of workers, provided that they agree and the MISSM approves it.[251] But we should warn that the financial participation of workers should have a minimal scope. Therefore, mechanisms for benefit plans in which the recipients themselves decide to take them out, at their own expense, with an insurance entity cannot be considered voluntary improvements.
- Private management. Article 240(1) of the GSSA considers the possibility that voluntary improvements be managed by public entities, as it admits that companies could improve their benefits through the Social Security Administration itself. The thing is that the Public Management System contained in the aforementioned Article 240(1) of the GSSA has hardly been used. In practice, the management of voluntary improvements is private and is assumed: (a) either directly by companies, regarding improvements for temporary disability; or (b) indirectly through insurance contracts, mutual benefit schemes or pension plans concerning improvements for permanent disability pensions and concerning benefits due to death and for survivors.
- Legal system. Voluntary improvements are generally governed by the unilateral acts of employers, pacts, agreements or rules that they have established. Only when not expressly provided in said establishment instruments, will voluntary measures be regulated by the rules of the Social Security System, in order, for example, to define the concept of industrial accidents or the various degrees of permanent disability.
- In addition, voluntary improvements do not form part of the subsidiary liability of the National Institute of Social Security. The principle of automaticity of benefits is also not applicable to said improvements, and consequently the obligation to pay benefits in advance that characterize this principle cannot come into play either.

251. Article 239 of the GSSA.

- Similarly, they are also not subject to the rules on the limitation of the amount of pensions. The maximum figure, regulated in Article 57 of the GSSA and in budgetary regulations, is applicable in cases of multiple pensions. However, we should remember that said limitation only applies when the same holder has the right to two or more public pensions. Voluntary improvements, the purpose of which is precisely to cover the shortcomings and limitations of said system, are therefore excluded.
- Finally concerning voluntary improvements, the general rule on the incompatibility of benefits does not apply. The principle of one single benefit is included in Article 163 of the GSSA, but this only refers to public pensions in the General System, not covering pension supplements.

491. The majority of corporate collective agreements improve social security benefits due to temporary disability. Based on the statistical data published by the Ministry of Labour in 2021, 73.67% of corporate collective agreements provided supplements for temporary disability due to ordinary risks and 79.26% established improvements for industrial accidents and occupational diseases.

492. The trend for collective bargaining is to complement social security benefits relating to this specific situation of need irrespective of the cause (ordinary or work-related). However, it is important to highlight the clear special treatment that work-related risks receive compared to ordinary risks. This is special protection that translates, in practice, into greater coverage because the receipt of a higher payment percentage by workers is guaranteed, or because the items included in the calculation of the supplement are broadened, or because coverage is extended to a longer period of time.

493. In addition, the majority of collective agreements provide clauses for benefits in response to situations of permanent disability or due to death and for survivors. And the trend is that protection is established in the payment of a lump sum of a fixed sum or a certain number of monthly payments of the affected worker's salary. The personal circumstances of workers are not usually taken into account in the calculation of the sum.

Chapter 10. Civil Liability

494. In the event of an industrial accident or occupational disease, an employer can be sued for compensation for the damages caused. This reparation consists of a cash sum that an employer must pay to the victim to compensate for the damages caused by a breach.

§1. Requirements So That the Civil Liability of an Employer Is Applicable

495. Generally and strictly speaking, compensation for damages is not produced automatically because of a contractual breach; instead the following requirements need to be fulfilled:

(a) There must be actual damages: If an employer infringes health and safety at work regulations, but no harmful result arises from said breach for workers, no civil liability arises whatsoever.
(b) Damages must originate from the breach of health and safety obligations (existence of a causal connection).
(c) The employer must be responsible for said breach due to the existence of fault or negligence. Therefore, as employers are responsible for health and safety in an employment contract (as they are the ones that create risks), they must demonstrate that they have carried out all due diligence beyond regulatory requirements, having to protect workers even against their own carelessness or non-negligent reckless actions.

496. An employer is only not liable when the damaging result is caused by force majeure or an Act of God, by negligence that could not have been predicted carried out by workers themselves, or by the exclusive fault of third parties that could not be avoided by the employer, it being incumbent upon the employer to demonstrate these possible grounds for exemption.

§2. The Purpose of Civil Liability

497. The obligation to pay compensation has a dual purpose: (a) reparative or compensatory, in that it seeks the satisfaction of the injured party; and (b) preventive because it seeks to ensure that the breaching party will not wish to repeat the damaging act and also because it represents an example for society, which is a witness to the consequences of said conduct.

498. Common law differentiates between compensatory damages and punitive damages. The first compensate the damage caused. The second penalize those responsible. Considering the seriousness of the breach and disregarding the relationship between the damages and the compensation, the liable party must pay the victim a sum that is far higher than it would have to if the purpose of the payment were purely as compensation for the damages suffered. However, it continues to be a compensation that, as such, is paid to the injured party.

499. However, punitive damages do not appear to have support in the Spanish legal system, as Article 1101 of the Spanish Civil Code solely provides reparation for damages caused, which appears to fulfil a function that is solely compensatory, not punitive.

500. To this end, reparation includes:

- Pecuniary or material damages: This is what victims suffer to their assets and financial rights, which is then divided into consequential damages and loss of profits. Consequential damage is the value of the loss suffered. Loss of profits is the value of income that has ceased to be obtained.
- Non-pecuniary damages are in turn divided into bodily harm (injury to the physical or psychological well-being of a person that causes harm to an asset, such as health) and pain and suffering (an injury to a purely psychological asset).[252]

§3. Compensation Amount

501. As the purpose of compensation is to compensate for the damages suffered by a worker, its amount must be the sum at which said damages are valued. Therefore, when damages are assessed, the amount of the compensation is pre-established by the legislator and this must be independent of the actual scope of the damage. However, when damages are not assessed, the amount of the compensation will be the result of applying the following rules and principles for the valuation of damages.

I. Rules

502.

(a) Who should demonstrate the extent of damages? In general, the person who alleges the damages must provide the factual basis for the amount of compensation claimed. The quantification of pain and suffering is only required in the event of an infringement of a fundamental right (Article 179(3) of the Labour Jurisdiction Act).

(b) Who quantifies damages? The quantification of damages is entrusted to the Court of First Instance and the amount it establishes cannot be revised unless it is clearly disproportionate.

(c) How are damages valued? Pecuniary damage can be valued financially, according to the market value of the damaged property. Non-pecuniary damage cannot be compensated in the strictest sense, as it is to assets that do not have a market

252. Supreme Court Ruling of 15 Apr. 2013, Register No. 1114/2012.

value. As there is no replacement for the lost asset on the market, the compensation focuses on compensating for the suffering caused. And, for this purpose, the courts usually resort by analogy to the existing scale for traffic accidents.

II. Applicable Principles in the Valuation of Damages

503.

(a) The full compensation of damages: The purpose of compensation for damages is to achieve full compensation for them, to provide the injured party with full compensation for the damaging act.

(b) The principle of proportionality: Compensation must be adequate and in proportion to the damages and must therefore not entail unfair enrichment. This principle applies as the maximum sum in the determination of the amount for the compensation of damages.

(c) The principle of compatibility between various compensation channels: In the event of an industrial accident or occupational disease, the reparation for damages is organized through various fully compatible channels: social security benefits, voluntary improvements, supplementary benefits and compensation for civil liability.

III. Time Limit

504. The time limit to initiate a claim for damages arising from an industrial accident or occupational disease is one year from the determination of the injuries, as until that time an individual does not know precisely what the consequences will be or the damages that said events would cause.

Chapter 11. Accumulation Rules

505. The compatibility of benefits with individual earnings: the legal system concerning the compatibility or incompatibility of benefits with work does not differ from what is established in the case of ordinary risks, the study of which we have referred to. However, we should highlight one exception: if the permanent disability arises from an occupational disease, Article 43 of MO of 15 April 1969[253] makes the benefit compatible with any job, provided that the relevant prior authorization is obtained from the managing entity.

506. The compatibility of benefits with other channels for the reparation of damage: we have already seen that, in the event of an industrial accident or an occupational disease, the reparation for the damages is made through various channels: social security benefits, the payment of supplementary benefits and compensation through civil liability. That is precisely why coordination is required, starting from a general principle of compatibility.

507. This criterion of compatibility determines that, for the purposes of establishing the amount of additional compensation for damages, social security benefits and voluntary improvements amount should be deducted from total compensation sums. However, this deduction excludes supplementary benefits.

508. Therefore, taking into account that damages have various components (physical and psychological injuries, pain and suffering, consequential financial damage and loss of profits), the coordination of the various channels for reparation should be carried out using similar criteria, meaning that, in the event of social security benefits that compensate losses of profits because of an inability to earn them, the only way to compensate them is through the recognized compensation payments for loss of profits.

253. Order of 15 Apr. 1969 establishing rules for the application and implementation of disability benefits in the General Social Security System (BOE No. 110 of 8 May 1969).

Part VII. Unemployment

Daniel Pérez del Prado

Chapter 1. Provision of Work

509. Since the 1970s, unemployment has been one of the most significant social problems in Spain. Except for 2008, the moment in which the Spanish unemployment rate converged to the European average, the country has always been above the level of the rest of the European countries. The Great Recession 2007–2013 affected Spain significantly, increasing the unemployment rate from 8% up to more than 26%. Nevertheless, the recovery is driving the country to a completely different scenario, closing 2022 around the level of 12%.

510. Aside from the reforms on the labour market, Spanish Governments have traditionally dealt with unemployment by using two different tools. On the one hand, passive employment policies focused on guaranteeing social protection during unemployment; on the other hand, active employment policies aimed to facilitate access to a new job. Whereas passive policies will be analysed in the following chapter, this will go into the details of the active ones.

511. From a financial point of view, actives are more important than passives because Spain spends more money on the first ones than on the second ones, what is one of the characteristics of the Spanish Employment System. As Figure 1 shows, before the crisis, the expenditure on passive policies (categories 8–9) more than duplicate the expenditure on active ones (categories 1–7).

Figure 1 Expenditure on Employment Policies

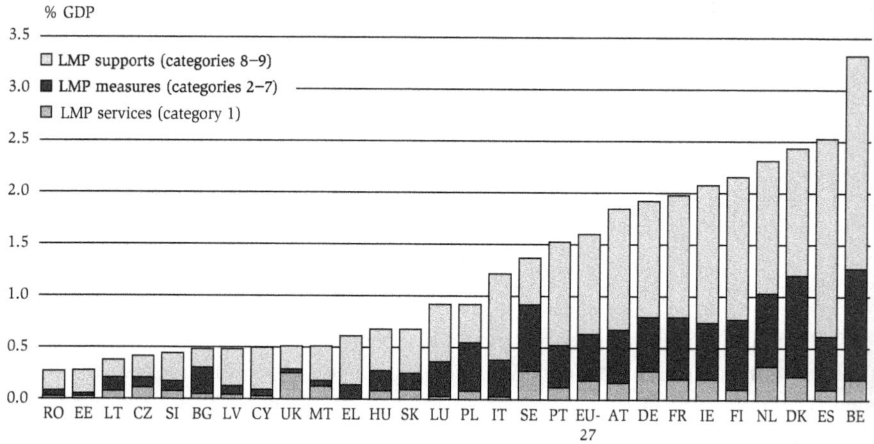

Source: Eurostat, 2008.
Note: GDP: Gross Domestic Product; LMP: Labour Market Policies.

512. Concerning active employment policies, up to the financial crisis, there were some explicit signals about Spanish determination of improving employment services:

> An appropriate response to new challenges means to be capable of creating new jobs, giving new competences, greater adaptation capacity and mobility to our labour force […]. Future entails more flexibility and mobility in professional careers. Public Employment Services is going to play an essential role in this new dynamic, in which there will be a bigger number of employment transitions thought the professional life. Actually, they are the instruments to get easier those transitions, through proper measures of prospecting, orientation, activation and traineeship. Therefore, Public Employment Services activity is important, both crisis periods and expansion times, to accompany and promote the changes related to access and improvement of employment and make easier the continuous adaptation of employees to the new productive model towards to this new model we want to advance.[254]

513. Fortunately, the recovery is permitting to reinitiate this trend. In this sense, it is important to take into account the competence framework of Spanish employment policies, which is distributed as follows: passive policies belong to the State, active policies are on CCAA hands mainly, whereas municipalities have a subsidiary role since their activity depends on others. Actually, Spanish municipalities do

254. Rojo Torrecilla, E., 'Servicios Públicos de Empleo. Una Mejora Inaplazable Para Afrontar El Presente y El Futuro,' *Relaciones Laborales: Revista Crítica de Teoría y Práctica,* 2 (2010): 1231–1240 (author's translation).

not have any competence in active labour employment policies, but they develop them in practice as a sort of social or economic policy.

514. Despite the main role concerning active employment policies played by CCAA, the State coordinates the whole National Employment System through two main tools. On the one hand, the Spain's Activation Strategy for Employment,[255] which determines the conceptual and organizational framework to which all the actions carried out within the National Employment System must refer in terms of activation policies, setting the principles, common objectives, the instruments to be used, and the financial resources that are expected to be available for the fulfilment of these objectives and actions. On the other hand, the Annual Employment Policy Plan, which is the operational instrument to develop and translate into actions that set out in this Strategy for every year.

515. Additionally, the State does coordinate employment policies not only within Spain but also with the rest of Europe. As part of the EU, Spain's Strategy must follow the lines set at the European Employment Strategy (EES),[256] the guideline that establishes a set of common objectives and targets for employment policy through the EU. The final result is a multilevel structure in which the State coordinates from the European stage to the local one.

516. In this structure, the role of social partners is very limited and frequently focused on an advisory role. Despite this, they are frequently represented in advisory bodies in the different levels of management of employment policies; the most effective instrument of participation is through tripartite social dialogue. By different social Pacts, social partners have influenced Government reforms and, consequently, the way in which employment policies have been articulated and implemented.

517. Within this framework, Article 36 of Royal Legislative Decree 3/2015 of 23 October, approving the consolidated text of the Employment Law, distinguishes several types of active employment policies:[257] information and job guidance, education and training, employment promotion, self-employment promotion, geographical mobility or employment inclusion. Nevertheless, some of them must be highlighted.

§1. Labour Mediation

518. Labour mediation is one of the most important employment policies in order to promote an adequate balance between supply and demand in the labour market. According to the Fiscal Responsibility Independent Authority's evaluation,

255. The current version has been set for the period 2017–2020. For more info: http://www.lamoncloa.gob.es/lang/en/gobierno/councilministers/Paginas/2017/20171215_councilministers.aspx.
256. In detail: https://ec.europa.eu/social/main.jsp?catId=101&langId=en.
257. BOE No. 77 of 31 Mar. 2015.

only 2.1% of workers find a new job, thanks to the help of Public Employment Services.[258] This does not only suggest a significant inefficiency on public mediation but also promotes other ways to find a new job, being informal tools the most significant ones. Concretely, some research studies suggest that 'using relations with relatives and friends' is the most frequent way to find a new job.

519. The general decline of importance of Public Employment Services on employment mediation started the abolition of its monopoly in 1994. Since this time, non-profit employment agencies were allowed to intervene in the labour market to match offers and applications for employment. Recently, the participation of private entities has been enlarged. In 2011, for-profit private agencies were included as new agents in the labour market. In 2012, temporary employment agencies were authorized to act as intermediators as well. This increasing number of entities acting in the labour market is due to the huge number of unemployed people, which forced to find new subjects to help them to find a new job. Nevertheless, this news strategy also produced discoordination and the logical consequences of agency problem.

§2. Vocational Training

520. Vocational training is regulated by Organic Law 3/2022, of 31 March, of organization and integration of vocational training.[259] It focuses on both employed and unemployed people, involving all public administrations, undertakings and social partners. Actually, both social partners and collective bargaining have a central role. They are the parties who are closer and know best, the productive reality, what permits them to design a system of vocational training that responds effectively to the real needs of companies and workers.

521. The system of vocational training is based on a multi-annual strategic planning scenario which is elaborated previewing the economic trends and requires the adaptation and upgrading of employees, economic sectors with growth potential or the upward transversal skills. All these elements are used to design a vocational training system that is coherent with the present and future necessities of employers and employees.

522. The system includes some specific services and actions which must be highlighted: (a) the so-called vocational training account (*cuenta formación*) was created in order to certify the employees' educational curriculum and drive the offer of vocational training programmes to the increase of their employability; (b) telelearning is also promoted as a tool that will provide efficiency and flexibility to the

258. http://www.airef.es/es/informes-orden/.

259. BOE No. 78 of 1 Apr. 2022. Law 30/2015, of 9 September, which regulates the Vocational Training System for employment in the workplace is in force insofar as it does not contravene Organic Law 2/2022.

system, taking over the rigidities of the official academic calendar, which is conditioned by the administrative procedure; (c) vocational training in the workplace consists of: on the one hand, courses given by the company itself if it has an adequate infrastructure; or, on the other hand, by a third party (social partners, joint organisms, etc.), whether it is legally accredited or registered; (d) regarding training for unemployed people, the so-called teaching-cheque (*cheque formación*) tries to permit that unemployed people can choose the entity that is going to provide their vocational training courses, notwithstanding the Public Employment Service's advice and control.

523. The fight against fraud is strengthened by the publishing of bad practices and illegalities but, especially, by the creation of a special unit, within the Labour and Social Security Inspectorate, to control vocational training activities. This unit will have the capacity to sanction these kinds of irregularities. Penalties include, among others, the impossibility of developing vocational training activities financed by the public administration during five years.

524. Finally, despite the advances in regulation, the most important problem of vocational training in Spain is still the lack of enough investment and financing.

§3. Direct Work Provision

525. Direct work provision includes both the promotion of small and medium enterprises (for instance, public works projects, subsidies) to increase labour demand and direct hiring by public administrations. This type of employment policy has been seriously limited by austerity measures applied during the Great Recession and, even, after that.

§4. Other Active Labour Market Policies

526. Nevertheless, the most important employment policy from a financial point of view is hiring incentives or hiring subsidies. This consists of the reduction of taxes or social security contributions or the provision of a specific amount of money in case of hiring someone who has been classified as a subject with difficulties in the access to the labour market or to find a new job.

527. According to Figure 2, around one in EUR 2 expended on active LMP in Spain were used to finance hiring incentives. The success of this policy in Spain is due to its easy and rapid implementation. Nevertheless, there is both national and international studies, which shows that this kind of employment policy does not help to create employment, but to focus the employment already created on certain groups. This is owed to the so-called 'deadweight effect' which means that incentives are financing jobs which would be created in all circumstances.

Figure 2 Expenditure on Active Employment Policies in Spain

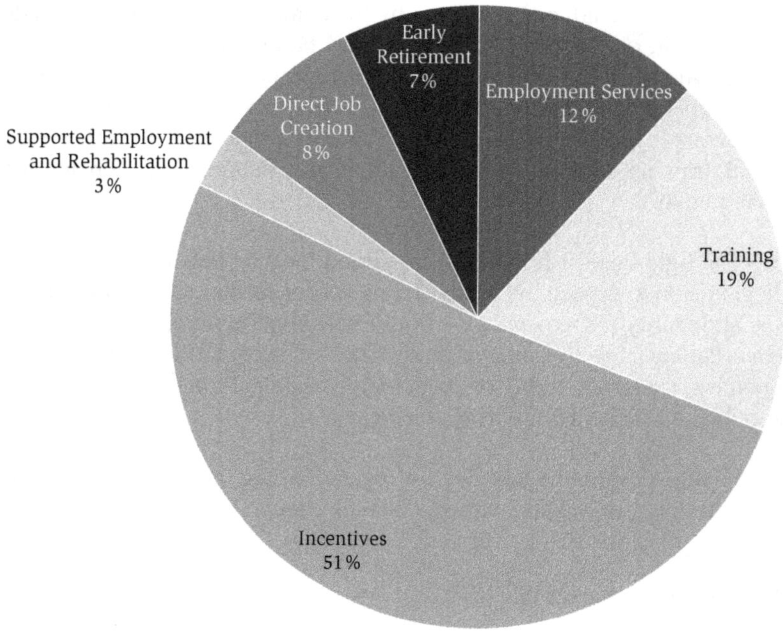

Source: Own elaboration based on OECD databank 2015.
Note: GDP: Gross Domestic Product; LMP: Labour Market Policies.

Chapter 2. Unemployment Benefits

528. Concerning passive employment policies, they are provided by the so-called unemployment protection system. Since the 1990s, it is included in the social security; despite it having some special characteristics which makes it different from other benefits. Nowadays, it is regulated in the GSSA and covers, not only employed but also self-employed people.

§1. Field of Application

I. Territorial

529. The regulation and management of unemployment protection system is competence of the State, 'without prejudice to implementation of its services by the CCAA' (Article 148(17) of the SC). Despite this mention, CCAA do not have a significant role in the management of this type of passive employment policy. Actually, as mentioned above, there is a clear distinction between its competences on active employment policies and the State's competence on passive ones. This separation frequently produces cases of discoordination. In spite of the effort to overcome these difficulties, the services in charge of dealing with active and passive employment policies are different.

530. Additionally, it must be considered that CCAA have competences on 'social assistance' (Article 149(20) of the SC). On the basis of this power, they have created a large variety of subsidies whose limits with unemployment protection is not clear. In some cases, these allowances are combined with programmes for reinsertion into the labour market, which puts them even closer to the unemployment system. This is clearly another source of discoordination and inefficiency because subjects and resources involved are partially overlapped.

II. Personal

531. From a subjective point of view, all person who fulfil the requirements set by the GSSA will be covered by the unemployment system. In this sense, the definition set by the Spanish Law is not very different from other comparable legal systems. Hence, it is unemployed the person who wants and can work but has lost his job. Traditionally, this definition has been divided into three main elements:

(1) Willingness to work: The system covers only persons who want to work, excluding those who carry out other activities, such as studying, family caring, etc.
(2) Capability to work: The system gives protection to those who are able to work. People with disabilities which do not permit them to develop a professional activity are covered by a different social security scheme, the different benefits included in the incapacity.

(3) Unintentional loss of a previous job: It is required not only to have the will and capacity but also to have lost a previous job. This means that first job searching, such as students who have finished their studies, are not covered by the system. Resignation and other types of intentional termination of the employment relationship are not covered either.

532. In addition to the general definition of unemployed person, the GSSA also includes as a contingency covered by the system, the suspension of the contract and the reduction of working time. These are measures of internal flexibility, adopted by undertaking in order to overcome any kind of difficulty or to adapt themselves to the competition or the changing circumstances of the markets. As an alternative to external flexibility, the internal flexibility permits the company to keep its workforce. In order to strengthen this kind of policies, avoid the terrible effects of dismissal and smooth the diminution of revenues, the unemployment system includes these two cases as a type of unemployment despite there is no a real case of loss of job, because the employment relationship is still alive. This permits to provide income support to compensate for the decrease of revenues produced by the suspension of the contract or the reduction of the working time. Consequently, it would be possible to combine the perception of the salary with an unemployment subsidy.

533. This exception permits to distinguish between the concepts of total unemployment and partial unemployment. The first one is defined as the situation in which the employee ceases to work, temporarily or permanently, and loses his salary as a consequence. It must be noted that this situation can be produced when the employment relationship is finished, is suspended or is reduced by affecting complete days in a week. The second one is defined as the situation in which the employee reduces his daily working time from at least 10% to 70% as maximum. This means that only the reduction of working time which is produced within the day and between those limits is considered as partial unemployment, to prevent from both minimum and excessive reductions. Partial unemployment is compatible with the reduced salary received in this case.

534. Finally, the GSSA specifies some circumstances in which the person is unemployed from a legal point of view. Hence, unemployment may be produced by dismissal, suspension of the contract or reduction of working time, death, retirement or incapacity of the employer, voluntary termination of the employment relationship when it is caused by the employer's fault, termination of a fixed-term contract, termination during the probationary period by employer's will,[260] periods of inactivity in the case of seasonal workers (*trabajadores fijos discontinuos*), returned emigrants when they finished an employment relationship abroad, employee's incapacity and cessation of a political or representative position.

260. It is required that the previous employment relationship has been terminated by a different cause or occurred three months before it.

III. Levels of Protection

535. From an objective point of view, the protection provided by the system varies depending on the 'level' of protection. The Spanish unemployment system has two levels of protection, which are connected to the two most common models of social security. On the one hand, the so-called contributory level is based on the contributory system; that is, the coverage and protection depend on previous contributions and it is aimed to provide an income substitutive of the salary. On the other hand, the 'assistance level' is inspired by the non-contributory or assistance model. In this case, the protection is due when the subject is in a state of need frequently connected to the lack of (enough) income and its main objective is to provide an allowance to prevent that state of need.

536. The use of the term 'level' probably shows that the relationship between them is not balanced. On the contrary, the assistance level has been configured as a complement of the contributory one. Hence, it usually operates when the contributory benefit is exhausted or when it is not possible to access to the protection of the contributory level.

537. Paradoxically, despite each level is inspired in a different model of social security, as in other legal systems, the distinction is not completely pure. Consequently, it is possible to find elements from the assistance model in the contributory level. At the same time, it is also frequent to find characteristics of contributory benefits in the assistance level. Maybe, the clearest example is the so-called 'contributory subsidy' (*subsidio contributivo*), which requires not only a certain level of income but also previous contributions (*see* §2.II). In order to avoid misunderstandings, the term 'benefit' will be used for the contributory level (*prestación contributiva*), whereas the term 'subsidy' for the assistance protection (*subsidios asistenciales*).

538. Apart from these two traditional levels, it would be possible to say that third level of protection has been created during the last decades. Nevertheless, this level is neither homogeneous nor coherent with the traditional structure and functioning of the Spanish unemployment system. Concerning the first notion, the third level of protection is formed by several allowances inspired by different purposes, which are not connected among them or with the rest of levels of protection. Regarding the second point, this third level has been brought outside the social security and, consequently, serving to the same aims of the unemployment system but without forming part of it from a legal and formal point of view.

539. This third level of protection was born with the name Active Insertion Income (*Renta Activa de Inserción* – RAI). It was created in 2000 as a new allowance, which incorporates some active employment measures in order to help unemployed persons older than 45 years old to find a new job. Since then, its subjective scope has been extended to other groups with difficulties to find a new job, such as people with disabilities, victims of gender-based violence or migrants. Nowadays, the main requirements in order to be entitled to this programme are:

- General Requirements: (a) be registered as a job seeker for at least twelve months and searching employment actively; (b) be under 65 years old; (c) the unemployed person's level of income cannot exceed EUR 712.50 per month and the total monthly income of your entire household, divided by the number of members of the same, cannot exceed the same amount; (d) have exhausted previous unemployment benefit and/or subsidies and not be entitled to them; (e) the unemployed person cannot have been a recipient of the RAI in the 365 calendar days preceding your application, except in the case of victims of gender-based violence or domestic violence and people with a disability; and (f) and he cannot have been a recipient of three previous RAI allowances.
- Special requirements. As it focuses on certain groups, some special conditions are required in order to determine which are those beneficiaries. As a consequence, in order to be covered by this Income, these persons must: (a) be older than 45 years old, (b) be a person with disability, (c) be a returned emigrant; or (d) be a victim of gender violence.[261]

540. Fulfilling these requirements, the unemployed person will be entitled to an allowance of EUR 480 per month (the 80% of the IPREM, *see* §3.II)[262] during a maximum period of eleven months.

541. In addition to the RAI, recently, new special programmes have emerged, expanding this level of protection, as a direct consequence of the last economic crisis. The Great Recession showed the limitations of the Spanish unemployment system, which was not able to keep the level of protection for a long period. As a consequence, the coverage rate, that is, the percentage of beneficiaries of an unemployment scheme compared to the whole population of unemployed people, diminished from around 90% to close to 50%. In order words, the system was not capable of preventing that one in two unemployed persons did not have any coverage.

542. In order to ameliorate this situation, the Government passed different programmes[263] whose main objective was to increase the coverage of the system. They were created with a temporary nature and, frequently, outside the limits of social

261. For the last two cases, it is not required to be registered as unemployed person during at least twelve months.
262. This is an indicator created in 2004 (RD-Law 3/2004 of 25 June, to rationalize the minimum wage and to increment its amount, BOE No. 154 of 26 Jun. 2004) in order to substitute the minimum statutory wage as an indicator to determine the amount of certain benefits or the access to them. The evolution of the quantity of this indicator can be found here: http://www.seg-social.es/wps/portal/wss/internet/Trabajadores/CotizacionRecaudacionTrabajadores/10721/10957/9932/730#47860.
263. The first one was the 'Temporary Programme for Unemployment and Insertion' (Programa Temporal para el Empleo y la Inserción – PRODI), created in 2009. This was substituted by the 'Professional Requalification Programme' (Programa de Recualificación Profesional – PREPARA) in 2011, which was followed by the 'Activation Programme for Employment', created in 2011 and renewed up to 2017. Nevertheless, the Constitutional Court declared these last programmes unconstitutional because they invaded Autonomous Communities' competences on employment policies. Consequently, both of them were not renewed (nevertheless, it remains active for those who were receiving it in that moment) but substituted by a new one, the so-called 'extraordinary subsidy' in 2018. This was included, for the first time, in the GSSA, but with a temporary base.

security as well. As a consequence, they provide a conjectural and partial solution for a structural problem of the Spanish unemployment system. Generally speaking, they have been provided an exiguous aid (around EUR 430.27 per month) for a limited period of time (as a rule, six months which were not renewable).

543. The COVID-19 pandemic put the unemployment system under pressure as well. Despite new subsidies similar to the previous ones were created to protect certain groups – artists, bullfighters, temporary agricultural workers, etc. – the most important role played by the unemployment system was as a complement of the temporary suspension of the contracts and the reduction of working time (ERTEs is the acronym of this programme in Spanish). Hence, the unemployment benefit was used to cover the lack of income whereas the contract is suspended or for the percentage of working time which was reduced.

§2. Conditions

I. Unemployment Benefits

544. In order to be entitled to the unemployment benefit (*prestación de desempleo*), it is necessary: (a) to be registered with the social security (or in a similar situation); (b) to have at least 360 days of contributions in the last six years and be registered at an employment office (these two requirements are connected to the idea of losing a previous job); (c) to be unemployed (in the sense explained above), registered such as at the employment office and searching actively for a new job (this is related to the idea of willingness to work); and (d) to be below the ordinary age to access to a retirement pension (this is linked to the capacity to work).

545. The most important requirement in this level of protection is the previous social security contributions. In this sense, it is necessary to highlight that social security contributions are paid by both sides of the employment relationship:

- Insured person: The contribution is calculated by applying a percentage to the so-called 'CB'. The contribution is based on the monthly earnings, so the amount is quite similar. Nevertheless, GSSA sets a minimum of EUR 1,150.00 and a maximum of EUR 4,495.50 (amounts for 2023). Concerning the percentage, it is 1.55% for indefinite contracts and 1.6% for fixed-term contract.
- Employer: The calculation is exactly the same, but the percentage differs. It is 5.5% for indefinite contracts and 6.7% for fixed-term contracts.

546. Despite the obligation of contributing is shared by the employer and the employee, the duty of paying the money to the TGSS is effectively posed on the employer. So, he is in charge of depositing the money in a special fund.

547. Whereas contributions will be considered to calculate the money in which the benefit consists (*see* §3.I), the number of days contributed by the parties will be taken into account in order to determine the access and the duration. Concerning the access, as it was mentioned before, it is necessary, at least 360 days of contribution. For full-time work, every day worked is counted as a day contributed. In the case of part-time workers, the days accounted will be natural days in order to avoid discrimination between vertical and horizontal part-time employment (*see* §4.I). In case of various part-time jobs, it will be counted the days related to the job which was terminated.

548. Additionally, the rule also sets a reference period of six years. When the employee has worked continuously, this period is not applied, because it only makes sense when there is a number of fractionated periods of work. In those circumstances, it will be accounted for all the periods within the reference of six years before the termination of the employment relationship. The rules concerning the accountability of the days to access to the benefit are applied automatically; that is, the unemployed person will be entitled just for working during that period and even when the employer has not fulfilled his duty of depositing the contributions (without prejudice his responsibility for this).

II. Unemployment Assistance

549. Concerning unemployment assistance, there is a set of common requirements which affect the different kinds of subsidies, besides the specific conditions related to each type of subsidy. The common requirements are: (a) be registered as unemployed at the employment office, (b) for at least one month (waiting period), (c) searching employment actively and not rejecting an adequate job offer, and (d) monthly income must not exceed 75% of the statutory monthly minimum wage.[264] This last condition must be respected not only in the moment to access to the subsidy but also when he is receiving it.

550. On the other hand, the following are the different types of unemployment subsidies and the conditions related to each one.

A. *Pure Assistance Subsidies*

551. In this category, it is included a package of different subsidies which match perfectly with the legal nature of the assistance level, because no contributory conditions are required. Nevertheless, the protection is focused on certain groups of unemployed people, which means the adoption of additional requirements:

- Subsidy for family responsibilities (*subsidio por responsabilidades familiares*): It requires having family responsibilities and having exhausted the contributory benefit. The subsidy aims to extend the protection given by the system taking into consideration the protection of the family. In this sense, family responsibilities are defined from a pure economic perspective. Family responsibilities are defined as

264. For 2020, the statutory minimum wage is set at EUR 950, so the mean test is at EUR 721.50.

having a spouse, children younger than 26 years old or older with disabilities who are economically dependent from the unemployed person. At the same time, the economic dependence is produced when household's income divided by its members, including the unemployed person, is below 75% of the statutory minimum wage salary. This last condition, as the means-test, must be respected not only in the moment to access to the subsidy but also when the unemployed person is receiving it.

- Subsidy for people older than 45 years old (*subsidio para mayores de 45 años*): It requires having exhausted the contributory benefit and being older than 45 years old. The subsidy is configured as a complement of the contributory level, prolonging the protection owed to the especial difficulties finding a new job of elder people.
- Subsidy for returned emigrants (*subsidio para emigrantes retornados*): It requires being Spanish emigrant worker who returns from a country not a member of the European Economic Space or with which there is no international agreement on unemployment protection; having worked for at least twelve months within the last six years since leaving Spain; and not being entitled to unemployment benefit. This subsidy aims to facilitate the return of emigrants by means of a guarantee.
- Subsidy for rehabilitated workers (*subsidio para incapaces rehabilitados*): It requires having been declared capable to work from a previous declaration of incapacity. This subsidy focuses on permitting the transition from incapacity to work.
- Subsidy for persons released from prison (*subsidio para liberados de prisión*): It requires, besides leaving the prison definitely, not being entitled to unemployment subsidy and having been imprisoned for more than six months. This subsidy also includes persons who have undergone a treatment for drug addiction during their imprisonment if it has lasted at least six months.

B. Contributory Subsidy (Subsidio Contributivo)

552. This subsidy works not as a complement but as a substitute to the contributory benefits. As it was mentioned before, it is a mix of the two models of social security because, in addition to the typical requirements as assistance subsidy (including one month of waiting period), that is the general conditions, it also requires: at least three months of contributions in case of having family responsibilities; or at least six months of contributions, for those who have no family responsibilities. Consequently, it is configured as a second option for those who do not have enough contributions to access to the unemployment benefit, being covered, but with a lower amount (*see* §3.II). It must be noted that family responsibilities are used to facilitate access to this subsidy, so unemployed people with family may be covered with less previous social security contributions. These are defined as in the case of the subsidy for family responsibilities (*see* previous section).

C. *Pre-retirement Subsidy (Subsidio de Prejubilación o Para Mayores de 52 Años)*

553. It is called 'pre-retirement' subsidy because it focuses on elderly workers who have difficulties trying to find a new job precisely because of their age. Assuming that, in the worst situation, it is quite probable that they do not find a new job, it tries to be a 'bridge' to retirement. This is another subsidy in which elements from contributory and non-contributory protection are mixed. So, in addition to the general conditions mentioned above, these ones are also required: being at least 52 years old, at least six years of contributions for unemployment during his whole working life and fulfilling all the requirements to access to retirement pensions except for the age.

III. Unemployment Benefits for Self-Employed Workers: Cease of Activity

554. Self-employed people are also covered by the unemployment system, but with a scheme included in its Special Regime (RETA). Without a doubt, the unemployment protection of self-employed persons has particular characteristics which makes it different from the employees' one. The most important special note is the fact that, in his case, there is not a third person who put an end to a previous relationship. In other words, the note of 'unwillingness' is put in doubt here and must have a different configuration.

555. These differences explain the specialities of its regulation. With this, three important points must be highlighted. First, the scheme was born outside social security, despite it is included within GSSA nowadays.[265] Second, it was born as a contributory scheme and has been kept this nature so far. Finally, unemployment protection for self-employees receives different names and definition. According to GSSA, it is called 'cease of activity', which is defined as the temporal or definitive cease of the activity which permitted the incorporation into the RETA. Additionally, the Law also sets a list of cases in which the cease of activities crystallizes: (a) when it is caused by economic, technical, productive or organizational reasons; (b) when it is caused by force majeure temporarily or definitively; (c) when it is caused by the withdrawal of an administrative authorization which is indispensable for the development of the activity; (d) when it is caused by gender-based violence; or (e) when it is caused by divorce or legal separation when the spouse worked at the familiar business.[266]

---

265. It was created by Law 32/2010 of 5 August, which sets the specific scheme of cessation of the activity of self-employed people (BOE No. 190 of 6 Aug. 2010). Nowadays, it is regulated under the Title V of the Ch. III of the GSSA.

266. These conditions are modified for certain types of self-employees, such as the so-called 'economic dependent self-employees', that is, those who (1) they are formally self-employed; and (2) they depend on a single employer for their income (according to the Spanish regulation, at least 75% of their income).

556. When one of these circumstances arise, the protection of the system is due. Moreover, since 2019, insurance against this specific risk is obliged for all self-employees, so all of them are included under its coverage. However, in order to be insured, some particular requirements must be fulfilled: (a) to be registered (or in a similar situation) in the Special Regimen for Self-Employed; (b) to have at least twelve months of contributions in the last forty-eight months (four years);[267] (c) to be in situation of 'cease of activity' (unemployed), registered such as at the employment office and searching actively for a new job; (d) be under the age for retirement (65 or 67, depending on the situation) except for when they do not fulfil the requirements to access to the retirement pension; and (e) have paid their (and their employees) social security contributions.

557. As in the case of the unemployment benefit, the most important requirement in this level of protection is the previous social security contributions but, obviously, in this case, they will be paid by the self-employee according to the following rules:

- The contribution is calculated by applying a percentage to the so-called 'CB'.
- The CB is exactly the same as for other contingencies.
- It is chosen by the self-employed person according to its monthly earnings but within the minimum limit of EUR 751.63 up to the maximum EUR 4, 138.40.[268] Concerning the percentage, it is 0.9%.

558. These contributions will be used to calculate the amount in which this benefit consists and its duration. As it was mentioned above, it is necessary at least twelve months of contributions during the last forty-eight months.

§3. Amount of the Benefits

I. Unemployment Benefits

559. As it was mentioned before, the amount of the benefit is calculated taking into consideration the contributions, which are linked to the monthly earnings.[269] Nevertheless, in order to encourage job searching the amount is reduced to 70% for the first 180 days; and 60%, thereafter.

560. Nevertheless, the GSSA also sets a minimum amount with the objective of covering the minimum needs; and a maximum, as materialization of the principles of solidarity and progressivity. These limits are calculated using the IPREM, which

267. It must be noted that, in contrast to the unemployment benefit, here the regulation uses 'months' instead of 'days' and 'years', despite the periods are quite similar.
268. There are special rules for self-employed people older than 47 years.
269. Technically, the amount is equal to the RB multiplied by 70% or 50%, depending on the moment. The RB is equal to the average CB in the last six months, which is calculated according to the monthly earning days when working.

was set at EUR 600 for 2023 by the Government. The indicator must be incremented by one-sixth. Thus, the minimum amount is equal to 80% IPREM, except for if the unemployed person who has at least a dependent child[270] (107%);[271] whereas the maximum amount is 175% IPREM, except for if the unemployed person has one dependent child (200%) or two or more dependent children (225%).[272]

561. Hence, the minimum monthly unemployment benefit is EUR 560, whereas the maximum monthly unemployment benefit is EUR 1,225. Additionally, the minimum amount will be increased up to EUR 749 if the unemployed person has dependent children, while the maximum amount is EUR 1,400 with one dependent child; and EUR 1,575 with two or more dependent children. Curiously, varying the amount depending on the family circumstances is a characteristic, which is proper to assistance protection, but it has been included in the contributory one. Paradoxically, this does not avoid that the minimum limit is below the poverty threshold (*see* next section).

562. In the case of part-time employment, the following rules must be taken into consideration:

- The general rule is that the amount does not need any adaptation, because the previous earnings were already reduced.
- When there are previous periods of full-time and part-time work, the maximum and the minimum amount must be adapted by using the average earnings of the last 180 days, pondering, within that period, those for part-time and full-time work.
- When the employee has two part-time contracts and loses one of them, the amount of the benefit will be calculated as the average of the earnings from both jobs in the last six months and the maximum and minimum amount will be adapted following the rules explained above.

563. In case of partial unemployment, the amount is calculated taken into consideration the proportion of reduction applied to the working time. The worker will receive the whole amount in case of reduction of working time for family care purposes or victims of gender-based violence or terrorism.

564. Besides these two forms of receiving the benefit, there is a third option which is not so common in other countries.[273] GSSA permits the so-called 'single

270. 'Dependent child' is defined as someone younger than 26 years old or older with disabilities whose monthly income is below the 75% of the statutory minimum wage salary. Additionally, it is required that household's income divided by its members, including the unemployed person, is below the 75% of the statutory minimum wage salary.

271. (EUR 600 × 1/6) × 80 = 560; (EUR 600 × 1/6) × 107 = 749.

272. (EUR 600 × 1/6) × 175= 1,225; (EUR 600 × 1/6) × 200 = 1,400; (EUR 600 × 1/6) × 225= 1,575.

273. The European Economic and Social Committee highlighted the cases of Italy and Spain as good practices in the field of activation of passive employment policies. European Economic and Social Committee, 'Opinion of the European Economic and Social Committee on Economic Diversification in the Accession Countries – Role of SMEs and Social Economy Enterprises' (2004/C 112/27)'

payment of unemployment benefits' (*pago único de prestaciones*). This is a case of 'activation' of unemployment benefits because it permits to receive the whole amount of the benefit in order to use it for an entrepreneurial purpose. It is an exception to the general rule which sets that the perception is monthly base which is permitted as a way to encourage self-employment and, consequently, to find a new job or activity.

565. Single payment consists of starting work as a self-employed individual or joining existing or newly created cooperatives or worker-owned or commercial companies as a worker-member or working partner by using the whole benefit as investment. In order to use this possibility, some conditions must be fulfilled: (a) to have at least three months of unemployment benefit left; (b) not to have been the beneficiary of a single-payment scheme for four years prior to the claim; (c) to use the money for becoming self-employee or constitute or incorporate into a cooperative or worker-owned or trade company; and (d) to start the activity within one month following notification that the allowance has been granted, which in any case must be after the date of the application.

566. The unemployed person is not free to use the money received in whatever activities. Depending on the type of entrepreneurial activity, the application of the single payment can vary. Consequently, there are different options or purposes which can be covered.

567. As self-employed, it is possible to use the single payment: (a) to cover the amount justified as the investment necessary to start the activity (up to 100% of the current value of the benefit); (b) if the entire benefit is not exhausted, it is possible to simultaneously ask for the outstanding amount to be paid in order to meet the cost of the monthly social security contributions while working; (c) alternatively, it can receive the exact total outstanding benefit for the purpose of paying your monthly social security contributions; (d) alternatively or complementary, it is possible to cover duly justified investment amount. Regarding the last one, the unemployed person can use up to 15% of the capitalized benefit to pay for specific consultancy, training and information services related to the activity he will be starting or to pay the incorporation and setting-up expenses of a company, as well as to pay taxes and rates.

568. As worker-member or stable working partner in an existing or newly created cooperative, there are the following options: (a) to cover the membership fee and any obligatory and voluntary contributions that you have already paid;[274] (b) to pay the membership fee and the obligatory and voluntary contributions subscribed; (c) additionally, it is also possible to use the exact total outstanding benefit for the purpose of paying your monthly social security contributions; and (d) to use the single payment of the benefit to pay for the incorporation and setting-up expenses

(European Economic and Social Committee, 30 Apr. 2004): https://eur-lex.europa.eu/LexUriServ/LexUriServ.do?uri=OJ:C:2004:112:0105:0112:EN:PDF.

274. The future or deferred payments cannot be financed.

of the company, as well as to pay taxes and the price of specific consultancy, training and information services related to the activity you will be starting.

569. As a worker-member or stable working partner in an existing or newly created worker-owned company, there are the following possibilities: (a) to cover the cost of purchasing the required shares in the company;[275] (b) to pay the cost related to the purchase of the required shares of the company; (c) additionally, it is also possible to receive the exact total outstanding benefit for the purpose of paying the monthly social security contributions; and (d) to pay for the incorporation and setting-up expenses of the company, as well as to pay taxes and the price of specific consultancy, training and information services related to the activity you will be starting.

570. Finally, in addition to the amount of money that the unemployed person receives, there is another benefit included. Whereas the subject is perceiving the unemployment benefit, the SPEE is obliged to pay social security contributions for all contingencies. When the unemployment is caused by the termination of the employment relationship, contributions for unemployment, work hazards, insolvency fund and training are excluded.

II. Unemployment Assistance

571. As in other legal systems, unemployment subsidies in Spain, as a consequence of its assistance nature, are set by the GSSA without considering any previous professional circumstances. Particularly, the Law establishes that the amount of the unemployment subsidies will be equal to 80% of the IPREM. Reminding that this indicator has been set at EUR 600 for 2023, the amount of the unemployment subsidies for that year is EUR 480 per month (EUR 5,760 per year).[276] In contrast to other countries, this amount does not vary depending on family circumstances. This is rather paradoxical, not only from a comparative point of view but also taking into consideration its assistance nature and that this is permitted for the unemployment benefit in the contributory level.

572. Additionally, there is another consequence of the 'rigidity' of the assistance level to family and personal situation. The Organisation for Economic Co-operation and Development (OECD) has criticized that these amounts are below the poverty threshold.[277] In Spain, the poverty threshold[278] is EUR 9,009.2 per year (EUR 750.76 per month) for one-person households and EUR 18,919.3 per year

275. The benefit cannot be used to fund capital enlargements, or meet future or deferred payments.
276. In this case, the GSSA does not set any increase, so the IPREM is taken without any amelioration: EUR 700 x 0.8 = EUR 480.
277. OECD, 'OECD Employment Outlook 2011' (Paris: OECD, 2011).
278. A total of 60% of the median annual income per consumption unit (modified OECD scale), using the distribution of persons. Income per consumption unit is obtained by dividing the total household income by the number of consumption units.

(EUR 1,576.6 per month) for two adults and two children.[279] Consequently, unemployment subsidies are not preventing from poverty and, actually, unemployment (even, protected unemployment) is one of the most important sources of poverty and social exclusion.

573. Finally, as in the case of the unemployment benefit, in addition to the amount of money that the unemployed person receives, there is another benefit included. Whereas the subject is perceiving the pre-retirement subsidy, the State's Public Employment Service is obliged to pay social security contributions for retirement. This rule is also applied, with some particularities, to seasonal workers (*trabajadores fijos discontinuos*). Except for this case, no other groups of unemployed people receive this complementary scheme, despite GSSA habilitates the Government to extend it to other cases.

III. Unemployment Benefits for Self-Employed Workers: Cease of Activity

574. As it was mentioned above, the amount of the benefit is calculated taking into consideration the monthly contributions. Particularly, it will take into consideration the average of CBs during the last continuous twelve months immediately before the cease of activity. As in the case of the contributory benefit, in order to encourage job searching, the amount is reduced, but here there is only one percentage, which is 70%.

575. Nevertheless, the GSSA also sets a minimum amount with the objective of covering the minimum needs; and a maximum, as materialization of the principles of solidarity and progressivity. The calculation is quite similar to the one applied in the contributory benefit. First, both of them are calculated taking the IPREM as reference. Second, the indicator must be incremented by one-sixth. Finally, it will apply a percentage which varies depending on the family circumstances.

576. Using these rules, the minimum monthly unemployment benefit is 80% of IPREM (EUR 560); whereas the maximum monthly unemployment benefit is 175% of it (EUR 1,225). Additionally, the minimum amount is being increased up to EUR 749 (107% of the indicator) if the unemployed person has at least a dependent child;[280] while the maximum amount is EUR 1,400 (200%) with one dependent child and EUR 1,575 with two or more dependent children (225%). The same criticism shown for the unemployment benefit can be translated here.[281]

279. *Source*: Instituto Nacional de Estadística (INE): http://www.ine.es/jaxiT3/Tabla.htm?t=9964&L=1.

280. *See* footnote No. 262. In this case Art. 339(3) of the GSSA regarding 'dependent child' does not mention the family income but expressly requires that the child must live with the unemployed person.

281. Calculation using the IPREM for 2023.

577. Finally, as in previous cases, in addition to the amount of money, the cease of activity benefit includes the State Public Employment Service's obligation of paying social security contributions to the RETA.

§4. Duration of the Benefits

I. Unemployment Benefits

578. The duration of the unemployment benefit depends on the number of days worked within the period of six years before the termination of the employment relationship. As it was mentioned before, the reference period of six years is only used when existing several intervals of short work, which have to be counted together. From the minimum period of 360 days and depending on the period of work accredited, the GSSA sets different levels of duration, which are shown in Table 1.

Table 1 Duration of Unemployment Benefit

Contribution Period (Days)	*Duration (Day)*
From 360 to 539	120
From 540 to 719	180
From 720 to 899	240
From 900 to 1,079	300
From 1,080 to 1,259	360
From 1,260 to 1,439	420
From 1,440 to 1,619	480
From 1,620 to 1,799	540
From 1,800 to 1,979	600
From 1,980 to 2,159	660
From 2,160	720

Source: Author's Own.

579. It is possible for the Government to change this table, that is the duration of the unemployment benefit, taking into consideration the unemployment rate and financial possibility, besides the opinion of the SPEE. However, this possibility has never been used.

580. In order to determine the number of days previously worked, it does not take into account the period used or consumed in previous benefits or subsidies (when contributions are required). In case of part-time employment, it counts the number of days in which the company is obliged to pay social security contributions. This is a new rule introduced in 2018 as a consequence of *Espadas Recio*.[282]

581. According to the former regulation, for part-time employees, every day worked was considered as a day of contribution concerning the access and the duration of the unemployment benefit (and the so-called contributory subsidy), without considering the number of hours effectively worked. This rule was introduced to promote part-time employment, guaranteeing access to unemployment protection easily. Nevertheless, the rule does not affect part-time employees in the same way.

582. As *Espadas Recio* shows, Spanish regulation did not respect Article 4 of Council Directive 79/7/EEC of 19 December 1978 on the progressive implementation of the principle of equal treatment for men and women in matters of social security because, in the case of 'vertical' part-time work (work carried out only on certain days of the week), the rule excluded days not worked from the calculation of days in respect of which contributions have been paid, and therefore reduces the unemployment benefit payment period.[283]

583. Consequently, in order to avoid this discrimination, the rule was changed to take into account the whole period of work, without considering if the days comprehended within it were worked completely, partially or not worked, that is excluding the type of part-time work. This rule is also applicable for the so-called contributory subsidy in the assistance level.

584. Concerning the consumption of the benefit, in the case of full unemployment, every day in which the benefit is received is considered as consumed. It is possible to suspend the perception of the benefit in case of finding a new job if its duration is shorter than twelve months.[284] For partial unemployment, the benefit is consumed per hours instead of days. In this case, the time consumed will be equivalent to the percentage of reduction of working time applied by the company.

585. The GSSA also includes a rule of option for the case in which the worker generates a new period of at least 360 days (which is the minimum period to access to the unemployment benefit), having a former contribution period which had not been consumed completely. A typical case is an unemployed person who is receiving the benefit but finds a new job before expiring its right. In that case, the subsidy is suspended until the new employment relationship is finished. At this moment, the right to opt emerges, permitting the employee to opt between the former period (in the same conditions and for the time which was not consumed) or the new one. Opting for one of this option means that the other one becomes automatically cancelled.

282. Judgment of the Court of Justice of the EU (Fifth Chamber) of 9 Nov. 2017, C-98/15. ECLI: EU:C:2017:833.
283. In contrast to 'horizontal' part-time work (work carried out only in some hours of all days in a week), for whom all days were accounted.
284. In case of longer duration, the benefit is cancelled, except for it is saved by the right to option.

II. Unemployment Assistance

586. Concerning the duration of unemployment subsidies, there is a general rule and some exceptions. The general rule sets that duration will be six months, renewable for periods of six months up to eighteen months. As a consequence, the maximum duration, as a general rule, is eighteen months, except for some cases in which, taking in consideration the special difficulties to access to a new job or his personal and family situation, the duration of the unemployment subsidy may be enlarged even for a longer period if needed or, otherwise, it is also possible to shorten it. Those exceptional cases are the following ones:

- Subsidy for family responsibilities: (a) for unemployed people older than 45 years, having exhausted a contributory benefit of at least 120 days, the maximum duration will be twenty-four months; (b) for unemployed people older than 45 years having exhausted a contributory benefit of at least 180 days, the maximum duration will be thirty months; (c) for unemployed people younger than 45 years, having exhausted a contributory benefit of at least 180 days, the maximum duration will be twenty-four months.
- Subsidy for people older than 45 years: The duration will be six months that cannot be extended.
- Contributory subsidy: If the unemployed person does not have family responsibility and have contributed at least six months (but less than twelve months),[285] the duration is six months that cannot be extended; if he has family responsibilities, the duration depends on the previous contributions according to Table 2.

Table 2 Duration of the Contributory Subsidy

Social Security Contributions	*Duration*
3 months	3 months
4 months	4 months
5 months	5 months
6 months or more	21 months

Source: Author's Own.

In both cases, the contributions used for accessing this subsidy will not be used for being entitled to the unemployment benefit.

Pre-retirement Subsidy: The maximum duration of the subsidy is up to the age in which the unemployed people may access to the contributory retirement pension (65 or 67 years old depending on the years of contributions). Consequently, the duration is coherent with its definition as a 'bridge' to retirement.

285. In this case, he would be entitled to the contributory benefit.

587. The GSSA permits the Government to modify the duration of the unemployment subsidies taking into consideration the unemployment rate, the financing possibilities and the SPEE. Nevertheless, this possibility has not been ever used.

588. Subsidies can be suspended or extinguished by the same situations of the unemployment benefit. Nevertheless, there is a single type, the perception of income above the maximum level. In these circumstances, the subsidy will be suspended, whereas the situation is kept and up to twelve months. Beyond this limit, the subsidy is terminated.

III. Unemployment Benefits for Self-Employed Workers: The Cease of Activity

589. The duration of the cease of activity benefit depends on the previous social security contributions. As it was mentioned above, the GSSA requires at least twelve months of contributions within the last forty-eight months before the cease of activity. Additionally, those twelve months must be continuous and contributed immediately before the cease of activity.

590. Consequently, here, the requirements are harder than in the case of employees and the two periods work has a little difference: whereas in the case of the unemployment benefit, it would be possible to collect the minimum twelve months of contributions within the six years (seventy-two months) before the termination of the employment relationship; in the case of the cease of activity, within the reference period, which is shorter and, thus, makes more difficult to have the months required, it will be possible to collect more months than the minimum period, because these twelve months must have been contributed immediately before the cease activity.

591. From that minimum limit, the duration of the benefit varies according to Table 3. It must be noted that, in contrast to the unemployment benefit, the duration is expressed on months (instead of days) and the number of stages is lower, so it is more difficult to pass from one to another, despite the minimum and maximum duration is exactly the same one.

Table 3 Duration of the Cease of Activity Benefit

Contributions (Months)	*Duration (Months)*
From 12 to 17	4
From 18 to 23	6
From 24 to 29	8
From 30 to 35	10
From 36 to 42	12

Contributions (Months)	*Duration (Months)*
From 43 to 47	16
More than 48	24

Source: Author's Own.

592. The GSSA sets some special rules concerning the accountability of the monthly contributions in order to be taken into consideration for determining the duration and the access to the benefit.

593. First of all, it is not possible to ask for a new benefit after a waiting period of eighteen months after the recognition of the right to the benefit (assuming that the rest of the requirements are fulfilled (*see* §2.III)). Second, only contributions for cease of activity are admitted, so contributions for unemployment benefits are excluded, in other words, transfers between regimes are not allowed despite the fact they are both types of unemployment protection. Third, contributions can be used if they have not been exhausted for previous benefits and they will be accounted for by complete months. Finally, there is no parallel 'right to opt' for self-employed, so contributions used for a certain benefit cannot be used in another one posterior.

594. The cease of activity benefit may be suspended or terminated by similar circumstances as the previous schemes (expiration, retirement, etc.). Those particularly related to this type of protection, such as the development of an activity as self-employee or as an employee (below the limit of twelve months the benefit is suspended, whereas above that limit is terminated) or the voluntary renunciation must be highlighted.

§5. Administration

595. The governance of employment policies in Spain is based on a multiple base approach, in which different administrative bodies or organisms are involved. In order to analyse them, it is useful to distinguish between active and passive employment policies. As it was mentioned above, whereas passive policies belong to the State, active policies are managed by CCAA mainly.

596. Concerning active employment policies, despite the main role is played by CCAA, the State coordinates the whole National Employment System, connecting local and regional level to the EES. The MLSE provides this general supervision and coordination.

597. Regarding passive employment policies, they are mainly managed by the State. It has two administrative bodies for dealing with unemployment protection issues. On the one hand, the TGSS, which administers the economic resources of the Social Security System, registers employers and insured persons and collects contributions, and, on the other hand, the SPEE, which is a self-governing body attached to the MLSE.

598. The SPEE is in charge of three main activities:

(1) Coordination: It cooperates with the State in its function of coordinating the whole National Employment System by planning and promoting employment policy proposals in all types of areas: professional guidance, job training, employment promotion programmes, etc.
(2) Unemployment benefits: This is its main role and consists in managing and monitoring unemployment benefits. Consequently, unemployed people must ask for their benefits at the State Public Employment Service's offices. The activities of control and supervision also take place there.
(3) Researching: It additionally develops researches, studies and analyses on the labour market situation, as an objective base to try to improve employment policies all over the country.

599. As it was mentioned above, in this structure the role of social partners is very limited and frequently focused on an advisory role. Despite they have representation in different advisory bodies, the most effective instrument of participation is through tripartite social dialogue. By different Social Pacts, social partners have influenced Government reforms and, consequently, the way in which passive employment policies have been articulated and implemented. The most recent one is the reform of the pre-retirement subsidy in 2019. It agreed with trade unions, and it was focused on eliminating the harder conditions set during the crisis, coming back to the regulation before that.

Part VIII. Pensions

María Arántzazu Vicente Palacio

600. The financial sustainability of the Spanish Social Security System has been questioned for decades. As all systems based on a financial distribution technique, this sustainability is highly conditioned by the evolution of two variables, namely an ageing population and unemployment, and the fact that neither is 'healthy' in Spain, no future improvements are expected given this scenario.

601. Spain still has very high unemployment rates compared to other European countries. According to data from the National Statistics Institute, the third quarter of 2022 closed with an unemployment rate of 12.67%, with 32.6% for those under 25 years of age. By sex, the unemployment rate for women was four points higher (14.84% compared to 10.74%), the same difference as for those under 25 (33.43% for women; 29.01% for men). Such high unemployment rates mean having to pay high unemployment benefits, which especially reduces the income from social security as the number of taxpayers lowers. Although unemployment rates have considerably lowered after the financial crisis (it had reached 26%), it is true that the Spanish economic model, and also its labour market, present specificities that make them particularly vulnerable: the high occupational seasonality of many occupational activities (agriculture; tourism); loss of relevance in the industrial sector to favour the services sector; the increasing importance of the building sector, among many other reasons. The Spanish labour market has been traditionally characterized by high temporary work and workers' rotation, and also by a very marked underground economy and the difficulty of youths' employability.

602. Spain's demographic evolution also has its peculiarities. First, because its demographic explosion took place ten years after the rest of Europe as Spanish *baby boomers* were born in the 1960s and 1970s, who will become pensioners in the next two decades. At the same time, birth rates were about 20 per thousand, and even reached 22 per thousand (1964), with fertility rates over 2.90% and even 3% (1964). It is also necessary to consider that Spain has had one of the world's lowest birth rates for decades and continues as it is still below 10 per thousand (in the 1990s and during 2012–2015). In 2022, Spain's birth rate was 7,12 per thousand, with very low fertility rates (the lowest were recorded in the 1990s: 1,9). The complete lack of birth-related policies simply, women in Spain enter the labour market later than they do in the rest of Europe, youths having difficulties finding jobs and the precariousness of work all account for these rates. Birth rates have improved because immigrants have arrived with more children rather than making policies that encourage children to be born. Moreover, Spain is one of the countries with the longest life expectancy in the world, with a mean of 83.07 years; 85.83 years for women and 80.27 for men in 2021. This trend is also growing as studies show that Spain will have the world's longest life expectancy in 2040.

603. The reforms made in recent decades have led to this scenario, which makes it hard to defend the various measures that have generally been taken to reduce the protection offered by the public Social Security System, especially as far as pensions are concerned. The last of these reforms (2011) is still being implemented and affects several highly relevant matters. The most striking one is that the minimum retirement age has gone from 65 years (which has been in force since 1919) to 67, unless the worker can justify having worked a long contributory career (thirty-eight years and six months). However, this reform was not the only one: a sustainability factor was introduced that links the amount of a pension to the generational life expectancy; the link between revaluing pensions and the CPI (for instance, increased cost of living) has been removed, although both reforms have been reversed and pensions are currently revalued according to the CPI, and the sustainability factor has been eliminated; the contributory period used to calculate the amount of pensions has been prolonged; modifications have been made to include gaps and minimum pension supplements, etc. In short, several important measures have been introduced that impact social security expenditures and aim to lower the 'high' replacement rates which, according to some people, apply to public pensions in Spain. Some sources (OECD) place this (mean) rate at 83.3%.

604. Some of these people are not neutral. In recent years, pressure has redoubled by a change of model that also allows capitalization systems to enter the public model, albeit with private management. One of the most well-defended proposals (by the Business Insurance Association, and the Association of Institutions for Collective Investment and Pension Funds) is a three-pillar one, of which the last two pillars are capitalization: the second pillar falls within the employment framework and would be compulsory and of an appointed kind by the Special Social Security Scheme for Sea Workers; the third would be the current 'free' type; for example, employment or individual or associated. The second pillar would be financed by tax payments, which would amount to 4% of salaries: 2% paid by the company, which would lower the payment in the first pillar, and 2% that workers pay by either lowering the current tax payments made by workers or increasing workers' contributory participations. The third pillar would remain free by proposing that both parties maintain tax incentives, and by even introducing a state subsidy of the same amount as the tax payments paid by workers. The proliferation of catastrophic predictions about today's pensions system's sustainability in the mass media owned by financial institutions or investment/pension funds is no chance occurrence. A very profitable business is at risk, and the power of intervention in political powers is enormous and will increase if they accumulate more resources.

605. Currently, the Spanish labour force is 20,545,700 people (January 2023). By social security schemes, in March 2023 the General Scheme (employees) had 16,906,358 (March 2023), the RETA had 3,328,402 workers and the Special

Scheme for Sea Workers had 60,526 contributors between employees and the self-employed. The total contributions of these workers practically cover the contributory pensions of the current pensioners in the social security system. In January 2023, there were 9,994,836 pensioners, of whom 6,302,297 received retirement pensions, 2,356,613 widow's and widower's pensions, 341,311 orphan's pensions and 44,834 receive other family pensions. In addition, 949,781 were permanent disability pensions.

606. The presentation below indicates the requirements and conditions that have resulted from the last reforms, and which have not yet been fully applied. For those matters for which a temporary scheme exists, this circumstance is briefly presented and no details of the complex temporary regulation are provided.

Chapter 1. Pensions for Wage Earners (General Scheme)

§1. Retirement Pensions

I. Beneficiaries

A. Territorial Field of Application

607. Social security norms are based on the territoriality principle: a worker has to carry out his/her occupational activity in Spanish territory, although there are exceptions (e.g., those workers sent by their company to work abroad). Many coordination norms about social security matters exist and include the principle of totalizing the tax payments made in different States to access a retirement pension. The following are especially important given their very wide subjective scope in which they apply: Regulation No. 883/2004 of 29 April (and Regulation No. 978/2009 of 16 September) and the Multilateral Latin American Social Security Agreement. Bilateral agreements about social security also widely apply.

B. Personal Field of Application

608. The retirement pension for wage earners includes workers from the private sector, and also from the public sector when their work services are subject to occupational legislation (Workers' Statute). It also applies to many civil servants (subject to Administrative Law). However, some civil servants are still included in the Special Civil Servant Scheme (*see 'Contributions for Public Sector Workers', supra*). This Special Scheme is currently being phased out (no new taxpayers can join it) as far as protection by pensions is concerned (passive classes).

609. The beneficiaries are the above-cited workers, who have to be of the minimum age set in each case and meet the previously set contributory requirements. Generally, access to retirement is always voluntary, save two exceptions: (a) if it is thus established in the applicative collective agreement, with certain legal job creation demands (a novel aspect that came into effect on 1 January 2019); (b) in the public sector, where the minimum retirement age is outlined as forced retirement.

610. A wide range of minimum ages exists to access retirement. Early retirement can also be applied for, which implies reducing the quantity of the retirement pension while it is paid. Partial retirement is another possibility, which can also be early retirement or, conversely, after reaching the minimum retirement age. In the latter case, it is taken as a way to prolong someone's working life beyond the minimum set age. This option is framed within various policies to promote prolonging one's working life during the ageing process.

II. Conditions

611. There are two expected conditions to access a (contributory) retirement pension: having reached the minimum set age and having paid a complete given contributory period. The contributory period is also used to establish the applicable percentage to determine the amount of someone's retirement pension.

A. *Minimum Age(s) and Early Retirement*

612. Apart from the above-cited exceptions, retirement is always voluntary for workers after they have reached the minimum legally set age when several assumed situations apply.

613. The minimum age in a generally assumed case depends on the tax payments that workers accredit. As of 1 January 2027 (when the transition period ends), workers are expected to have reached the age of 67, but this minimum age drops to 65 years for those workers who can accredit a contributory period of 38 years and 6 months (without computing any tax payments made for any extraordinary payments). From 2013 to 2026, provisional rules apply to operate the transition from the previously expected minimum age of 65 years to the present-day regulation.

614. Nonetheless, lower minimum ages exist and are indicated for objective (e.g., hazardousness, toxicity, insalubrity) or subjective (disability) reasons.

Younger minimum age in assumed cases of hazardous, toxic, or even unhealthy, job posts that accredit high mortality and morbidity indices

615. In such circumstances, workers have the recognized right to access retirement at a younger age than the general set minimum age. To establish this younger age, some reducing coefficients apply in certain cases to determine the age at which retirement can be accessed for those activities set in due form; in any other cases, the regulation directly establishes a younger age.

616. Reducing coefficients are applied to the minimum age to access retirement for maritime workers (RD 1311/2007),[286] coal mining workers (RD 3255/1983 and RD 2366/1984),[287] firefighters in the service of public administrations/organisms, flight personnel (RD 1559/1986),[288] and some State Security Forces and Bodies, such as the Ertzaintza (the Autonomous Basque Police; Additional Provision No. 20 of the GSSA) or the Local Police Force (RD 1449/2018).[289] The coefficients used to lower age are applied according to the occupational activity performed in the

286. BOE No. 255 of 24 Oct. 2007.
287. BOE No. 3 of 4 Jan. 1984 and BOE No. 13 of 15 Jan. 1985.
288. BOE No. 182 of 31 Jul. 1986.
289. BOE No. 302 of 15 Dec. 2018.

foreseen activities and apply to the period worked. This results in the number of years by which the minimum retirement age lowers. Maximum limits exist to lower this age.

617. Norms directly set a minimum younger age that generally applied to other groups. The minimum retirement age of some artists (singers, dancers and trapeze artists) is 60, provided they meet the contributory requirements. Some bullfighting professionals can retire at 55 (bullfighters, mounted bullfighters, apprentice bullfighters, bullfighters who use *banderillas*, picadors and comic bullfighters), provided they officially work and meet the contributory requirements.

Younger minimum age for people with a degree of disability that equals or exceeds 65%

618. In these cases, the minimum retirement age lowers after applying age-reducing coefficients: 0.25% or 0.50% if, apart from accrediting 65% disability, workers require a third person to help them perform essential activities of daily living. These coefficients contemplate the period during which workers with disability have worked (RD 1539/2003 of 5 December).

People with a degree of disability that equals or exceeds 45% affected by the disabilities determined by law

619. In this case, the retirement age can lower to 56 years (RD 1851/2009 of 4 December). The norm lists the disabilities to which this case applies. It is also necessary for disability to reach a degree that equals or exceeds 45%.

Early retirement

620. Spanish legislation allows retirement to be accessed at a younger age to the applicable minimum age as previously indicated, and is known as early retirement. In this case, workers pay the cost of early retirement because the quantity of their retirement pension undergoes a variable reduction depending on the accredited contributory period and the number of monthly periods by which workers wish to access their retirement early. This reduction in the amount is maintained while the early retirement pension is paid. Two assumed cases exist according to the 'voluntary' role that workers play to access early retirement:

(a) For causes not attributable to workers.[290] Workers can retire earlier than the minimum set age by as much as four years when they have involuntarily lost their job for business reasons. Dismissal is considered 'a non-attributable cause' by economic, technical, organizational or (collective or individual) production causes; the business employer's death, retirement or disability; a legal sentence as the result of insolvency proceedings; force majeure reasons; the work relationship cannot continue. It also includes the termination of the contract at the will of the female worker who is a victim of gender-based violence. Workers are also expected to: (i) sign on as seeking work for at least six months prior to

290. Article 207 of the GSSA.

applying; (ii) can accredit a minimum contributory period of at least thirty-three years (without computing one-off payments). Apart from these two demands, any compulsory military service or replacement social allowance periods can be calculated with a maximum one-year limit.

(b) For workers' exclusive willingness-[291] Workers can retire early by as much as two years at the most compared to the minimum set age, and it will apply according to their accredited exclusion period. The expected requirements include: (i) accredit a minimum contributory period of thirty-five years (without computing one-off payments). Accordingly, periods of compulsory military service or replacement social allowance can be calculated with a maximum one-year limit; (ii) the quantity of the retirement pension to be paid has to be higher than the quantity of the minimum pension that would correspond to the interested party given his/her family situation when reaching the age of 65.

Other assumed cases of early retirement that derive from provisional norms

621. Many provisional assumed cases exist because of the different reforms made to laws on retirement pensions. In general terms, most forecasts are ineffective because the workers they applied to have retired or died. Some of these cases were used until quite recently as channels to access retirement pensions from the age of 60 (e.g., retirement for those who were Workers Association Members before 1 January 1967).

Early part-time retirement

622. Retirement is not necessary due to the complete working day that workers used to work.[292] For some time now, the Spanish legal system contemplates the possibility of part-time retirement, which can start from the minimum set age or earlier. Early part-time retirement is a measure taken to encourage employment. Early retirement can be achieved before the minimum set age if, simultaneously to retirement, a takeover contract is signed with someone unemployed or if a company contracts someone on a part-time basis to replace part of the working day previously worked by someone who has taken early retirement.[293] This 'take over contract' must continue for at least the time that the replaced workers have to wait until they reach the minimum retirement age applicable to them. While the early retirement period is underway, the company and workers must continue paying the contributory base that would have corresponded to them if they had worked full-time (this demand is also expected to be gradually met: Temporary Provision No. 10(3) of the GSSA). The requirements in this case are:

(a) Age: The worker taken over must have reached the age of 65, or 63 and can justify having paid tax for thirty-six years and six months. These ages are those expected as of 1 January 2027. From 2013 to 2026, provisional norms apply (Temporary Provision No. 10).

---

291. Article 208 of the GSSA.
292. Article 15(2) of the GSSA.
293. Article 12(7) of the Workers' Statute.

(b) Length of service: The worker taken over must accredit a minimum six-year length of service in the company. These six years must have been worked immediately prior to the date that (s)he takes part-time retirement.
(c) Previous tax payments: The worker taken over must accredit having paid taxes to the social security for thirty-three years at the time (s)he takes part-time retirement (without computing one-off payments) or for twenty-five years if the worker has a degree of disability that equals or exceeds 33%. Accordingly, any period of compulsory military service or replacement social allowance can be calculated with a maximum limit of one year.
(d) A shorter working day: The reduction of a replaced worker's working day must lie between 25% and 50% (or 75% if the worker taken over or substituted has signed an indefinite full-time contract).
(e) Equivalence between the contributory bases of the part-time retired person and the substitute worker. The substitute worker's contributory base cannot be less than 65% of the average contributory bases that correspond to the last six months of the base period regulating the part-time retirement pension.

623. Provisional norms exist (Temporary Provisions Nos 4, 5 and 6) that maintain the right to early part-time retirement in line with legislation before Law 27/2011 came into force, which was more favourable, for certain assumed cases.

Part-time (but not early) retirement[294]

624. Once workers have reached the minimum age that applies to them, and if they meet the requirements to obtain this right, they can retire part-time without having to sign a takeover contract. In this case, part-time retirement is contemplated as a way to (voluntarily) postpone workers' access to retirement, eases the financial pressure on the pensions system and allows people to work during the ageing process. Workers are paid a retirement pension for the part of the working day they do not work for being retired part-time pensioners, and they maintain the salary they are paid for part of the working day they still work. Both the cut in the working day to make it part-time and the subsequent retirement pension must lie between a minimum of 25% and a maximum of 50% of the working day.

B. Contributory Period

625. To the minimum age requirement, the need for workers to accredit a minimum fifteen-year contributory period must be added, of which at least two years must be worked during the fifteen-year period immediately before receiving a pension. In this case, no one-off payments are computed. If access to retirement takes place when workers do not work or in equivalent situations, this two-year period must fall within the fifteen years immediately before the date when the obligation to pay taxes ceased.

294. Article 215(1) of the GSSA.

626. As the Social Security System is composed of several regimes, being entitled to a retirement pension can fall in more than one of these regimes, provided workers meet the requirements expected in each one (known as 'pluri-activity'). In such cases, when workers do not work or are in equivalent situations in some of these regimes, to be entitled to two retirement pensions, it is necessary that the contributory period of each regime overlap for at least fifteen years.

Exclusion period and part-time workers

627. Since 1 October 2023, for the purposes of accrediting the contribution periods necessary for entitlement to the benefits for retirement, permanent disability, death and survival, temporary disability and birth and care of a minor, the different periods during which the worker has been registered with a part-time contract shall be taken into account, regardless of the duration of the work carried out in each of them.[295] Therefore, the unequal treatment of part-time workers for the calculation of the waiting period has been abolished, a regulation that the Court of Justice of the European Union and the Constitutional Court labelled as discriminatory on several occasions.

Exclusion period and contracted workers with temporary contacts that last or are less than five days

628. Quite recently (2019), a 'temporariness coefficient' came into being to calculate the exclusion period of workers with temporary contracts that last or are less than five days. The purpose of this coefficient is to help meet the tax-payment requirements set out to access social security benefits. In these cases, every day that a worker has paid tax is multiplied by 1.4, which means attributing 1.4 tax-working days to each worked day.

III. Calculating Pensions

629. Retirement pensions are calculated by applying a variable percentage to the average of the contributory bases of a given time period. As of 1 January 2023, the average is calculated over the last twenty-five years. If the calculated period contains months for which no tax payments were made (contributory 'gaps'), these months are calculated for a maximum of forty-eight months, with the system's minimum contributory base (this being the legal minimum monthly salary and the amount of one-off payments is proportionally distributed). Any other contributory 'gaps' are included with 50% of the aforementioned quantity. This issue has been amended again: from 1 January 2026, the regulatory base will be the quotient resulting from dividing by 378 the sum of the person's contribution bases for the 324 months preceding the month before the month in which the qualifying event occurred. These 324 months will be selected from the 348 consecutive months immediately preceding the month prior to the month before the qualifying event (these are the 324 contribution bases with the highest amount, after taking into

295. Article 247 of the GSSA.

account any gaps in contributions and updating the contribution bases for the 24 months preceding the month before the qualifying event, which are calculated at their nominal value). However, this reform is also applied progressively and gradually in the terms provided in D.T.40ª. According to this rule, the full application of this formula will take place from 1 January 2037.

630. The applicable percentage is in accordance with the contributory years accredited by workers. The 100% figure is reached after paying taxes for thirty-seven years (as of 1 January 2027; the period is now provisional). The minimum allowed contributory period (fifteen years) entitles workers to 50% of the RB, and the applicable percentage rises for each additional contributory month after the minimum fifteen-year period: the rule to be applied as of 1 January 2027 will be 0.19% for each additional month after these first 15 first years for months 1–248; and 0.18% for each additional month from months 1–248 for a maximum of 37 years.[296] Currently, the process is a provisional one.

631. In principle, exceeding the 100% regulatory basis takes place in the assumed case of workers accessing retirement at an older age than the set minimum age in each case, and provided that, at that time the minimum legally set contributory period has been met. In this case (not applicable to assumed cases of part-time or flexible retirement), workers are entitled to an additional amount. The law provides for two systems, at the choice of the interested party:

(a) An additional percentage of 4% for each full year of contributions paid between the date of reaching that age and the date of the event giving rise to the pension, without the amount of the pension ever exceeding the maximum limit established for public pensions. However, if the initial amount of the pension exceeds this maximum amount without applying the additional percentage (or if it is applied, but only partially), workers are entitled to receive, in addition to their retirement pension, an additional annual amount. This amount is the result of applying an additional percentage to the current maximum limit. The pension is paid monthly at the end of each month, in fourteen payments per year. There is an insuperable limit: the sum of this pension and other pensions to which the person concerned is entitled, calculated annually, may not exceed the amount of the maximum CB in force at any given time, which It is also calculated annually.
(b) A flat-rate amount for each full year of contributions made between the date on which the said age is reached and the date of the event giving rise to the pension. The amount shall be determined on the basis of the years of contribution credited on the first of the above dates, in accordance with the calculation formulae set out in the regulations.

632. The so-called 'sustainability factor' is applied to the pension amount resulting from the above rules. This mathematical index links the amount of pensions to

296. Temporary Provision No. 9 of the GSSA.

the evolution of pensioners' life expectancy by adjusting the amounts paid to pensioners when they retire under similar conditions at different times.

Although this condition was expected to be in force for pensions applied from 1 January 2019, it has not yet entered into force, and will not do so until an agreement is reached within the Commission for the Monitoring and Evaluation of Agreements of the so-called Toledo Pact, or until 1 January 2023, whichever comes first (LPGE-2018).

Reducing the quantity of pensions in assumed cases of early retirement

633. Access to early retirement determines some reducing coefficients being applied to the quantity of pensions. These coefficients are applied during each three-monthly period or fraction of each three-monthly period which, when someone leaves their job, (s)he has yet to reach the legal retirement age, which is to be applied in each case. The coefficients combine two variables: (a) voluntarily access to early retirement; (b) the exclusion period accredited by workers when they access early retirement.

634. Should the assumed retirement case be due to a cause not attributable to workers,[297] the coefficients are as follows:

	Contribution period: less than 38 years and 6 months	*Contribution period: equal to or more than 38 years and 6 months and less than 41 years and 6 months*	*Contribution period: 41 years and 6 months or more and less than 44 years and 6 months*	*Contribution period: 44 years and 6 months or more*
Retirement: Months ahead of schedule	*% reduction*	*% reduction*	*% reduction*	*% reduction*
48	30.00	28.00	26.00	24.00
47	29.38	27.42	25.46	23.50
46	28.75	26.83	24.92	23.00
45	28.13	26.25	24.38	22.50
44	27.50	25.67	23.83	22.00
43	26.88	25.08	23.29	21.50
42	26.25	24.50	22.75	21.00
41	25.63	23.92	22.21	20.50
40	25.00	23.33	21.67	20.00
39	24.38	22.75	21.13	19.50

297. Article 2017 of the GSSA.

	Contribution period: less than 38 years and 6 months	*Contribution period: equal to or more than 38 years and 6 months and less than 41 years and 6 months*	*Contribution period: 41 years and 6 months or more and less than 44 years and 6 months*	*Contribution period: 44 years and 6 months or more*
Retirement: Months ahead of schedule	*% reduction*	*% reduction*	*% reduction*	*% reduction*
38	23.75	22.17	20.58	19.00
37	23.13	21.58	20.04	18.50
36	22.50	21.00	19.50	18.00
35	21.88	20.42	18.96	17.50
34	21.25	19.83	18.42	17.00
33	20.63	19.25	17.88	16.50
32	20.00	18.67	17.33	16.00
31	19.38	18.08	16.79	15.50
30	18.75	17.50	16.25	15.00
29	18.13	16.92	15.71	14.50
28	17.50	16.33	15.17	14.00
27	16.88	15.75	14.63	13.50
26	16.25	15.17	14.08	13.00
25	15.63	14.58	13.54	12.50
24	15.00	14.00	13.00	12.00
23	14.38	13.42	12.46	11.50
22	13.75	12.83	11.92	11.00
21	12.57	12.00	11.38	10.00
20	11.00	10.50	10.00	9.20
19	9.78	9.33	8.89	8.40
18	8.80	8.40	8.00	7.60
17	8.00	7.64	7.27	6.91
16	7.33	7.00	6.67	6.33
15	6.77	6.46	6.15	5.85
14	6.29	6.00	5.71	5.43
13	5.87	5.60	5.33	5.07
12	5.50	5.25	5.00	4.75

	Contribution period: less than 38 years and 6 months	*Contribution period: equal to or more than 38 years and 6 months and less than 41 years and 6 months*	*Contribution period: 41 years and 6 months or more and less than 44 years and 6 months*	*Contribution period: 44 years and 6 months or more*
Retirement: Months ahead of schedule	*% reduction*	*% reduction*	*% reduction*	*% reduction*
11	5.18	4.94	4.71	4.47
10	4.89	4.67	4.44	4.22
9	4.63	4.42	4.21	4.00
8	4.40	4.20	4.00	3.80
7	4.19	4.00	3.81	3.62
6	3.75	3.50	3.25	3.00
5	3.13	2.92	2.71	2.50
4	2.50	2.33	2.17	2.00
3	1.88	1.75	1.63	1.50
2	1.25	1.17	1.08	1.00
1	0.63	0.58	0.54	0.50

635. In the assumed case of workers' early retirement being voluntary,[298] the coefficients to apply to the quantity of the retirement pensions are as follows:

	Contribution period: less than 38 years and 6 months	*Contribution period: equal to or more than 38 years and 6 months and less than 41 years and 6 months*	*Contribution period: 41 years and 6 months or more and less than 44 years and 6 months.*	*Contribution period: 44 years and 6 months or more*
Retirement: Months ahead of schedule	*% reduction*	*% reduction*	*% reduction*	*% reduction*
24	21.00	19.00	17.00	13.00
23	17.60	16.50	15.00	12.00

298. Article 208 of the GSSA.

	Contribution period: less than 38 years and 6 months	*Contribution period: equal to or more than 38 years and 6 months and less than 41 years and 6 months*	*Contribution period: 41 years and 6 months or more and less than 44 years and 6 months.*	*Contribution period: 44 years and 6 months or more*
Retirement: Months ahead of schedule	*% reduction*	*% reduction*	*% reduction*	*% reduction*
22	14.67	14.00	13.33	11.00
21	12.57	12.00	11.43	10.00
20	11.00	10.50	10.00	9.20
19	9.78	9.33	8.89	8.40
18	8.80	8.40	8.00	7.60
17	8.00	7.64	7.27	6.91
16	7.33	7.00	6.67	6.33
15	6.77	6.46	6.15	5.85
14	6.29	6.00	5.71	5.43
13	5.87	5.60	5.33	5.07
12	5.50	5.25	5.00	4.75
11	5.18	4.94	4.71	4.47
10	4.89	4.67	4.44	4.22
9	4.63	4.42	4.21	4.00
8	4.40	4.20	4.00	3.80
7	4.19	4.00	3.81	3.62
6	4.00	3.82	3.64	3.45
5	3.83	3.65	3.48	3.30
4	3.67	3.50	3.33	3.17
3	3.52	3.36	3.20	3.04
2	3.38	3.23	3.08	2.92
1	3.26	3.11	2.96	2.81

636. In short, early retirement (including both assumed cases) comes with a very high cost for workers although, logically, a lower cost when workers retire early if the reason is caused by the (involuntary) loss of their job for business reasons or gender-based violence. Nonetheless, companies frequently take early retirement measures by paying the economic cost involved by workers retiring early.

637. In both early retirement cases, complete periods (in years and months) are taken, and fractions of years/months are not included in calculations. The 'legal retirement age' is considered that workers would have reached if they had continued paying taxes during the period that goes from the date they left work to the date they reach the legal minimum retirement age, depending on which case applies.

Compatibility of retirement pensions with work (flexible retirement)

638. The latest legal reforms have made the retirement pension and work compatibility regime flexible. There are several reasons for this flexibility: the legislator tends to stress the will to encourage active ageing. Others point out reducing the quantity of retirement pensions as a result of the latest reforms and the subsequent need to allow pensioners to supplement their incomes with what they will possibly earn from performing another occupational or professional activity. Nonetheless, it would not be realistic to assume the access of pensioners to a labour market like the Spanish one with its high unemployment levels, unless pensioners work as self-employed workers. Two assumed cases appear.

639. As a general rule, the first one establishes that a retirement pension is incompatible with wage earners' work, unless it is part-time work (flexible retirement):[299] the result is to proportionally reduce the amount of a retirement pension to the work performed. If a pensioner does full-time work, the retirement pension is not paid until the worker leaves this work. The new (compulsory) tax payments do not affect the already calculated pension, which will once again be paid and at the same amount as initially calculated. Moreover, the retirement pension is always considered incompatible with occupying any public service job post with the same consequence: the retirement pension is not paid until the worker leaves this public service job post. However, the retirement pension is compatible with working as self-employed workers, provided that the income earned by this self-employed work is lower than the legal minimum monthly salary. In this case, pensioners are not obliged to pay tax payments for their self-employed professional work. In the assumed case that, after accessing retirement, a pensioner works as a part-time wage earner and this working activity falls within the foreseen working day limits, then the retirement pension is compatible with the salary paid for this new job (flexible retirement). New tax payments can be computed to recalculate the amount of the retirement pension (RB and applicable percentage). Evidently, the retirement pension paid for partial (at an early or standard retirement age) retirement is compatible with the salary that the pensioner earns in this case.

640. The second assumed case is called 'retirement and active ageing'.[300] In this case, the retirement pension is compatible with either working self-employed or as a wage earner (except for occupying a high or public sector job post), and either can be full-time or part-time, if the following requirements coincide: (a) access to retirement must take place at the minimum applicable age (without applying any

299. Article 213 of the GSSA.
300. Article 214 of the GSSA.

coefficients or assumed cases of early retirement age); (b) the percentage applicable to determine the quantity of the pension must be 100% of the RB. The work performed is exempt from paying taxes, except for temporary disability, work accidents, professional disease and 'solidarity tax payments' (8%), which is not included in calculations for allowances.

Gender Gap Supplement to Contributory Pensions[301]

641. On 2 January 2016, the maternity supplement entered into force. It applied to pensions (including retirement pensions) paid to women who have had biological or adopted children, i.e., for their 'demographic contribution'. The supplement was calculated by applying a variable percentage to the initial amount of the pension, depending on the number of children born or adopted before the qualifying event. For this purpose, a range was established between two children (5%) and four or more children (15%).

642. The Judgment of the ECJ of 12 December 2019 (Case C-450/18) held that this supplement was discriminatory on grounds of sex and therefore incompatible with EU law, because it is limited exclusively to women and excludes men unconditionally. Consequently, the Spanish regulation was amended by RD-Law 3/2021.[302]

643. Currently, the 'gender gap supplement to contributory pensions' (*complemento de pensiones contributivas para la reducción de la brecha de género*) is initially granted to mothers (biological or adoptive) but does not exclude fathers, who are eligible for the supplement if they meet additional requirements. The case where the parents are two women or two men is regulated, given that Spain recognizes the right to marriage and adoption for same-sex couples. With regard to surrogacy that has been carried out in other countries that accept it, the regulation admits its legal effects in Spain, which nevertheless prohibits this type of maternity.

644. The amount of the allowance is established annually by the LPGE. In 2023, it is EUR 30.40 per month (fourteen payments) for each child, with a limit of four times this amount.

645. The supplement is not paid in the case of voluntary early retirement and early partial retirement. However, the appropriate supplement will be paid when partial retirement is followed by full retirement, once the corresponding age has been reached.

Part-time workers

646. The RB is calculated according to the general regulations, with the characteristic that some gaps are included by using the applicable minimum contributory base at each time, and corresponds to the number of contracted hours as a last

301. Article 60 of the GSSA.
302. BOE No. 29 of 3 Feb. 2021.

resort. Moreover, to determine the contributory period that is computable to apply a table of percentages to help establish the quantity of pensions, the contributory period to be calculated after applying the part-time coefficient is multiplied by 1.5. The resulting number of days cannot exceed the worked part-time period. Additionally, regarding the rules on the determination of the computable contribution period for the application of the percentage table to the fixation of the amount of the pension, the Constitutional Court (STC 88/2019 of 3 July) has declared its unconstitutionality as discriminatory. In this regard, the GSSA stated that the computable contribution period after the application of the partiality coefficient would be multiplied by 1.5, without the resulting number of days exceeding the period registered on a part-time contract; consequently, nowadays after the minimum set up contribution period is credited (fifteen years), the retirement pension is calculated by applying the general scale to the corresponding RB, without taking into account the reduction established regarding the period with part-time contract. Similarly, Judgment of the ECJ of 8 May 2019 (Case Villar Láiz)[303] considered that this regulation regarded as indirect discrimination, and against the Directive 79/7/EEC of Council of 19 December, on the progressive implementation of the principle of equal treatment for men and women in matters of social security, insofar that it disfavours women with regard to male workers. The applicable percentage is the provided in the general rule, but if the interested party accredits a contribution period of less than fifteen years, considering the sum of the full-time days with the increased part-time days and the latter with the coefficient of 1, 5, the percentage applicable to the RB is the equivalent to that resulting from applying the percentage that represents the contribution period credited by the worker over fifteen years to fifty.

Minimum pension

647. A guarantee exists for a minimum pension quantity. 'Minimum pension supplements' are the quantity paid to ensure that the minimum pension established yearly is paid according to the type of pension and to the pensioner's person and family circumstances, provided that the pensioner does not exceed the set income limit. For 2023, the limit of income for a minimum pension is:

Limit of Income for a Minimum Pension (EUR)

Limit of Income (Not Including the Pension)	*Yearly Amount*
Does not need to take care of a spouse	8,614.00
Needs to take care of a spouse	10,048.00
Single (single-person family unit)	8,614.00

303. Judgment of the Court of Justice of the EU (Third Chamber) of 8 May 2019, C-161/18. ECLI: EU:C:2019:382.

648. For 2023, the quantity of the minimum contributory retirement pension is:

Minimum Contributory Retirement Pension (EUR)		
Retirement at Age 65	*Monthly Amount*	*Yearly Amount*
Does not need to take care of a spouse	743.30	10,406.20
Single (single-person family unit)	783.10	10,963.40
Needs to take care of a spouse	966.20	13,526.80
Retirement Younger Than 65		
Does not need to take care of a spouse	692.50	9,695.00
Single (single-person family unit)	732.60	10,256.40
Needs to take care of a spouse	905.9	12,682.60
Retirement at Age 65 Coming from Severe Disability		
Does not need to take care of a spouse	1,115.00	15,610.00
Single (single-person family unit)	1,174.70	16,445.80
Needs to take care of a spouse	1,449.30	20,290.20

Maximum limit for public pensions

649. The quantity established each year as the maximum limit cannot be exceeded for public pensions (one pension or more if compatible). For 2023, the maximum limit is EUR 3,058,81 per month, or EUR 42,823.30 per year.

Agricultural wage earners

650. Agricultural wage earners are included in the General Scheme (Special Agricultural System). For retirement pensions, the above-mentioned rules apply to them. However, for the assumed cases of early retirement (for causes not attributable to workers, ex Article 207 of the GSSA; and for workers' voluntary early retirement, ex Article 208 of the GSSA) to accredit the demanded minimum contributory period requirement, at least six years in the last ten contributory years corresponding to periods of having worked and been registered in the Special Agricultural Scheme are expected. Accordingly, the tax periods during which unemployment allowances in this Special Scheme are paid are also calculated.

Sea workers

651. To sea wage earners, the same rules that apply to general wage earners also apply. This is one of the workers' groups which accesses retirement at a younger age, given the added difficulty that this work entails. The time period that results from lowering these workers' retirement age by applying reducing coefficients cannot exceed ten years. This time is calculated as a contributory period, but only to determine the applicable percentage to calculate the quantity of their pension.

§2. SURVIVORS PENSION

I. Beneficiaries

652. When workers (or pensioners or people with permanent disability in their contributory regimes) die, their spouses (if legally married), registered partners (*parejas de hecho*),[304] and even former spouses (widows/widowers), or the underage children of the deceased of a certain age or their disabled children (orphans) are entitled to economic allowances. There is also the possibility of recognizing allowances to the deceased's family relations other than those indicated here given certain situations involving economic dependence (fathers/mothers, siblings, grandchildren) (allowances for other family relations).

II. Conditions

653. To access survivors' pensions (only those that derive from common disease), a former contributory period is expected: (a) if the worker is registered as working or is in an equivalent situation, then the deceased must have met a minimum contributory period of 500 days during the five-year period immediately before his/her death (one exception is orphans' pension entitlement); (b) if the worker is neither registered as a worker nor in an equivalent situation: fifteen years.

A. *Widows/Widowers Pensions*

654. From 1 January 2022, no distinction is made according to the type of affective relationship the deceased had with the survivor (marriage, registered partnership). The recognition of registered partnerships as a protected situation in widow's pensions is fairly recent (2008), and although initially it was required that the survivor be financially dependent on the deceased, this is no longer the case and they can access it under the same conditions as the survivors of married couples. The widow's/widower's pension has also been granted to ex-spouses since the first Spanish divorce law (1981), when there is financial dependence on the deceased. Since 1 January 2022, this right has also been granted to ex-partners.

655. Widow/widower pension or temporary allowance for the surviving spouse:[305] for any married person and now also for members of a registered partnership, no economic dependence is expected of the survivor in relation to the deceased. In Spain, marriage has the same requirements and effects when both spouses are of the same gender or not (Article 44 of the Civil Code).

304. In Spain, 'registered partners' *(parejas de hecho)* are defined as those couples who are listed in a special register, due to which they are entitled to certain rights similar, although not equal, to those who are married. Each Autonomous Community has their own regulatory system.

305. Article 219 of the GSSA.

656. Generally speaking, the marriage and the cohabitation of the unmarried partner is not expected to have a minimum duration. However, if the death is due to an illness known prior to the marriage, the marriage must have lasted at least one year or, alternatively, children must have been born during this marriage. A minimum duration is not required if, at the time of the marriage, a period of cohabitation with the deceased is proven which, added to the duration of the marriage, exceeds two years. In this case, however, there is not right to a life pension but a temporary widow's/widower's allowance of two years instead of an annuity. Registered partners are also entitled to a temporary allowance for two years in an amount equal to the amount that would have been payable as a pension, if at least two years have not elapsed since registration or the formalisation of the corresponding public document, provided that the other requirements are met.

657. Widowhood pension for 'registered partners': in these cases, the economic dependence of the survivor in relation to the deceased is expected. This economic dependence is measured in two (alternative) ways: (1) when his/her income during the previous calendar year was less than 50% of the sum of his/her own income and those of the deceased during the same period (or 25% if there are no child/children entitled to an orphan's pension); (b) when the survivor's income is 1.5 times less than the legal minimum monthly salary in force when the deceased died. This limit increases by 0.5 times the quantity of the legal minimum monthly salary in force for the child of both spouses, who is entitled to an orphan's pension and lives with the survivor.

658. A legal registered partnership definition exists by which merely living together and not having formalized the partnership does not give the right to a pension. Some requirements to formalize the partnership and the situation of the partners living together are demanded. For this purpose, a registered partnership is that with a similar emotional relationship to that of marriage, and one constituted by those not impeded to marry, have no matrimonial link with anyone else and can accredit that both partners have lived together in a stable and evident manner by means of the corresponding census register immediately before the deceased's death for an interrupted duration no less than five years, unless there are children in common, in which case registration is only required on the terms set out below. The fact that a registered partnership exists is accredited by having registered in any of the specific registers in Spanish CCAA or in the Town/City Councils where they live, or by any public document that accredits this partnership. Both the aforementioned registration and the formalization of this corresponding public document must have taken place at least two years before the deceased died.

659. Widow/widower pension in assumed cases of separation, divorce or nullity of marriage and registered partnership:[306] in these cases, the survivor is expected to economically depend on the deceased, but this economic dependence implies the surviving ex-spouse or ex-registered partner to be the beneficiary of a compensatory pension paid by the deceased, which ended with his/her death. A compensatory

306. Article 220 of the GSSA.

pension involves a spouse having the right to be paid a pension when the divorce implies an economic imbalance in relation to the other spouse's position, provided that this imbalance worsened the situation prior to the marriage taking place. It is judicially agreed or imposed within a divorce process. The above-cited terms expect the ex-spouse or ex-registered partner to have neither remarried nor formed a registered partnership. This requirement is not expected of those women who can accredit being a victim of gender-based violence at the time of legal separation or divorce.

660. A temporary regime exists for anyone legally separated or divorced before 1 January 2008 when no agreement had been reached about a compensatory pension. In this case, people can access the widow/widower pension by applying the regime in force prior to the reform.[307] Two assumed cases are considered: in both cases, the period between the date of the divorce or legal separation and the date when the deceased died cannot be longer than ten years. The assumed cases are:

(1) when the matrimonial link has lasted at least ten years and the beneficiary also coincides by fulfilling one of the following conditions: (a) children were born during the marriage; (b) the beneficiary is older than 50 years when the deceased died;
(2) if no children were born during the marriage, the beneficiary has to be aged 65 years or more, not be entitled to any other public pension and the marriage lasted no less than fifteen years.

B. *Orphan's Pension*

661. An orphan's pension is acknowledged for the children of the (working or pensioner) deceased. Orphanage is acknowledged for children under the age of 21, or older than 21 who are unfit to work. Those children of the (working or pensioner) deceased are also acknowledged if aged under 25 years, but do not occupy a job post as either wage earners or self-employed workers, or if they do, and their annual calculated income is less than the quantity of the legal minimum monthly salary in force at the time.

C. *Orphans Allowance*

662. This allowance is acknowledged for the assumed cases of death by violence against women when orphans are not acknowledged as being the beneficiaries of an orphan's pension. The beneficiaries are the deceased's children who find themselves in circumstances that are comparable to absolute orphanage. Children must be under the age of 21 (or 25 if they do not occupy a job post as wage earners or

307. Temporary Provision No. 13 of the GSSA.

as self-employed workers, or if they do, and their annual calculated income is less than the quantity of the legal minimum monthly salary in force at the time).

D. Allowances for Other (Consanguineous) Family Relations

663. Other family relations have acknowledged the right to a pension or temporary allowance. In this case, they need to accredit their economic dependence on the deceased. Life pensions or temporary subsidies exist.

664. A pension in favour of family relations can be acknowledged for the following (consanguineous) family relations:

(a) Children and siblings can be beneficiaries of contributory retirement or permanent disability pensions when: (1) they have lived with the deceased who has been responsible for them; (2) people aged more than 45 years, and single people, divorced people or widows/widowers; (3) they can accredit having cared for the deceased in the long term; (4) they have no own means of living.
(b) Grandchildren and siblings under the age of 18 or their capacity to work is reduced to a percentage scored as a degree of absolute permanent disability or severe disability, and are orphans of both mother and father when: (1) they have lived with the deceased and at his/her expense for at least two years before (s)he died; (2) if they are not entitled to a public pension; (3) they lack their own means of living and have no other family relations who are obliged to, and can, keep and feed them according to Civil Law. When grandchildren or siblings are aged over 18, and under 22 and do not occupy a job post as wage earners or as self-employed workers, or their income is less than 75 per 100 of the legal minimum monthly salary in force at the time.
(c) Mother and grandmothers, widows, married women whose husband is unfit to work, or single women, provided they fulfil the conditions cited for grandchildren and siblings.
(d) Father and grandparents who have reached the age of 60 or are unfit for work and fulfil the conditions cited for grandchildren and siblings.

665. The temporary subsidy in favour of family relations can be acknowledged for the deceased's children and siblings over the age of 22, or are widowed or single, who meet the above requirements for grandchildren and siblings under the age of 18.

III. Calculation

666. Like all contributory pensions, they are calculated according to the taxes paid by workers during the period defined by the norm. The RB is for any allowances for common disease or non-work accident (common risks) and for allowances for work accidents or professional disease (professional risks). Certain percentages apply to the corresponding RB. Only the new (2019) orphans allowance, which addresses the orphans born of women who have died as a result of violence against women, is calculated differently given its distinct legal nature.

A. *Widow/Widower Pension or Temporary Widow/Widower Allowance*

667. The RB: when death is by common disease or a non-work-related accident, the RB is the average of the taxes paid for twenty-four months running chosen by the beneficiary over the last fifteen contributory years. If death was caused by a work accident or was due to professional disease, the RB is made up of the payments made in the last year, including overtime. The RB of professional contingencies is, therefore, superior to that applicable for common contingencies. If the deceased was retired or had a permanent disability, the RB would be the same as that used to calculate his/her pension duly updated.

668. Applicable percentages: some percentages are applied to the previous bases, which vary according to the personal circumstances and/or family relations of the widow/widower. Several assumed cases exist. The general or ordinary (common) percentage is 52%, which increases to 60% when the beneficiary is aged 65 years or more, and provided that (s)he is not paid another public pension. If the widow/widower was responsible for family relations (younger than 26 years, or older if they are disabled) and their income is below the set limits, the applicable percentage rises to 70%.

669. The quantity of the pension and temporary allowance is the same: the difference lies in its duration. The former is for life, but ends if the beneficiary remarries or forms a registered partnership (some exceptions exist), or if other causes come into play. The latter lasts two years.

670. Maternity supplement:[308] to calculate the quantity of pensions (including widow/widower pensions), their quantity increases for those women who have given birth to biological children or have adopted to thank them for their demographic contribution. It is also granted to male parents, if certain conditions are met. In 2023, the pension supplement is 28 euros/month (14 payments) for each child, up to a maximum of four children.

671. Compatibility with a widow/widower pension: the widow/widower pension has a very flexible system that is compatible with work or with other pensions. It is compatible with any work or income that the pensioner may receive. It is also compatible with other pensions that the pensioner may be paid: the only restriction is that the sum of (public) pensions does not exceed the maximum limit of a public pension.

308. Article 60 of the GSSA.

B. Orphan's Pension, and Pensions or Subsidies That Favour Other Family Relations

672. The RB used to calculate these allowances is the same as that indicated to calculate the widow/widower pension. The applicable percentage is 20% for each pension.

673. Absolute orphan status: for cases of the absolute orphan status, the percentage of 52% of a widow/widower pension increases to favour these orphans.

674. Orphans in assumed cases of victims of violence against women: if the orphan/s is/are entitled to an orphan's pension, some mechanisms exist to improve the protection of child/children who is/are a victim/s of violence against women, such as increasing the widow/widower pension if the other parent is not entitled to one for being responsible for the death of the person that has resulted in the pension, or increase the applicable percentage to 70% when the income of the family unit living together, including the orphan/s, divided by the number of people forming the family unit does not exceed 75% of the annually calculated legal minimum monthly salary, after excluding the proportional part of one-off payments. If there is more than one beneficiary of this pension, the combined quantity of these pensions can rise to 118% of the RB, and cannot go below the minimum equivalent to a widow/widower pension for anyone responsible for family relations.

675. A joint limit exists for pensions by death and survival (not for orphans): they cannot exceed the amount of the corresponding RB. Orphans' pensions have preference over those pensions favouring other family relations, and an order or priority is set. One exception is when several orphans' pensions coincide with a widow/widower pension to which the applicable percentage is over 52%, and can exceed 100% RB as the sum of orphans' pensions cannot exceed 48% of this base.

C. Orphans Allowance

676. Given its peculiar legal nature, the regulatory basis cannot be calculated by considering the contributory bases of the person causing this allowance. Instead, a uniform RB is used for all possible beneficiaries: the minimum contributory base in force at each time is taken as the RB (namely the legal minimum monthly salary increased by the proportional part of extraordinary payments). To this amount, a percentage of 70% applies, provided that the income of the family unit living together, including orphans, divided by the number of people in the family unit does not exceed the annual calculation of 75% of the legal minimum monthly salary in force at any time, excluding the proportional part of one-off payments. If there is more than one beneficiary of this allowance, the joint quantity of their allowances can rise to 118% of the RB, but cannot go below the minimum equivalent to a widow/widower pension of anyone in charge of family relations.

D. *Flat-Rate Special Compensation for Death by Work Accident or Professional Disease*

677. As a result of the privileged nature of protection from professional risks in the Spanish Social Security System, when death is caused by a work accident or professional disease, an additional allowance is acknowledged for certain family relations. The spouse or survivor of a registered partner is entitled to compensation of six monthly payments according to the RB of a widow/widower pension. Orphans are entitled to a compensation of one monthly payment. If no other family members are entitled to pensions due to death or survival, this compensation can be acknowledged to ancestors, provided they were economically dependent on the deceased and are not entitled to allowances for family relations. In this case, the quantity equals nine months of the RB, or twelve months if both ancestors are entitled.

E. *Compensation for Death*

678. This is to help pay the deceased's funeral arrangements and comes to EUR 46.50 (paid as a single payment).

F. *Minimum Pension*

679. A guarantee exists for a minimum pension quantity. 'Minimum pension supplements' are the quantity paid to ensure that the minimum pension established yearly is paid according to the type of pension and to the pensioner's person and family circumstances, provided that the pensioner does not exceed the set income limit. These minimum pension supplements are paid while the pensioner legally lives in Spain; thus, exporting pensions is excluded from the general rule. A maximum limit also exists whose quantity cannot exceed the amount established yearly for non-contributory retirement or disability pensions (singular rules exist when a spouse lives off a pensioner). For 2023:

Limit of Income for a Minimum Pension

Limit of Income (Not Including the Pension)	*Yearly Amount (EUR)*
Does not need to take care of a spouse	8,614.00
Needs to take care of a spouse	10,048.00
Single (single-person family unit)	8,614.00

680. For 2023, the minimum quantity of pensions caused by death and survival are:

Minimum Contributory Survival Pension (EUR)		
Widow/widower	*Monthly Amount*	*Yearly Amount*
Needs to care for family relations	905.90	12,682.60
Aged 65 years or with =>65% disability	783.10	10,963.40
Between the age of 60 and 64	732.60	10,256.40
Under the age of 60	593.30	8,306.20
Orphans		
Per beneficiary	239.50	3.353.00
Per beneficiary aged less than 18 with =>65% disability	470.90	6,592.60
Absolute Orphan Status		
One single beneficiary	832.80	11,659.2
Several beneficiaries (N)	239.50 + 593.30/N	3,353.00 + 8,306.20/N
In Favour of Family Relations		
For beneficiary	700	9,800,00º
If no widow or orphan exist		
A single beneficiary aged 65	578.50	8,099.00
A single beneficiary aged under 65	542.20	7,632.80
Several beneficiaries (N)	239.50 + 353.80/N	3,353.00 + 4,953.20/N

681. Maximum limit for public pensions: The quantity established each year as the maximum limit cannot be exceeded for public pensions (one pension or more if compatible). For 2023, the maximum limit is EUR 3,058.81 per month, or EUR 42,829.29 per year.

Chapter 2. Pensions for Self-Employed Workers

§1. Retirement Pensions

682. The same legal system for retirement matters applies to the self-employed workers in the RETA as that used for the Wage Earners' Scheme in the General Scheme.[309] There are some exceptions:

(a) No gaps are included: i.e., those periods during which no tax payments were made are not included to calculate the RB, which takes a value of 0.
(b) Currently, partial retirement does not apply to them (pending legal developments).
(c) There is no access to early retirement for the causes not attributable to workers set out in Article 207 of the GSSA.

683. The general rules are also applied for self-employed workers in the RETM, with the exceptions indicated below:[310]

(a) The minimum retirement age lowers by applying reducing coefficients to ages depending on the type of job post occupied by workers.[311] The time period by which the retirement work of workers lowers by applying reducing coefficients cannot exceed ten years. This time is calculated only for determining the applicable percentage to calculate the quantity of the pension. Coefficients are not applied when accessing retirement from a situation in which workers are not registered for work or are in an equivalent situation.
(b) Gaps cannot be included: those periods during which no tax payments were made are not included to calculate the RB, which takes a value of 0.
(c) Currently, partial retirement does not apply to them (pending legal developments).
(d) There is no access to early retirement for the causes not attributable to workers set out in Article 207 of the GSSA.

§2. Survivors' Pension

684. The same legal system for death and survival matters is applied to the self-employed worker in the Self-Employed Workers Scheme and those included in the Special Maritime Workers Scheme.

309. Article 318 of the GSSA.
310. Article 30 of Law 47/2005.
311. RD 1311/2007.

Chapter 3. Guaranteed Income for the Retired (Non-contributory Retirement Pension)

685. A non-contributory pension is recognized for people aged 65 years or more with less income or earnings than the quantity established for those who always live legally in the Spanish territory and have done so for ten years between the age of 16 and the age at which they are paid the pension; two of these ten years must be consecutive and immediately prior to them applying for this allowance. The limit of their income for 2023 is EUR 6,784.54 per year. If the beneficiary lives in a unit with other family relatives, even though their income is less than the cited amount, it is necessary to verify that the sum of all the annual incomes and earnings of the members of the economic unit living together is less than the following quantities for 2023:

	No. People Living Together	*EUR/Year*
(a) Lives only with spouse and/or second-degree consanguineous parents	2	11,533.72
	3	16,282.90
	4	21,032.08
(b) If consanguineous family relations include any parents or children	2	28,834.30
	3	40,707.25
	4	52,580.20

686. The quantity of an individual's pension is set according to his/her personal income and/or to that of the economic unit living together, and cannot be less than the minimum quantity of 25%. Special rules apply if more than one beneficiary of a non-contributory pension (retirement or disability) lives in the same family.

(a) Basic rule:

	EUR/Month	*EUR/Year*
Full	484.61	6,784.54
Minimum 25%	121.15	1,696.14

(b) Where more than one beneficiary entitled to a non-contributory pension lives in the same family, the individual amount of each of them is:

No. Beneficiaries	*EUR/Month*	*EUR/Year*
2	411.92	5,766.86
3	387.69	5,427.63

Part IX. Handicapped Persons

Carmen Jover Ramírez

687. The study of the 'Handicapped Persons' in the Spanish social protection system requires a previous terminological delimitation. Incapacity, disability and dependency are three terms that respond to different situations and find diverse protection within the system. In some cases, they are exclusionary terms and compatible or complementary in others.

688. 'Incapacity' into the Spanish social protection system is associated with the capacity of a person to work. On one side, the term 'temporary incapacity' is used to refer to the situation of those who, suffering from a health impairment, cannot temporarily perform their professional services. On the other, 'permanent disability' is relating to irreversible ailments and presumably definitive over time, making it impossible for the subjects to professionally provide their services, either in their usual profession or in any other profession even if different from the usual one. Instead, the 'non-contributory disability' refers to the protection of those who, not having contributed to the Social Security System, suffer from an illness that incapacitates them to provide their services, in addition to a lack of earnings or income.

689. Along with the term incapacity, the Spanish legal system incorporates the protection of both disabled and dependent persons. In a strict sense, these situations constitute disability and dependency.

Chapter 1. Social Integration

690. The Spanish legal system has for a long time been concerned about the social integration of people with disabilities, to whom this disability could lead to a situation of social exclusion and inequality of opportunities.

691. Faced with the situation of those affected by a physical, mental or sensory impairment, Law 13/1982 of 7 April on the Social Integration of Persons with Disabilities was the first legislative milestone in Spain,[312] which sought to guarantee the adoption of measures by the public authorities in different fields, in order to ensure the full integration of these persons.

692. Subsequently, Law 51/2003 of 2 December, on Equal Opportunities, Non-Discrimination and Universal Accessibility for Persons with Disabilities[313] gave priority to the establishment of measures to guarantee and give effect to the right to equal opportunities for persons with disabilities, in accordance with Articles 9(2), 10, 14 and 49 of the SC.

693. With the ratification on 3 December 2007 of the International Convention on the Rights of Persons with Disabilities – adopted on 13 December 2006 by the General Assembly of the UN – the policies of social integration of persons with disabilities in Spain received a new impulse. In consequence, Law 26/2011 of 1 August,[314] which proclaimed the regulatory adaption to the Convention on the Rights of Persons with Disabilities, was approved, causing important amendments in the regulations in force in order to comply with them. Among these measures, the Second Final Provision itself authorized the Government to draw up and adopt a consolidated text to regularize, clarify and harmonize the different existing statutory provisions on disability. As a result, Royal Legislative Decree 1/2013 of 29 November approved the Consolidated Text of the General Law on the Rights of Persons with Disabilities and Their Social Inclusion (hereinafter 'RPDA'), which constitutes the current regulation of the matter, recently amended by Law 6/2022 of 31 March, to establish and regulate cognitive accessibility and its conditions of requirement and application.[315]

694. The Preamble of the latter stresses the recognition of persons with disabilities as a large and vulnerable group that society, given its structure and functioning, has habitually maintained in well-known conditions of exclusion. This has led to a restriction of the fundamental rights and freedoms of these people, conditioning or hindering their personal development, and the enjoyment of resources and services available to the entire population, as well as the possibility of contributing with their capacities to the progress of society. It is therefore a priority objective, the need for the legislator to identify existing needs and propose the most appropriate solutions.

312. BOE No. 103 of 30 Apr. 1982.
313. BOE No. 289 of 3 Dec. 2003.
314. BOE No. 184 of 2 Aug. 2011.
315. BOE No. 78 of 1 Apr. 2022.

695. Accordingly, Article 1 of the RPDA highlights the objectives of guarantee to persons with disabilities the right to equality of opportunity and treatment, as well as the full and effective exercise of their rights, on an equal footing with other citizens. This may be achieved through the following actions: promotion of personal autonomy, universal accessibility and access to employment, inclusion in the community and independent living, and the eradication of all forms of discrimination. As a means of ensuring compliance, the act points to the need to establish a corresponding system of infringements and sanctions in order to guarantee the basic conditions of equal opportunities, non-discrimination and universal accessibility for persons with disabilities.

§1. DISABILITY

I. Disability and Disabled Persons

696. Disability – for the purposes of the RPDA – is the situation resulting from the interaction between persons with foreseeably permanent impairments and any type of barrier that limits or prevents their full and effective participation in society, on an equal footing with others. A person with a disability is one who has a physical, mental, intellectual or sensory impairment, that is foreseeable permanent and which, when interacting with various barriers, may prevent his or her full and effective participation in society on an equal footing with others.

697. Persons with disabilities are those who have been recognized by the competent body as having a degree of disability of 33% or more. However, it is legally presumed that social security pensioners with a total, absolute or serious permanent disability pension, and State pensioners who have been granted a retirement pension for permanent disability or incapacity for work, are considered to have a disability of 33% or more.

II. Recognition, Declaration and Qualification of the Degree of Disability

698. In order to guarantee citizens equal conditions of access to benefits, economic rights and services granted by public bodies, and to achieve national uniformity in the assessment and qualification of the degree of disability, RD 888/2022 of 18 October, on the procedure for the recognition, declaration and qualification of the degree of disability, was approved.[316] This norm, amended on occasion, regulates the recognition of the degree of disability, the establishment of applicable levels, the determination of the competent bodies to carry out said recognition and the procedure to be followed.

316. BOE No. 252 of 20 Oct. 2022.

699. As indicated above, the degree of disability responds to a series of unified technical criteria, established by means of the scale described in the applicable regulations. Impairments and limitations in activity and restrictions in participation presented by the person, such as, where relevant, contextual factors/environmental barriers, are subject to evaluation.

700. Annexes I to VI of the aforementioned RD contain the general rules and the basic overview of the scale components, as well as the body functions and structures/global person impairment) assessment scale (BDGP), the abilities/ activity limitations assessment scale (BLA), the performance/barriers to participation assessment scale (BRP) and the contextual factors/environmental barriers assessment scale (BFCA).

701. To determine the degree of disability, the percentage obtained in the assessment of the person's impairments, activity limitations and participation restrictions will be modified, where appropriate, by the addition of the score obtained in the Contextual Factors/Environmental Barriers scale.

702. The recognition of disability corresponds to each Autonomous Community, in accordance with the division of competences between these and the State, established by the SC.[317] In this way, the interested party must address his request to the competent administrative body, in accordance with the established procedure.

703. Multi-professional teams for the qualification and recognition of the degree of disability, competent technical bodies, shall issue the corresponding opinions for the recognition of the degree of disability. These teams are responsible for evaluating and qualifying the degree of disability and reviewing it for by intensification or mitigation or material or factual error. They must also determine the need for assistance from another person to carry out the essential acts of daily life and assess the mobility problems. It is also up to them to determine the time limit for requesting a review the degree of disability.

704. This evaluation and qualification will be carried out after the interested party has been examined. At the proposal of the multi-professional team, it may be agreed, by the body competent to decide, to require the cooperation of social disability organisations, in order to inform, help, assist or provide expert knowledge in all matters related to the assessment of disability. Minors (under 18) and persons with support measures for the exercise of their legal capacity shall have the right to be informed, heard and listened to without discrimination on the grounds of age or disability. Minors with disabilities shall exercise their rights on an equal basis with other minors, receiving assistance appropriate to their disability and age. The multi-professional team shall issue a proposal which must necessarily contain at least the diagnosis, type and degree of disability as well as, if necessary, the scores obtained by applying the different scales, the diagnosis codes, impairment, activity limitations, participation restrictions, environmental barriers, and any others that may be

317. Articles 148–149 of the SC.

established; the scores of the scales to determine the need to have the support of another person for the performance of basic activities and the existence of mobility difficulties by mass public transport. An express resolution will be issued by the heads of the competent body of the Autonomous Community on the recognition of the degree as well as the score obtained on the scales to determine the need for support from another person or mobility difficulties.

§2. Rights of Disabled People

I. Right to Equality

705. Article 14 of the SC enshrines the right to equality of Spaniards before the law, without any discrimination on the grounds of birth, race, sex, religion, opinion or any other personal or social condition or circumstance. It can be said that the right to equality of disabled people is itself recognized in the Constitution.

706. This right to equality is provided in the RPDA which establishes that 'persons with disabilities have the same rights as other citizens under our legal system'.[318] The law entrusts public administrations with the task of promoting the necessary measures to ensure a real and effective equal exercise of the rights of persons with disabilities in all areas of life. It concerns their rights in terms of equality between women and men, health, employment, social protection, education, effective judicial protection, mobility, communication, information and access to culture, sports, leisure and participation in public affairs. In this field, a special mention deserves those people or groups who are particularly vulnerable to multiple discrimination, such as children and women with disabilities, elderly people with disabilities, women with disabilities, victims of gender-based violence, people with multiple disabilities, or other persons with disabilities who are members of minorities.

II. Right to Health Protection

707. The right to health protection for people with disabilities provided by this law includes both disease prevention and health protection, promotion and recovery, without any discrimination on grounds of disability. In this area, special attention must be paid to mental health as well as the sexual and reproductive health of these people.

708. Within the scope of their competences, the public administrations pay specific attention to the needs of disabled people, in accordance with the general and sectoral health legislation in force. In particular, they must carry out an effective and efficient coordination between social and healthcare with respect to people affected

318. Article 7 of the RPDA.

by an impairment, who have health problems associated with it and require simultaneously or successively care. In addition, they must promote the necessary measures to ensure the access of such persons to services and benefits related to their health, on an equal footing with other citizens.

709. In this sense, the General Health Act 14/1986 recognizes in Article 10(1) the right of all users, before any public health administration, not to be discriminated against on the basis of their impairment, likewise, the right to accessible and understandable information regarding the health services for everyone.

710. The health activities of the National Health System include the promotion, expansion and improvement of early detection systems for disabilities, as well as services aimed at preventing and minimizing new deficiencies or the worsening of pre-existing conditions.[319] In addition, Royal Legislative Decree 16/2003 on Cohesion and Quality of the National Health System (hereinafter 'NHSA') states that the prevention of impairments must be added as one of the actions of the SPSs.[320]

711. The prevention of impairments and the aggravation of disabilities is a right and a duty of each citizen and of society as a whole. It must form part of the State's priority obligations in the field of public health and social services, taking into account the diversity of these persons, giving a differential treatment according to the specific needs of each person.[321] To this end, plans are promoted to prevent impairments and worsening disabilities, with particular emphasis on the following: family planning and counselling services; genetic counselling, prenatal and perinatal care; early detection and diagnosis and paediatric care; mental health of infants and young people; geriatric care; occupational safety and health; road safety; food hygiene and health control; and environmental pollution.

712. In the area of health protection, the multi-professional teams carry out the qualification and recognition of the degree of disability. They are the bodies responsible for assessing and qualifying situations of disability, for official recognition by the competent administrative body. They must have an appropriate, specialized training to provide interdisciplinary care to each person with disabilities who need it, guaranteeing their inclusion and full participation in society on an equal footing with others. Among its functions:

(a) issuing a standardized technical opinion on deficiencies and limitations in carrying out activities, as well as barriers to social participation, collecting the competences and skills for which the person needs support;
(b) orientations for the qualification and rehabilitation, with full respect for the autonomy of the person with disability, proposing needs, competences and possibilities of recovery, as well as their follow-up and revision;

319. Article 18(18) of the General Health Act 14/1986.
320. Article 11(2) d) of Law 16/2003.
321. Article 11 of the RPDA.

(c) the evaluation and qualification of the disability situation, determining the type and degree of disability in relation to the benefits, economic rights and services provided by law, without prejudice to the recognition of the right that corresponds to the competent administrative body.

713. NHSA recognizes expressly the accessibility of certain benefits, such as medical transport for persons with disabilities.[322] Facilitating access to health centres is a quality criterion that must be guaranteed by the National Health System. Thus, newly created health centres must promote accessibility and eliminate barriers of all kinds. Along these lines, public health administrations promote programmes for the elimination of barriers in health centres which, for reasons of age or otherwise, jeopardize users with mobility problems.[323]

III. Right to Comprehensive Care

714. The right to comprehensive care becomes relevant when the deficiency has an unquestionable impact on any aspect of a person's life. This attention includes 'processes or other intervention measures designed to enable persons with disabilities to acquire their maximum level of personal development and autonomy, achieving and maintaining their maximum independence, physical, mental and social ability, as well as their inclusion and full participation in all aspects of life, including obtaining adequate employment' (according to RPDA).

715. Comprehensive care programmes developed from the earliest possible stage may include medical-functional qualification or rehabilitation measures; care, treatment and psychological counselling, and education and support for professional activity.

A. *Medical-Functional Qualification or Rehabilitation*

716.

(a) Objective: To achieve maximum functionality of physical, sensory, mental or intellectual capacities.
(b) Planning: Detection and identification of the impairments and psychosocial needs of each person; monitoring until the attainment and maintenance of the maximum development and personal autonomy possible.
(c) Measures:
  – Medical-functional qualification or rehabilitation processes, necessary to improve and achieve a maximum personal autonomy, and to be able to attain with the necessary supports their personal development and full and effective participation in society on an equal footing with others.

322. Article 19 of the NHSA.
323. Article 28 of the NHSA.

- Possibility of home treatment or in the environment in which the disabled persons develop their life, being essential the community services existing in its environment.
- As complementary measures: the provision, adaptation, maintenance and renewal of assistive technologies, prostheses, devices, vehicles, and other auxiliary elements whose personal circumstances make this advisable.

B. *Care, Treatment and Psychological Counselling*

717.

(a) Objective: To achieve maximum autonomy and full development of their personality, as well as support for their immediate family environment.

(b) Planning, during the different phases of the interdisciplinary qualification or rehabilitating process: Facilitating since the detection of the impairment or the start of a pathological process, or when an unexpected circumstance may lead to a limitation in the activity.

(c) Measures: Care, treatment and psychological counselling based on the personal characteristics of the disabled persons, their motivations and interests as well as the family and social factors that may condition them. These measures shall aim at maximizing the use of their capacities and personal autonomy, taking into account their unique life project.

C. *Education*

718. This is characterized as an inclusive education (*see* 'Right to education' *infra*).

D. *Support for Professional Activity*

719.

(a) To guarantee disabled persons of working age the right to benefit from vocational and rehabilitation, job retention and return to work programmes.

(b) Planning: From the previous and necessary stages for incorporation into the labour market – such as training and guidance – as well as during the performance of this professional activity.

(c) Measures:
  - Qualification or medical-functional rehabilitation processes: these include the development of capacity and the use of products, technologies and assistive devices for better performance of work on an equal footing with others.
  - Professional orientation provided by the corresponding services according to the real abilities of the person with disability, the training received and to be received, the existing employment possibilities in each case and the

attention to their motivations, aptitudes and professional preferences. Support is provided for seeking, obtaining, maintaining and re-entering work.
– Vocational training, retraining or rehabilitation: including basic general prior training, encouraging the acquisition of work experience in the labour market. It is carried out in accordance with the personal itinerary and previous professional orientation, according to the decision taken by the disabled person.

IV. Right to Education

720. What most identifies the right to education is its inclusive character. Thus, education administrations must ensure an inclusive education system at all levels of education, as well as lifelong learning. They must ensure a place in basic education for students with disabilities, paying attention to the diversity of their educational needs, regulating reasonable supports and accommodations for those who need special attention for learning or inclusion.[324]

721. To this end, the schooling of these pupils in centres or special educational units is carried out on an exceptional basis, when their needs cannot be met in ordinary centres, taking into account the opinion of the parents or legal guardians. However, in such cases, the necessary conditions are created to facilitate the connection between ordinary and special centres.

722. Indeed, such inclusion must be guaranteed at all stages of the educational environment in which the person with a disability can be incorporated. Thus, in the university environment, there exists the right of the persons with disability to request (and the universities to grant) more calls for examinations to compensate for their difficulty, without lowering the required level. In the same way, the evaluation tests carried out will be adapted, where appropriate, to the characteristics of the impairment presented by the interested party.

723. Specifically, children's hospitals, such as rehabilitation hospitals and those – public or private – with permanent paediatric services, must have a pedagogical section to prevent and avoid marginalization of the educational process of school-age patients.

724. However, inclusion in the educational environment requires the active participation of all parties involved. Hence, management teams, teachers and education professionals have awareness raising, information and continuous training programmes. Programmes aimed at their specialization in attending to the special educational needs of students with disabilities, so that they have the necessary

324. *See* Ch. IV of the RPDA.

knowledge and tools to do so. It also provides guidance support for schools, to facilitate pedagogical revitalization, quality and educational innovation.[325]

725. Such education must be free of charge, both in ordinary schools and in special centres.[326]

726. LO 2/2006 of 3 May on Education[327] urges to take into account the condition of disabled person in the educational field. It recognizes 'the equity' as the inspiring principle of a system that guarantees equal opportunities for the full development of the personality through education, educational inclusion, equal rights and opportunities, that help to overcome any discrimination and universal access to education, and acts as a compensating element for personal, cultural, economic and social inequalities, with special attention to those deriving from any type of impairment. However, its objectives include 'education for the respect of fundamental rights and freedoms, equal rights and opportunities for men and women, and equal treatment and non-discrimination for persons with disabilities'. With regard to pupils with special educational needs, the Law mentions the need to adopt flexible measures and alternative methodologies in teaching and assessment at different educational stages, and in specific subjects, such as foreign language.

V. Right to Independent Life

727. The RPDA recognizes the right of persons with disabilities to live independently and participate fully in all aspects of life.[328] To this end, public authorities must ensure universal accessibility and equal opportunities for all persons with disabilities. Any reference to accessibility and universal accessibility in this law is understood to include cognitive accessibility, to enable easy understanding, communication and interaction for all persons. This will be achieved through a range of measures in different areas:

(a) In terms of housing and construction, accessibility requirements for buildings and environments: elimination of barriers in facilities, adaptation of equipment and instruments and appropriate signposting, as well as access to and use of urban public spaces. Furthermore, technical building standards are required to include the minimum conditions of all buildings in order to allow accessibility for people with disabilities. Standards must be included in the drafting phase of basic works and partial projects, denying the corresponding official visas if either professional bodies or the supervisory offices of the competent public administration breach them.

325. Article 21 of the RPDA.
326. Article 19 of the RPDA.
327. BOE No. 106 of 4 May 2006.
328. Articles 22–29 of the RPDA.

(b) In the field of products and services related to the information society and the media, as well as ancillary services for communication (enhancer and alternative systems, Braille, easily accessible multimedia devices, support systems for oral communication and sign language, tactile communication systems and other communication-enabling devices).
(c) In the transport sector, facilitate access to and use of means of transport. In particular, local authorities should act appropriately to facilitate the parking of motor vehicles belonging to persons with serious mobility problems because of their disability.
(d) In the area of relations with public administrations, accessibility and non-discrimination must be ensured in public offices, facilities and services for citizens, including the administration of justice, participation in political life and in electoral processes.
(e) The making available to the public of goods and services, therefore, outside the scope of private and family life, shall respect the principle of equal opportunities for persons with disabilities, avoiding direct or indirect discrimination on the grounds of disability. Differences of treatment shall be admissible only where they are justified by a legitimate aim and where the means of achieving the differences are adequate, proportionate and necessary.

VI. Right to Employment

728. Article 14 of the SC enshrines the principle of non-discrimination on the grounds of any personal condition or circumstance. Likewise, Article 17 of the Workers' Statute provides for the nullity and ineffectiveness of regulatory precepts, clauses in collective agreements, individual agreements and unilateral decisions of the employer, which give rise to direct or indirect discrimination on the grounds of disability, in employment, remuneration, working hours and other working conditions. In addition, the RPDA includes the right to work of persons with disabilities under conditions that guarantee the principle of equal treatment and non-discrimination, referring to the specific regulations on the subject and including the general concepts of direct and indirect discrimination and equal treatment in this matter.[329]

729. This law also includes specific employment measures, which identify different types of employment through which persons with disabilities can exercise their right to work: regular employment in enterprises and public administrations, including supported employment services; sheltered employment in special employment centres and work enclaves, as well as self-employment.

730. Finally, there are numerous aids, subsidies and other measures for persons with disabilities and their employers, to promote the employment of persons with disabilities (*see* 'Social Allowances' *infra*).

329. Article 35 of the RPDA.

VII. Right to Social Protection

731. The broad concept of social protection in Spain includes not only the protection provided by the Social Security System in its contributory and non-contributory modality but also the assistance benefits. Specifically, the protection of permanent disability in its contributory modality, referred in another section, is outside our study.

732. The 'right to social protection' refers to the right of persons with disabilities and their families to have 'social services and benefits that satisfy their needs with guarantees of sufficiency and sustainability, oriented towards the development of their personality and their inclusion in the community, increasing their quality of life and social welfare'.[330] Services are provided by both public administrations and non-profit entities, through the necessary human, financial and technical resources.

733. In particular, these services can be both in kind and economic benefits.[331] On the one hand, the former include: social services to support the family, prevention of impairments and worsening of disabilities, promotion of personal autonomy, information and counselling, home care, residences, support in their environment, residential services, cultural activities, sports, leisure and free time. On the other, economic benefits are set out by autonomous legislation to persons with disabilities and their families who lack the resources to deal with situations of need (*see* 'Financial Allowances' *infra*).

VIII. Right to Participate in Public Life

734. Persons with disabilities may exercise the right to participate in political life and electoral processes on an equal basis with other citizens. They can also participate fully and effectively in public decisions that affect them, on an equal footing with other citizens. To this end, public administrations shall make available to them the means and resources they need.[332]

735. It is worth mentioning the modification introduced by LO 2/2018 of 5 December, amending LO 5/1985 on the general electoral system,[333] to guarantee the right to vote of all persons with disabilities. The amendment takes into account the recommendation made by the Committee on the Rights of Persons with Disabilities of UN of 23 September 2011, regarding the possibility of restricting the voting rights of persons with intellectual or psychosocial disabilities if the person concerned has been deprived of his/her legal capacity or placed in an institution.

330. Article 48 of the RPDA.
331. Article 50 of the RPDA.
332. Articles 53–54 of the RPDA.
333. BOE No. 147 of 20 Jun. 1985.

736. That law proceeds to repeal Article 3(1) b) and c) of LO 5/1985, relating to the lack of voting rights of those declared incapable by virtue of a final judicial sentence. Hereinafter, the judge expressly must declare the incapacity to exercise the right to vote of those detained in a psychiatric hospital with judicial authorization, during the period of their internment and provided that in the authorization.

737. With the entry into force of this amendment, the limitations on the exercise of voting rights established by court decision on the basis of the repealed Articles shall cease to be in force. Persons whose voting rights have been restricted or annulled for reasons of disability shall be fully rehabilitated by the Ministry of Justice.

Chapter 2. Financial Allowances for Disabled People

738. Any person who has been recognized as disabled, in accordance with the established procedure, is entitled to a wide range of disability-related financial support. Those benefits are characterized by their plurality and diversity, according to their purpose.

739. Both the State and the CCAA assume competences in this area, which makes it difficult to establish a unique and uniform list of such benefits for people with disabilities.

§1. Beneficiaries

740. Beneficiaries are those who hold the condition of disabled persons according to the law. First, persons recognized as having physical, mental, intellectual or sensory impairments, which are predictably permanent, and which, by interacting with various barriers, may prevent their full and effective participation in society, on equal terms with others. Second, and for all purposes, beneficiaries are those who are recognized as having a degree of disability equal to or more than 33%. Under this situation, there are total, absolute or serious permanent disability pensioners; likewise, State pensioners retired due to permanent disability or incapacity for work.[334]

§2. Conditions

741. The plurality and diversity of the benefits granted to people with disabilities makes it necessary to analyse the requirements demanded in each case. It is possible to include these requirements in two sections: (1) have a recognized degree of disability of 33% or more, and (2) have the condition of 'dependent person', in accordance with the provisions of Law 39/2006 of 14 December, on the promotion of personal autonomy and care for dependent persons (hereinafter 'LPAD').

742. The maintenance of the dependent status gives rise to the right to recognition of the benefits provided for in the aforementioned standard. 'Dependency' is understood as the permanent state of persons who, due to disability and linked to the lack or loss of physical, mental, intellectual or sensory autonomy, require the attention of another or other persons, or important aids for the development of basic activities of daily life; in particular, in the case of persons with intellectual disability or mental illness, the need of having other supports for their personal autonomy.[335]

334. Article 4 of the RPDA.
335. Article 2 of the LPDA.

§3. BENEFITS

743. The benefits for disabled person are, on the one hand, economic benefits, which encompass any financial amount received directly by the disabled person due to his/her condition as such, or by the person in charge of them, if this is the case. On the other hand, they have in-kind benefits, which are not intended to be financial support for disabled persons, whose materialization is either not economic, or is not so in the strict sense of the word, when it became in aids, subsidies etc.

I. Social Allowances

744. Non-economic benefit or non-economic benefits in the non-strict sense constitute the widest range of disability-related benefits. Listed below are those that are recognized at State level, regardless of the Autonomous Community of residence, without overlooking the fact that they will also receive the autonomous aid that, for the latter reason, corresponds to them.

A. *Social Services*

745. The objective of social services is to satisfy the needs of people with disabilities with guarantee of sufficiency and sustainability, and promote the development of their personality and their inclusion in the community, increasing their quality of life and social welfare.[336] Social services include the following:

- Social support services for family guidance and information to families.
- Emotional support, training and formation to attend stimulation, maturation and physical development.
- Mental and intellectual development of children and disabled people.
- Adequacy of the family and immediate environment to their needs.
- Social services for the prevention of impairments and worsening of disabilities, and the promotion of personal autonomy.
- Social counselling and information services that make it easier for people with disabilities and their families, to become aware of the benefits and services at their disposal.
- Social home care services, residences, day and night centres, supervised housing.
- Social services related to sports, cultural, leisure and free time activities, so that these activities are developed whenever possible, in accordance with the principle of universal accessibility to facilities and with ordinary means at the service of the citizens.

746. Special mention should be made to the social services provided in the case of people with disabilities who have been recognized as 'dependent', in particular:

336. Article 48 of the RPDA.

- Services for the prevention of situations of dependency and the promotion of personal autonomy.
- Remote assistance service.
- Home support service, care for both household needs and personal care.
- Day and night centre services (for the elderly, under sixty-five years and specialized care) as well as residential care service (care home for dependent elderly persons and care centre for persons in a dependency situation), according to the various types of disability.[337]

747. The norm establishes a regime of compatibility and incompatibility between these benefits among themselves, and with the economic benefits aforementioned.[338]

B. Housing

748.

- Grants and loans with interest subsidies are recognized to carry out the changes at home that people with disabilities or the family units with a member with a disability need to make it accessible.[339]
- Assignment of a series of houses that meet accessibility requirements for people with disabilities. In social housing projects, as well as housing projects of any other nature constructed, promoted or subsidized by public administrations and other entities dependent on the public sector, a minimum of 4% shall be programmed with the appropriate construction and design characteristics to ensure safe and comfortable access and development for persons with disabilities.[340]

C. Employment

749. As far as employment is concerned, the aid indirectly affects people with disabilities, since its objective is to facilitate their right to employment on equal and non-discriminatory terms.

750. In this way, aid is established to facilitate the labour market insertion of people with disabilities. An adequate aid is necessary to promote their insertion, in particular the promotion of cooperatives and other social economy entities, among others: subsidies or loans for hiring, for the adaptation of jobs, the elimination of barriers that hinder their access, mobility, communication or understanding in production centres, for their establishment as self-employed workers or subsidies for social security contributions.[341]

---

337. Article 15 of the LPAD.
338. Article 25bis of the LPAD.
339. Articles 33–34 of the RPDA.
340. Article 32 of the RPDA.
341. Article 39 of the LPAD.

751. For example, aids can be reductions in employers' social security contributions in the case of indefinite hiring of a person with a disability; or reductions in temporary contracts with unemployed people with a disability; or reductions for the replacement of disabled workers in situations of temporary incapacity; or aids in the hiring of a disabled worker in a special employment centre.[342] With regard to self-employment, reductions in social security contributions are recognized for self-employed workers with a degree of incapacity of 33% or more. In this case, the reduction is applicable from the date of registration in the RETA, when it is the first registration or if they have not been registered in the two immediately previous years.[343]

752. Similarly, another measure is to set a reserving job quota for people with disabilities. A quota of not less than 7% is thus set for public employment offers. The reservation of this minimum percentage is made in such a way that, at least, people who can prove an intellectual disability cover 2% of the places offered, and the rest to people who can prove any other type of disability.[344]

753. Likewise, public and private companies employing fifty or more workers are required to have 2% of disabled workers. If they apply alternative measures agreed collectively (sectorial and state, or lower), or by unilateral decision of the employer duly communicated to the labour authority, these companies may exceptionally be released in whole or in part from that obligation.[345] These alternative measures include the following: First, the conclusion of a commercial or civil contract with a special employment centre, or with a self-employed worker with a disability, for the supply of raw materials, machinery, capital goods or any other type of goods necessary for the normal development of the company's activity. This measure may serve the normal development of the company's activity, such as provide services to third parties Second, donations and sponsorship actions, always of a monetary nature, for the development of labour insertion activities and job creation for people with disabilities, when the beneficiary entity of said actions is a foundation or a public utility association, whose social object is, among others, professional training, employability or the creation of employment for people with disabilities. Finally, their integration into the labour market, the constitution of a labour enclave, following the signing of the corresponding contract with a special employment centre.

---

342. Law 43/2006 of 29 December, for the improvement of growth and employment, BOE No. 312 of 30 Dec. 2006, in accordance with the provisions of the fifth additional provision of Royal Decree-Law 1/2023, of 10 January, on urgent measures regarding incentives for labour recruitment and improvement of the social protection of artists, BOE No. 9 of 11 Jan. 2023.
343. Article 38ter of Law 20/2007 of 11 July, of the Statute of the Self-Employed Worker, BOE No. 166 of 12 Jul. 2007.
344. Article 59 of Royal Legislative Decree 5/2015 of 30 October, approving the revised text of the Organic Law of the Basic Statute of Public Employees, BOE No. 261 of 31 Oct. 2015.
345. Article 42 of the RPDA. Such exceptionality and the corresponding alternative measures are provided for in Royal Decree 364/2005 of 8 April, which regulates the alternative exceptional compliance of the reserve quota in favour of workers with disabilities (BOE No. 94 of 20 Apr. 2004).

754. With the same purpose, establishing economic compensation for special employment centres is possible, so that those can fulfil the required social function.[346]

D. Taxes

755. There are many tax advantages and privileges for people with disabilities. Generally, the tax exemptions are granted for certain economic benefits, directly or indirectly related to the disability of the beneficiary, as well as for certain income from work in kind. Therefore, income exempt from this tax is as follows:

- Economic benefits received from public institutions, due to the reception of persons with disabilities.
- Economic aid granted by public institutions to persons with disabilities with a degree of 65% or more, to finance their stay in residences or day centres.
- Income derived from benefits in cash obtained as persons with disabilities.

756. There are also reductions in the net return on their activities; reductions in benefits and contributions to social security systems established for people with disabilities; or reductions in contributions to protect the patrimony of people with disabilities.

757. Tax reductions are applying to transactions related to vehicles used for the transport of persons with reduced mobility. Likewise, they affect vehicles registered in the exclusive name of disabled persons.

758. Finally, reduced Value Added Tax (VAT) rates apply to delivery, intra-community acquisition or imports of goods, in particular, in the following cases: vehicles for disabled persons with reduced mobility; wheelchairs for the exclusive use of disabled persons; vehicles used as self-drive taxis, or special self-drive vehicle for the transport of disabled persons in wheelchairs; motor vehicles commonly used for the transport of disabled persons in wheelchairs, or with reduced mobility; prostheses, orthosis and internal implants.[347]

II. Financial Allowances

759. The following benefits in cash are granted to those who have the status of disabled persons:

(a) Contributory pensions of the Social Security System: Persons entitled to permanent, total or serious disability pension are those integrated into the Social Security System who have contributed and meted the appropriate requirements. The

346. Article 44 of the LPAD.
347. Valued Added Tax Act 37/1992 of 28 December (BOE No. 312 of 29 Dec. 1992).

amount of these economic benefits will depend on the RB of the beneficiary and the degree of disability recognized (*see* Part V, Chapter 5, *supra*).

(b) Non-contributory Disability Pension: It is granted to persons between 18 and 65 years of age, affected by a disability or by a chronic illness, in a degree equal to or more than 65%. They must lack sufficient income, legally reside in Spanish territory, and have done so for five years, two of which are immediately prior to the date of application for the pension (*see* Part X, *infra*).

(c) Financial allowances for dependent children (*see* Part IV, *supra*).

(d) Guaranteed minimum income allowance and carer's allowance: The beneficiaries of both will continue to be entitled to receive those as long as they meet their requirements and do not opt for any of the non-contributory disability pensions, or an economic allowance for dependent children.[348] The guaranteed minimum income allowance 'consists of a periodic economic benefit designed to meet the basic needs, such as food, clothing and housing, of those who, lacking the necessary means for their subsistence, are not able to, due to the degree of their disability'.[349] The carer's allowance is a periodic financial benefit for people with a disability who, due to anatomical or functional losses, need the daily assistance of a third party to dress, move, eat or perform similar functions. A multidisciplinary team qualifies this situation. The Government, in the LPGE and Pension Revaluation, shall annually set the amount of the benefit.

(e) Mobility allowance and allowance to compensate for transport costs: Disabled persons who have difficulties using collective transport and meet the conditions laid down are entitled to a mobility allowance, and an allowance for transport costs to cover travel expenses away from their usual residence. This amount shall be set annually in the LPGE.

(f) Economic benefits for dependents: There are three different types. First, the 'economic benefit linked to the service' of a periodic nature, for cases where access to a public service or subsidized assistance is not possible. It is granted according to the degree of dependency and economic capacity of the beneficiary, in accordance with the provisions of the agreement between the General State Administration and the corresponding Autonomous Community. Second, 'financial allowance for care in the family environment and support for non-professional carers', which is exceptionally recognized, when the beneficiary is being cared for by their family environment and the conditions established by regulation are met. Third, the 'personal assistance allowance' to promote the personal autonomy of dependent persons, at any level. It makes possible hiring personal assistance, for a number of hours, which allows the beneficiary access to education and work, as well as a more autonomous life in the exercise of the basic activities of daily life. The Territorial Council of the System for Autonomy and Care for Dependency establishes its amount, which is published in a Royal Decree.

---

348. While Law 13/1982 of 7 Apr. 1982 on the Social Integration of Persons with Disabilities was repealed by the Single Exceptional Provision of the RPDA, the Single Transitional Provision of the RPDA retains the guaranteed minimum income support and carer's allowance exceptionally.
349. Royal Decree 383/1984 of 1 February, which establishes and regulates the special system of social and economic benefits provided for in Law 13/1982 (BOE No. 49 of 27 Feb. 1984).

Part X. Minimum Income Benefits

Thais Guerrero Padrón

760. The evolution of social security, from its initial stage, was based on a simple rule of reciprocity: work-contribution-benefits. As in its historical conformation, time has shown the need to attend to other basic needs in addition to this simple syllogism. In Spain, the issue is addressed with a non-contributory level of protection that includes family allowances, retirement and disability pensions, unemployment benefits, and minimum supplements to contributory pensions (which are non-contributory in nature). Moreover, the CCAA themselves provide allowances of different amounts and causes and in an unequal manner.

761. In 2020, a new non-contributory social security benefit called 'minimum vital income' was created in Spain by RD-Law 20/2020[350] and currently, it is regulated by Law 19/2021 of 20 December, establishing the Minimum Vital Income.[351] This benefit is based on Article 41 EC and aims to deal with the risk of poverty and social exclusion in Spain of those people living in our country without sufficient economic resources to meet their basic needs, trying to guarantee a certain level of income for all households in a situation of economic vulnerability. In addition, the minimum vital income benefit aims to be a tool that facilitates the transition of people from social exclusion due to lack of resources to full participation in social and economic life, breaking the link between structural lack of resources and lack of access to opportunities in the labour, educational or social sphere.

762. The minimum vital income benefit is legally qualified as a genuine subjective right to an economic benefit, which guarantees a minimum level of income for people living alone or in a cohabitation unit, when they are in a situation of economic vulnerability. Therefore, it is not a guaranteed basic income for all citizens regardless of their financial means, but beneficiaries must prove, among other requirements, that they have an income below the poverty threshold.

763. It is defined as a periodic benefit that is paid for as long as the situation of economic vulnerability persists and the beneficiary continues to meet the requirements that gave entitlement to it. As it is a non-contributory benefit, its granting is

350. BOE No. 154 of 1 Jun. 2020.
351. BOE No. 304 of 21 Dec. 2021.

not conditional upon the completion of periods of insurance, employment or self-employment, and it is financed exclusively by the State, through transfers to the social security budget.

764. The minimum vital income is configured as a 'floor' benefit that is compatible with other benefits of similar characteristics recognized by the CCAA and also with employment and self-employment. Consequently, it not only tries to protect unemployed or inactive persons, but also those who are active and those who are job seekers registered as such in the public office, which is intended to avoid becoming a disincentive to participation in the labour market.

765. Therefore, the minimum vital income benefit is distinguished by the following:

(a) It guarantees a minimum level of income by covering the difference between the total financial resources of the individual beneficiary or the cohabitation unit, and the guaranteed income in each case.
(b) Its protective action is differentiated according to whether it is addressed to an individual beneficiary or to a cohabitation unit.
(c) This benefit is paid for as long as the situation of economic vulnerability persists and the requirements that gave entitlement to it are maintained.
(d) It is envisaged as a protective network aimed at enabling the transition from a situation of exclusion to one of participation in society. To this end, it is linked to employment and inclusion incentives, involving different administrations.
(e) It is non-transferable. It may not be offered as a guarantee for obligations, nor may it be the object of total or partial assignment, compensation or discount, retention or seizure.[352]

766. Although the minimum vital income benefit was approved as an emergency measure to reach a large number of people and households immediately, the complexity of its conditions and procedure, and the difficulty of its management, are preventing many of its potential beneficiaries from accessing the benefit.

352. Article 3 of Law 19/2021.

Chapter 1. Beneficiaries

767. Nationality is not a requirement for receipt of the benefit. In fact, it is aimed at people who are legally resident in Spain in a situation of economic vulnerability, whether they are Spaniards, citizens from countries where EU law is applicable or third-country nationals. In particular, the beneficiaries of the minimum vital income benefit will be the following:[353]

(a) Persons integrating a cohabitation unit. It means that in the same home reside several persons who are united by family ties (marriage, registered partnership, relatives up to the second degree by consanguinity, affinity or adoption) and persons living with them in a situation of guardianship for the purpose of adoption or foster care. It is also considered a cohabitation unit if these persons, instead of having a home, are registered in collective establishments, or in a fictional residence in the case of homeless persons who habitually reside in a municipality. Any case, clarifying that the same person may not form part of more than one cohabitation unit.[354]
    For the purposes of this benefit, the consideration of home as the place of residence is extended to special cases in which an individual or a cohabitation unit accredits by some legal title the individualized use of a hotel room or the exclusive use of an area of a dwelling.
(b) Persons who do not form part of a cohabitation unit, with the following specifications:
    - They must be persons at least 23 years old, provided that they are not married or in a registered partnership, unless they have initiated separation or divorce proceedings.
    - In the case of women who are victims of gender-based violence or human trafficking and sexual exploitation, the age limit does not apply.
    - Persons between 18 and 22 years old coming from residential centres for the protection of minors or absolute orphans.
(c) Temporary users of a residential service of a social, health or social-health nature. The aforementioned benefit may be permanent in the case of women who are victims of gender-based violence, or victims of human trafficking and sexual exploitation.

768. In addition to the beneficiaries, Law 19/2021 details which persons are entitled to the minimum vital income benefit, i.e., who can apply for and receive it in their own name as individual beneficiaries, or on behalf of the household, in which case it is the beneficiary.[355]

769. In general, the right holder must be at least 23 years old, but there are exceptions to this requirement. This is the case for minors under 23 who are of legal age or emancipated minors (16 years old), if they have children or minors in foster

353. Article 4 of Law 19/2021.
354. Article 6 of Law 19/2021.
355. Article 5 of Law 19/2021.

care for the purpose of adoption or permanent foster care or absolute orphans, in cohabitation units in which none of the members reaches the age of 23. Also exempt from the age requirement are women who are victims of gender violence, victims of human trafficking and sexual exploitation (adults or emancipated minors), or persons who have been in child protection centres in the three years prior to reaching the age of 18.

770. As a speciality, if people without family ties live together in the same household, those who are at proven risk of social exclusion may be entitled to the minimum vital income benefit.

Chapter 2. Conditions

771. Beneficiaries must meet the following two requirements in order to qualify for the minimum vital income benefit: Have legal residence in Spain and be in a situation of economic vulnerability.[356]

Residence in Spain

772. Residence in Spain must be legal and effective, continuously and uninterruptedly, for at least one year prior to the submission of the application.

773. Some people are not required to have a minimum period of prior residence in Spain. For example, minors incorporated into the cohabitation unit by birth, adoption, family or permanent foster care, or victims of human trafficking and sexual exploitation and women victims of gender-based violence.

774. However, this requirement is aggravated for beneficiaries under 30 years of age who are not married or in a registered partnership, who must have resided legally in Spain for the two years prior to the application, have lived independently (i.e., in a different address from that of their parents or guardians) and have been registered with the Social Security for at least twelve months, whether continuously or not. The aforementioned period of prior residence in Spain does not apply to persons between 18 and 22 years of age coming from residential institutions for the protection of minors in CCAA. In the case of beneficiaries over 30 years of age on the date of application for the benefit, they must prove that during the year prior to that date their address in Spain has been different from that of their parents, guardians or foster parents.

775. For the purposes of maintaining entitlement to this benefit, a person is considered to be habitually resident in Spain even if he/she has made short stays abroad of a maximum of ninety days in a one-year period, or duly justified absences due to illness.

776. The right of residence in Spain of EU citizens, citizens of the EEA and Switzerland is accredited by registering in the central register of foreigners. Third-country nationals can prove it by means of the EU citizen's family card or residence permit. The requirement of legal residence causes illegal migrants to be excluded from the personal scope of this benefit.

777. Notwithstanding, the requirement of legal residence in Spain should be clarified with regard to the citizens to whom the EU law applies. By its nature and characteristics, the minimum vital income benefit is a matter governed by Article 3 of Regulation 883/2004. It is a non-contributory social security benefit to which the

356. Article 10 of Law 19/2021.

principle of coordination of accumulation periods applies. Thus, the aforementioned prior period of residence requirement can be met when the person has been living not only in Spain but also in another State where EU law is applicable.

Situation of economic vulnerability[357]

778. In any case, entitlement to the benefit is conditional on a situation of economic vulnerability. It is measured on the basis of the economic capacity of the individual beneficiary or, where applicable, of the cohabitation unit as a whole. Thus, the monthly average of all their annual income (except for the social wage and minimum income granted by the CCAA) and the previous year's income must be, at least, EUR 10 less than the monthly amount of the income guaranteed by this benefit

779. It is also required that their assets, excluding the habitual residence, be lower than the limits established by Law 19/2021. Then, an individual beneficiary whose assets, excluding the main residence, are equal to or greater than three times the income guaranteed by the minimum living income is not considered to be in a situation of economic vulnerability.

This amount varies according to the size of the cohabitation unit.

Likewise, the application for the benefit is allowed when the requirement of economic vulnerability was not met in the previous year, but this has arisen during the current year.

780. For these purposes, the amount of pensions and benefits, whether contributory or non-contributory, public or private, is computed as income. However, income from self-employment or employment is not computed, which is explained as a measure to encourage the participation of minimum vital income beneficiaries in the labour market. Nor are the CCAA minimum income allowances, which are compatible with the minimum vital income.

357. Article 11 of Law 19/2021.

Chapter 3. Amount of the Benefit

781. The minimum vital income is a monthly benefit to be paid for as long as the situation of economic vulnerability persists and the beneficiary fulfils the requirements and obligations established in the regulations.

782. The amount of benefit for an individual or a cohabitation unit is the difference between their previous year's income and the guaranteed income, which is determined on a case-by-case basis.[358] Thus:

(a) For an individual beneficiary, the guaranteed income is equal to 100% of the annual amount of non-contributory pensions (fixed in the LPGE), divided by 12. In 2023: EUR 565.37. This amount is increased by the disability supplement of 22% if the recipient has a degree of disability equal to or greater than 65%.

(b) For cohabitation units: the above-mentioned amount is increased by 30% for each additional member from the second onwards, up to a maximum of 220%. For 2023, the amounts are:
   - EUR 734.99 (one adult and one minor or two adults).
   - EUR 904.60 (one adult and two minors, two adults and one minor or three adults).
   - EUR 1,074.21 (one adult and three minors, two adults and two minors or three adults and one minor or four adults).
   - EUR 1,243.83 (one adult and four or more minors, two adults and three or more minors or three adults and two or more minors, or four adults and one minor.).

(c) Single-parent cohabitation units: the monthly amount set out in paragraph (b) is increased by a supplement of 22% on the amount provided for in paragraph (a). For this purpose, single-parent cohabitation unit is considered to be:
   - a single adult who lives with one or more descendants minors up to the second degree over whom he/she has sole custody and guardianship;
   - a single adult who lives with one or more minors in permanent foster care or pre-adoption guardianship when he/she is the sole foster parent or guardian, or when the other parent, guardian or foster parent is in prison or in a hospital for an uninterrupted period of one year or more;
   - a woman who has suffered accredited gender violence and one or more kindred minors up to the second degree over whom she has custody or, where appropriate, one or more minors in permanent foster care or pre-adoption guardianship.

     For 2023, the monthly amounts are:
     - EUR 859.37 (one adult and one minor).
     - EUR 1,028.98 (one adult and two minors).
     - EUR 1,198.60 (one adult and three minors).
     - EUR 1,368.21(one adult and four or more minors).

358. Article 13 of Law 19/2021.

(d) The disability supplement of 22% is applied to the monthly amount corresponding to the cohabitation unit, if any member has a degree of disability equal to or greater than 65%.

(e) In addition to the above-mentioned amounts, a monthly child allowance will be paid for each child in the household (at the date of application), depending on the age of the child on 1 January of the year in question. For 2023:
   - Up to three years old: EUR 115.
   - From three to six years old: EUR 80.50.
   - From six to 18 years old: EUR 57.50.

783. In any case, and regardless of the income of the person living alone or of the cohabitation unit in the previous financial year, if the applicant or any member of the family unit receives Social Security pensions (contributory or non-contributory) or unemployment benefits for the over 52s, the amount of the minimum vital income benefit may not exceed the difference between the amount of these benefits and the applicable guaranteed income. On the other hand, when the monthly amount of these benefits is equal to or higher than the monthly amount of the applicable guaranteed income, entitlement to the minimum vital income will not be recognised.

Chapter 4. Claims and Administration

784. Access to the financial benefit requires the interested person to make the corresponding application, providing the documentation required to accredit compliance with all the requirements.

785. The INSS is the competent body for the granting and control of the minimum vital income benefit. This does not prevent the CCAA and local authorities from intervening in the management of this benefit, in which case it is necessary to have previously signed an appropriate agreement. In this way, these entities may initiate and process the administrative enquiry, which in any case will be resolved by the INSS.

Chapter 5. Reclaiming of Benefits Paid

786. The INSS may review ex officio, to the detriment of the beneficiaries and within a maximum period of four years, the actions relating to this benefit, being able to declare and demand ex officio the return of the benefits unduly collected.[359]

787. At any time, the INSS may rectify any material or factual and arithmetical errors it notices, review any omissions or inaccuracies in the beneficiary's declarations and reclaim any amounts received unduly.

788. In certain cases, the beneficiary is obliged to repay the amounts unduly received. This occurs when the INSS decides either to terminate the entitlement, or to reduce the amount of the benefit due to a change in the circumstances that determined its calculation.

789. The reimbursement of benefits is carried out through the special procedure set out in RD 1415/2004, which provides a voluntary period for payment of the amount owed, after which the corresponding surcharges and interest for late payment are applied.

790. For the reimbursement of benefits unduly received, declared and claimed as from 28 December 2022, in each financial year, amounts not exceeding 65% of the monthly amount of non-contributory pensions shall not be claimable, when at least one beneficiary who is a minor is included in the cohabitation unit. Only if the amount unduly received by the cohabitation unit exceeds 65% of the aforementioned indicator, will the INSS initiate the procedure for the reimbursement of unduly received benefits.

359. Article 19 of Law 19/2021.

Part XI. Claims and Adjudication

Thais Guerrero Padrón

Chapter 1. Claims

§1. Introduction of Claims

791. The access to protection is possible when the contingency occurs and the beneficiary fulfils the general legal requirements of affiliation, registration and contribution, and the specific ones of the benefit itself.[360] In this case, the claim must be submitted to the competent entity responsible for the benefit, which is the Managing Body, the MCSS or the TGSS, who will recognize formally the entitlement to protection, after having verified the compliance with the aforementioned requirements.

792. In special scenarios, the company may be liable for the payment of the benefit. This is the case under the General Scheme when the company has failed to comply with the obligations of affiliation, registration, deregistration or contribution with respect to its employees. In these situations, the managing entity or MCSS anticipates the payment of the benefit to the worker, subrogating the rights and actions of such beneficiary. In no case may the advance payment of benefits exceed the amount equivalent to two and a half times the amount of the IPREM in force at the time of the contingency.[361]

793. Once the right to the benefit has been recognized, it must be exercised by the person concerned within five years of the occurrence of the contingency. If this period elapses without having exercised it, the right to recognition of the benefit prescribes (is lost).

794. Notwithstanding, the prescription may be interrupted for certain legal reasons, for example, by filing a complaint with the Social Security Administration or by virtue of a file handled by the Labour and Social Security Inspectorate in relation to the case in question. In consequence, the interruption determines that the calculation of the period is restarted from zero.

360. Article 165 of the GSSA.
361. Article 167(3) of the GSSA.

795. If the right to recognition of the benefit is exercised late in relation to the time from which it was possible to do so (i.e., when the protected situation arises), the beneficiary may lose the benefits prior to the application, except for those of the three months prior to the application.[362]

796. The general prescription rule does not apply to all benefits. In particular, exceptions should be made for retirement and widowhood, orphanhood and family pensions, which are benefits whose entitlement is imprescriptible and may be exercised at any time from the date on which the contingency arises.

797. Finally, once the entitlement to the benefit has been recognized, it must be paid by the liable entity or person. Depending on the benefit, the beneficiary has a certain expiry period to claim its payment. This period may be suspended for established reasons, continuing on the day on which it was suspended. However, if this period elapses without the entity having paid the benefit, the right to receive it expires and it is no longer possible to receive it.[363]

§2. Protection Against Seizure and Transfer

798. In accordance with the GSSA, financial benefits of the social security have the following characteristics:

- They are non-transferable and non-waivable benefits since beneficiaries cannot transfer or waive their entitlement to them, irrespective of the exercise of the right to choose in the event of incompatibility of benefits.
- They enjoy guarantees against third parties; in other words, they cannot be subject to withholding, compensation or discount, except in established cases (maintenance obligations, debts to the social security, etc.).
- They are preferential benefits that have the nature of credits with a general preference.
- Lastly, they have a specific tax treatment, given that they are subject to taxation according to the terms set forth in the regulations for each tax.

799. Financial benefits of the social security can only be seized according to the terms and amounts set by the Law on Civil Procedure for pensions and wage income.[364] In particular, deductions will be made by applying the scale set out in Article 607 of the Civil Procedure Act, if the amount of the benefit is higher than the minimum professional wage at any time. If the pensions were taxed with permanent or temporary discounts of a public nature according to fiscal, tax or social security law, the net amount received by the entitlement holder, having deducted the above, will be used to govern the amount confiscated.

362. Article 53 of the GSSA.
363. Article 54 of the GSSA.
364. Law 1/2000 of 7 January, on Civil Procedure (BOE No. 7 of 8 Jan. 2000).

800. The general rule will exclude those cases where the judgment orders the payment of maintenance allowances whenever the obligation for paying them comes directly from the law, including rulings given in annulment, separation or divorce processes on maintenance allowances due to the spouse or children. In these cases, as well as relevant precautionary measure cases, the legal body will determine the amount that can be seized.

§3. Legal Capacity to Receive Benefits

801. As stated above, the constitution of the legal relationship of social security requires to complete administrative acts. By this way, the subjects included in its scope have access to protective action. At contributory level, active workers and persons treated as such must fulfil the general conditions (affiliation, registration and contribution) and those specific to each benefit in order to be entitled to them. On the other hand, there are 'non-contributory' benefits tending to protect situations of need; even without the common working conditions, the possible beneficiaries have to meet other personal conditions (residence, income limit) that will allow their recognition.

802. In Spain, persons who have full capacity to act in accordance with the provisions of the Civil Code (commonly persons over 18 years of age) have full capacity to work, so they automatically generate social security rights.

803. Regarding the legal capacity to receive benefits, there are special rules for workers under the age of 18. Given that the minimum age for employment in Spain is 16, young people should draw up a work contract when they live independently with the consent of their parents or guardians, or with the authorization of the person or institution in charge of them.

Chapter 2. Adjudication

804. The prosecution of benefits included in the protective action of social security follows basic rules defined by a simple request addressed to the competent management entities. These are the INSS as Managing Body, the MCSS, and the TGSS as common service. The rejection or silence of such a request makes it necessary to make a prior administrative complaint to them, which is a necessary requirement to bring an action before the bodies of labour jurisdiction.

805. Competence in matters of social security pertains to the bodies of labour jurisdiction, which are structured as follows: first, Labour Courts (*Juzgados de lo Social*), which are located in the capital of each province, having general jurisdiction at first instance. Second, the Labour Chamber of the High Courts of Justice of each Autonomous Community (*Tribunales Superiores de Justicia*), with competence at first instance and also over appeals against decisions issued by the Labour Courts of its territory. Third, the Labour Chamber of the National Court (*Audiencia Nacional*), which has general jurisdiction at single instance over proceedings whose resolution affects a territory superior to one Autonomous Community. Lastly, the Labour Chamber or Fourth Section of the Supreme Court, which has general jurisdiction over cassation appeals and over other extraordinary appeals provided for by Law.

§1. The Prior Administrative Complaint

806. To file a lawsuit regarding social security benefits, Law 36/2011 of 10 October, which regulates the social jurisdiction (hereinafter 'LJS'), requires completing a prior complaint with the competent Managing Body. Nevertheless, this requirement does not apply to administrative decisions issued by the competent Managing Body, by which it declares medical discharge in temporary incapacity proceedings after the 365-day period has expired.

807. In general, the prior claim shall be made within thirty days from the notification of the corresponding decision. In the challenge of medical discharges not included in the above case, the period will be eleven days. The refusal of the previous claim opens the judicial way.

808. It must be stressed that the aspects adduced in the prior administrative complaint will be unalterable in the lawsuit, except for when new facts or facts that were not known before the date of the complaint arise. Likewise, the Managing Body is bound by the reasoning and facts contained in its resolution, unless the new facts are intimately connected with them. In any case, the prior complaint interrupts the limitation periods and suspends the expiry periods.

§2. The Procedural Modality in Social Protection Claims

809. The LJS does not regulate specific modalities for the treatment of claims relating to social security benefits. It is presumed that the structure of the lawsuit is practically a copy of the prior administrative complaint, with the details that could be incorporated after having been rejected. In any case, the core of the challenge would be based on the particular aspects of each claim. Due to the complexity of some technical or mathematical aspects, the interested party may request the competent entity by judicial means to provide the administrative file. This one may be necessary for its study and defence and be useful also for information and knowledge of the judicial authority.

810. Some precisions should be made in the event of medical discharge challenge process in temporary incapacity situations. The claim shall be directed exclusively against the Managing Body and, where appropriate, against the MCSS. The process will be urgent and preferential, and the hearing will take place within five days following the admission of the claim. Finally, the sentence will not have an appeal, and its effects will be limited to the impugned medical discharge.[365]

811. Finally, in the challenge to unemployment benefits, the LJS establishes a typical corporate responsibility case. It occurs when in the four years immediately preceding an application for unemployment benefits it is found that the worker has received benefits for the termination of several temporary contracts with the same company. If the repeated temporary contracts are abusive or fraudulent, the Managing Body may ex officio request the employer to be declared responsible for its payment, and be ordered to return those benefits and the corresponding contributions. The sentence will be immediately enforceable and brought to the attention of the Labour and Social Security Inspectorate.[366]

§3. Appeals

812. As it was mentioned above, appeals are heard by the Social Courts of the High Courts of Justice and of the Supreme Court. The first one shall decide appeals against the resolutions issued by the Social Courts of their district. This appeal – called *recurso de suplicación* – is appropriate, for instance, in proceedings concerning the recognition or denial of the right to social security benefits as well as the degree of permanent disability applicable.[367]

813. The Supreme Court hears appeals against judgments and other decisions delivered in a single instance by the Social Chambers of the High Courts of Justice

365. Article 140 of the LJS.
366. Article 147 of the LJS.
367. Article 190 of the LJS.

and by the Social Chamber of the National Court (*recurso de casación*).[368] Additionally, the Supreme Court hears the 'appeal in cassation for the unification of doctrine' (*recurso de casación para la unificación de doctrina*).[369] Its objective is to unify different or contradictory decisions when dealing with the same litigants, or different litigants in the same situation, on the basis of substantially the same facts, grounds and claims. The appeal tries to unify the doctrine on the occasion of sentences dictated in supplication by the Social Chambers of the High Courts of Justice, which are contradictory among themselves, with that of one or more other Chambers of the aforementioned High Courts, or with sentences of the Supreme Court. Likewise, the contradiction can exist with sentences coming from the Constitutional Court and the jurisdictional bodies instituted in the international agreements and treaties on human rights and fundamental freedoms ratified by Spain. The doctrine established in the judgments of the ECJ in interpretation of European Law may also be invoked.

814. Finally, a brief word about provisional enforcement of social security judgments: sentences appealed, which condemn the payment of periodic payment benefits, are enforceable. During the processing of the appeal, the condemned subject (usually the employer) is being obliged to pay the benefit. If the higher court overturns the sentence, the beneficiary will not be obliged to reimburse the amounts received, keeping this right until the new sentence is final.[370]

815. When the judgment determines the payment of a lump sum, the beneficiary will have the right to apply to the Court for provisional enforcement while the appeal is being processed, obtaining advances on account at the expense of the defendant. If the higher court overturns the judgment, the beneficiary (or the worker) must repay the sums received. In any case, the State will be jointly liable for the reimbursement to the employer. If the new sentence confirms the appealed sentence, the beneficiary/worker will be entitled to receive the differences between the quantum of the sentence and the sums received in advance.[371]

368. Article 205 of the LJS.
369. Article 219 of the LJS.
370. Article 294 of the LJS.
371. Article 295 of the LJS.

Selected Bibliography

Aragón Gómez, C. *La prestación contributiva de Seguridad Social.* Valladolid: Lex Nova (2013).

Aragón Medina, J. et al., *La Situación de Las Personas de 55 a 64 Años En Relación Al Mercado de Trabajo y Sus Trayectorias Laborales.* Estudios de la Fundación. Madrid: Fundación Primero de Mayo (2009).

Arriba, A. & Moreno, L. *Spain: Poverty and 'Safety-Nets'.* In *Welfare State Reform in Southern Europe: Fighting Poverty and Social Exclusion in Greece, Italy, Spain and Portugal*, edited by M. Ferrera. London: Routledge, 2005.

Blasco Lahoz, J.F. & López Gandía, J. *Curso de Seguridad Social.* Edition No. 10, Valencia: Tirant lo Blanch (2018).

Blasco Lahoz, J.F. *La protección por contingencias profesionales en el régimen especial de la seguridad social de los trabajadores por cuenta propia o autónomos (RETA).* Revista de información laboral, No. 1 (2018): 65, 79.

Blasco Lahoz, J.F. *Ley de dependencia y normas de desarrollo.* Valencia: Tirant Lo Blanch (2010).

Boeri, T. & van Ours, J. *The Economics of Imperfect Labour Markets.* Princeton, New Jersey: Princeton University Press (2008).

Campoy Cervera, I. *Los derechos de las personas con discapacidad: perspectivas sociales, políticas, jurídicas y filosóficas.* Madrid: Dykinson (2004).

Cavas Martínez, F. & Fernández Orrico, F.J. *La cobertura de las contingencias profesionales en el sistema español de Seguridad Social.* Cizur Menor (Navarra): Thomson-Aranzadi (2006).

Desdentado Bonete, A. & de la Puebla Pinilla, A. *La responsabilidad del empresario por los accidentes de trabajo y el recargo de prestaciones por infracción de normas de seguridad: Algunas reflexiones sobre las últimas aportaciones de la Jurisprudencia.* Tribuna social: Revista de seguridad social y laboral, No. 125 (2001): 13, 27.

Desdentado Bonete, A. & Mercader Uguina, J.R. *El Desempleo Como Situación Protegida: (Un Estudio Sobre Los Problemas de Acceso a La Protección En El Nivel Contributivo y En El Asistencial)* (Estudios de Derecho Laboral; 24). Madrid: Civitas (1996).

Desdentado Bonete, A. *El recargo de prestaciones de la Seguridad Social y su aseguramiento. Contribución a un debate.* Revista de derecho social, No. 21 (2003): 11, 28.

Selected Bibliography

Desdentado Bonete, A. *Problemas de coordinación en los procesos sobre responsabilidad empresarial por los accidentes de trabajo.* Relaciones laborales: Revista crítica de teoría y práctica, No. 2 (2008): 357, 395.

Esteban Legarreta, R. *La Renta Activa de Inserción* (Colección Laboral; 172). Valencia: Tirant lo Blanch, 2006.

European Economic and Social Committee. 'Opinion of the European Economic and Social Committee on Economic Diversification in the Accession Countries – Role of SMEs and Social Economy Enterprises' (2004/C 112/27).' European Economic and Social Committee, 30 April 2004, https://eur-lex.europa.eu/LexUriServ/LexUriServ.do?uri=OJ:C:2004:112:0105:0112:EN:PDF.

García Garnica, M.C. *Estudios sobre dependencia y discapacidad,* Pamplona: Aranzadi (2011).

García Mainar, I. & Toharia Cortés, L. *Prestaciones Por Desempleo y Búsqueda de Empleo.* Revista de Economía Aplicada, No. 23 (2000): 5, 33.

García Sabater, A.B. *Necesidades especiales de apoyo laboral en colectivos con discapacidad, en particular, el empleo,* Pamplona: Aranzadi (2018).

Gonzalez Ortega, S. & Barcelón Cobedo, S. *Introducción al Derecho de la Seguridad Social.* Edition No. 12, Valencia: Tirant lo Blanch (2018).

Guerrero Padrón, T. *El trabajo autónomo en el Derecho comparado europeo desde la perspectiva española.* In: *El trabajo autónomo en España tras la crisis. Perspectivas y propuestas,* Gómez Muñoz, J.M. (dir.). Albacete: Bomarzo (2019): 409, 440.

Guerrero Padrón, T. *El derecho de residencia como factor limitativo del acceso a prestaciones de seguridad social*, Revista General de Derecho del Trabajo y de la Seguridad Social, IUSTEL, No. 49 (2018): 259, 293.

Guerrero Padrón, T. *Ingreso mínimo vital y nacionales británicos en España en tiempos del Brexit,* e-Revista Internacional de la Protección Social, vol. 5, No. 2 (2020): 60,76.

Guerrero Padrón, T. & Sánchez-Rodas Navarro, C. *The Spanish Old Age Security System in 2020,* Max Planck Institute for Social Law and Social Policy (2021) https://www.mpisoc.mpg.de/en/social-law/research/research-projects/pension-maps/project-website/spain/.

González Rodríguez, R. *Discapacidad versus dependencia, Terminología diferencial y procedimiento para su reconocimiento*, Index de Enfermería, 26, No. 3 (2017).

Homs, O. *Social and Employment Policies in Spain.* In-Depth Analysis for the EMPL Committee, 36 (2017).

Malgesini Rey, G. *EMIN Context Report SPAIN.* EMIN Context Report, 46 (2017).

Martín Jiménez, R. & Sempere Navarro, A.V. *El recargo de prestaciones: puntos críticos.* Revista del Ministerio de Trabajo e Inmigración, No. 53 (2004): 395, 437.

Mercader Uguina, J.R. *Indemnizaciones derivadas del accidente de trabajo. Seguridad Social y derecho de daños.* Madrid: La Ley-Actualidad (2001).

Monereo Pérez, J.L. & Fernández Avilés, J.A. *Determinación de contingencias de la Seguridad Social: (revisión crítica del sentido político-jurídico y de la delimitación técnica de las contingencias profesionales) I.* Aranzadi Social, I, No. 19 (2009): 69, 112.

Monereo Pérez, J.L. & Fernández Avilés, J.A. *Determinación de contingencias de la Seguridad Social: (revisión crítica del sentido político-jurídico y de la delimitación técnica de las contingencias profesionales) II*. Aranzadi Social, I, No. 20 (2009): 71, 114.

Monereo Pérez, J.L. & Molina Navarrete, C. *Manual de Seguridad Social*. Edition No. 14, Madrid: Tecnos (2018).

Monereo Pérez, J.L. *Manual de Derecho de la dependencia*. Madrid: Tecnos (2014).

Morón Prieto, R. & Moreno Solana, A. *Las rentas básicas y la protección por desempleo*. In *Reflexiones y Propuestas Sobre Protección Social y Empleabilidad Para Jóvenes y Parados de Larga Duración*, edited by Mercader Uguina, J.R. & Pérez del Prado, D. Valencia: Tirant lo Blanch (2017).

OECD. *Crisis Squeezes Income and Puts Pressure on Inequality and Poverty. New Results from OECD Income Distribution Database*. Nota para España. OECD (2013).

OECD. *OECD Employment Outlook 2011*. Paris: OECD (2011).

Pérez del Prado, D. 'Comparing Denmark and Spain: Two Different Kinds of ALMP Decentralization'. *Spanish Labour Law and Employment Relations Journal* 2, Nos 1–2 (2013): 41, 54.

Pérez del Prado, D. *Prestación Por Desempleo: Intensidad, Duración y Control*. Valladolid: Lex Nova – Thomson Reuters (2014).

Quintero Lima, M.G. *El derecho de los extranjeros extracomunitarios en situación irregular a las prestaciones de Seguridad Social derivadas de contingencias profesionales*. In: *La protección social de los extranjeros en España*. González Ortega, S. (coord). Valencia: Tirant lo Blanch (2010): 239, 277.

Rey Pérez, J.L. & Mateo Sanz, L. *El empleo de las personas con discapacidad*, Madrid: Dykinson (2018).

Ribes Moreno, I. *La incidencia del salario 'a la parte' sobre la Seguridad Social*. In: *Protección social en España, en la Unión Europea y en el derecho internacional*. Garrido Pérez, E. & Sánchez-Rodas Navarro, C. (coords); Aguilar Gonzálvez, M.C.; Cervilla Garzón, M.J., Ferradans Caramés, C.; Guerrero Padrón, T.; Jover Ramírez, C. & Ribes Moreno, I. (dirs.). Murcia: Laborum (2017): 133, 148, http://hdl.handle.net/11441/65904.

Ribes Moreno, I. *La necesaria reformulación del sistema de cotización de régimen de autónomos: una reflexión al hilo de las últimas novedades legislativas y perspectivas comparadas*. In: *El trabajo autónomo en España tras la crisis. Perspectivas y propuestas*, Gómez Muñoz, J.M. (dir.). Albacete: Bomarzo (2019): 475, 516.

Ribes Moreno, I. *La problemática derivada de la aplicación del Reglamento de coordinación de sistemas de Seguridad Social 883/2004, y del Convenio multilateral iberoamericano de Seguridad Social al personal que presta servicios a bordo de buques*. In *El derecho del trabajo y la seguridad social en la encrucijada: retos para la disciplina laboral*. Chocrón Giráldez, A.M.; Ramírez Bendala, M.D.; Sierra Benítez, E.M. & Cervilla Garzón, M.J. (coords); Sánchez-Rodas Navarro, C. & Garrido Pérez, E. (dirs). Murcia: Laborum (2016): 151, 166, https://idus.us.es/xmlui/bitstream/handle/11441/34282/derecho%20del%20trabajo.pdf?sequence=1&isAllowed=y.

Ribes Moreno, I. 'The Problems Derived from Applying a Social Security System to Personnel Serving on Board of Vessels'. *e-Revista Internacional de la Protección Social* 1, No. 1 (2016): 23, 55.

Rodríguez Cabrero, G. *Assessment of Minimum Income Schemes in Spain.* Peer Review in Social Protection and Social Inclusion and Assessment in Social Inclusion (2009).

Rohlfer, S. 'Perspectives on Social Pacts in Spain: Social Dialogue and the Social Partners'. *Management Revue* 23, No. 1 (2012): 48, 64, https://doi.org/10.5771/0935-9915-2012-1-48.

Rojo Torrecilla, E. *Servicios Públicos de Empleo. Una Mejora Inaplazable Para Afrontar El Presente y El Futuro.* Relaciones Laborales: Revista Crítica de Teoría y Práctica, 2 (2010): 1231, 1240.

Sánchez Pérez, J. *Las contingencias profesionales.* In: *Tratado de Derecho de la Seguridad Social.* Maldonado Molina, J.A., de Val Tena, A.L. and Monereo Pérez, J.L. (dir). Murcia: Laborum, Tomo I (2017): 501, 517.

Sempere Navarro, V. *Comentario Sistemático a la Ley de dependencia,* Pamplona: Aranzadi (2008).

Toharia Cortés, L. (dir), Arranz, J.M., Cebrián, I. García Serrano, C. Hernanz, V. & Pitarch, J. *El Efecto de Las Bonificaciones de Las Cotizaciones a La Seguridad Social Para El Empleo En La Seguridad Social: Un Intento de Evaluación Macroeconómica, Microeconómica e Institucional.* Ministerio de Trabajo e Inmigración. Secretaría de Estado de Seguridad Social (2008).

Valdés Dal-Ré, F. *Cooperación y coordinación entre los servicios públicos de empleo.* Relaciones laborales: Revista crítica de teoría y práctica, No. 1 (2009): 51, 62.

VV. AA., Cabra de Luna, M.A. (coord), *Comentarios al Texto Refundido de la Ley General de derechos de las personas con discapacidad y de su inclusión social,* Madrid: Dykinson (2015).

VV.AA., Barranco Avilés, Mª. C. (dir), *Situaciones de dependencia, discapacidad y derechos: una mirada a la ley 39/2006 de promoción de la autonomía personal y atención a las personas en situación de dependencia desde la Convención Internacional de los Derechos de las Personas con Discapacidad,* Madrid: Dykinson (2011).

VV.AA., Guilarte Martín-Calero (dir), *Estudios y comentarios jurisprudenciales sobre discapacidad,* Pamplona: Aranzadi (2016).

Zárate Rivera, B. *La tutela de la dependencia en el ordenamiento jurídico español,* Pamplona: Aranzadi (2015).

Index

The numbers here refer to paragraph numbers.

Index

Index

www.ingramcontent.com/pod-product-compliance
Lightning Source LLC
Chambersburg PA
CBHW071434230926
51846CB00001B/230
9789403518480